HOLT Effective Business Communication
Style Guide

Prepared in cooperation with

HOLT, RINEHART AND WINSTON
Harcourt Brace & Company

Austin • New York • Orlando • Atlanta • San Francisco • Boston • Dallas • Toronto • London

Shipley Associates

Shipley Associates, a division of Franklin Quest Co., is the premier provider of business and technical communication-skills training, consulting, and products. With over twenty years of experience in the training industry, Shipley helps individuals and organizations increase productivity with improved writing and communication skills. The *Shipley Style Guide* is the top business communication reference in America's largest corporations and universities. Shipley clients include a large number of the Fortune 500 companies.

Credits

Editorial Sigman Byrd, Mary Malone, Michael Neibergall, Barbara Sutherland; Kathy Blanchard, *Secretary*

Multimedia Kate Bennett

Design Pun Nio, *Senior Art Director*; Didona Design Associates, *Cover Design,*: Neel Heisel, *Designer, Packaging.*

Production Beth Prevelige, Rose Degollado, George Prevelige, Nancy Hargis

Copyright © 1996 by Holt, Rinehart and Winston, Inc. and Shipley Associates, a Division of Franklin Quest Co.

All rights reserved. No part of this publication may be reproduced or transmitted in any form or by any means, electronic or mechanical, including photocopy, recording, or any information storage and retrieval system, without permission in writing from the publisher.

Requests for permission to make copies of any part of this work should be mailed to Permissions Department; Holt, Rinehart and Winston, Inc.; 6277 Sea Harbor Drive; Orlando, Florida 32887-6777.

Portions of this work have been adapted from the *Style Guide,* Revised Edition, copyright © 1990 by Shipley Associates. All rights reserved.

Printed in the United States of America

ISBN 0-03-015593-2

5678 022 00 99 98

Table of Contents

Style Guide Table of Contents iii
How to Use the *Style Guide* v
Reference Glossary Table of Contents ix
English and Current Style x

Reference Glossary

Abbreviations 1–9
Active/Passive Voice 10–13
Agreement 14–17
Apostrophes 18–19
Bias-Free Language 20–24
Bibliography/Works Cited 25–28
Capitals 29–34
Citations 35–36
Colons 37–38
Commas 39–42
Conjunctions 43–46
Dashes 47–48
Ellipses 49–50
Emphasis 51–54
Graphics 55–60
Headings 61–63
Hyphens 64–67
Intellectual Property 68–70
Interviews 71–74
Letters 75–91
Lists 92–96
Memos 97–103
Numbers 104–107
Organization 108–114
Page Layout 115–125
Parallelism 126–127
Parentheses and Brackets 128–131
Persuasion 132–135
Plurals 136–138
Possessives 139–141
Quotation Marks 142–144
Résumés 145–160
Semicolons 161–162
Spelling 163–165
Titles 166–167
Tone 168–172
Transitions 173–174
Writing 175–184

Table of Contents

Model Documents

Model Documents Table of Contents 185

Job Applications/Résumés

Job Application, Completed 187–189
Job Application, Blank Form 190–192
Job Description 193–194
Résumé, Experienced Functional 195
Résumé, Experienced Chronological 196
Cover Letter, Experienced Applicant 197
Résumé, Inexperienced Functional 198
Cover Letter, Inexperienced Applicant 199
Thank You Letter 200

Letters

Commendation 201
Complaint 202
Persuasive Sales 203–204
Proposal 205
Proposal Acceptance 206
Proposal Rejection 207
Sales 208
Survey Data 209

Memos

Personnel Notice 210
Procedure 211–212
Recommendation 213
Report 214–217
Request 218
Request for Clarification 219

Others

Abstract, Descriptive 220
Abstract, Informative 221
Minutes, Action 222–223
Minutes, Traditional 224–225
Newsletter Item 226
Policy, Customer Service 227
Procedure, Incomplete Order 228
Shift Report, Computer Company 229

Index 230–241
Revising and Proofreading Symbols 243–245

How to Use the *Style Guide*

Sections of the *Style Guide*

This *Style Guide* is designed with helpful headings and signposts on every page. When you have a question about effective business writing, use the chart below and the illustrations on the following pages as guides to help you find the answer.

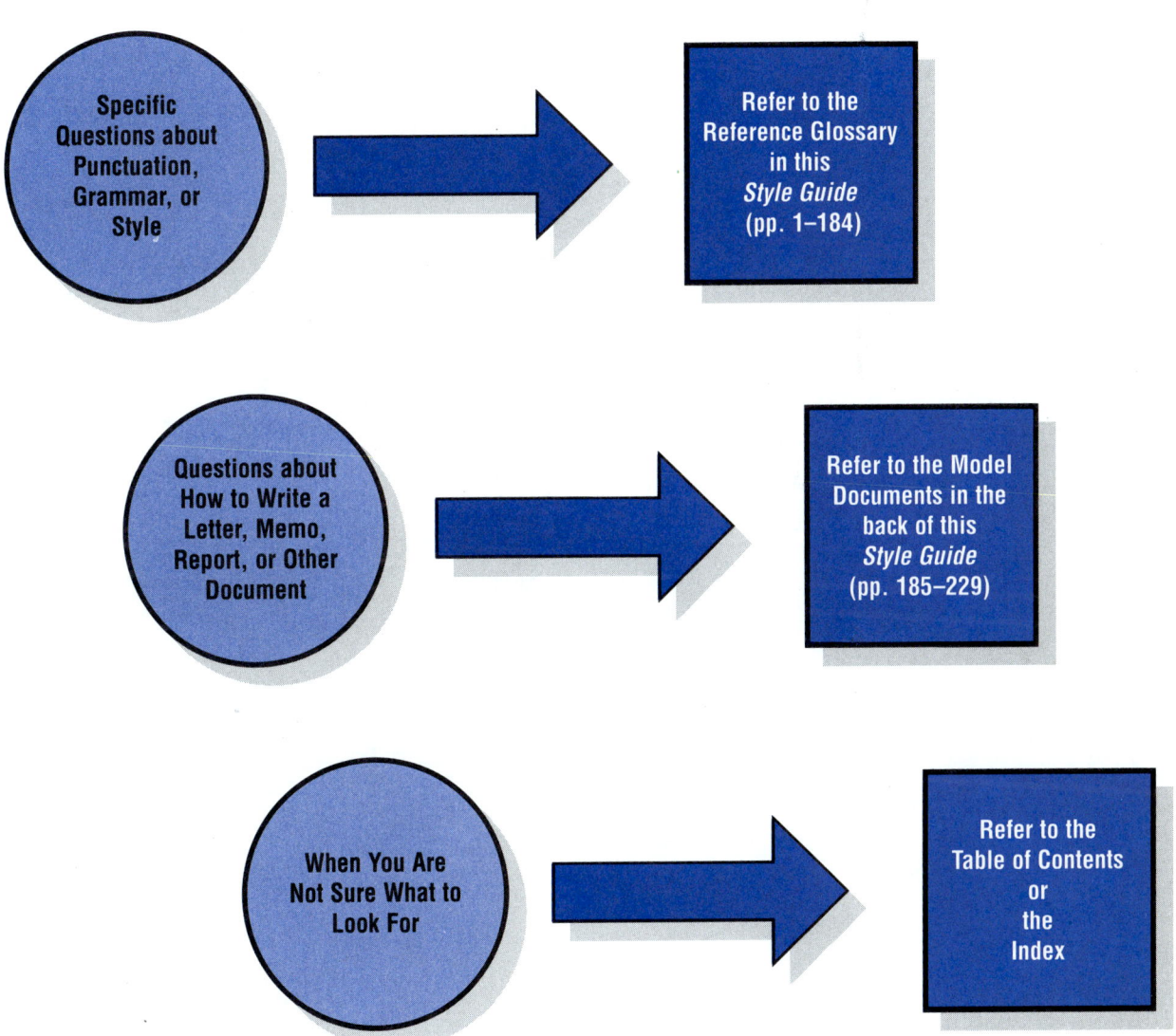

How to Use the *Style Guide*

Questions About Grammar, Punctuation, and Style

- Should I use a comma or a semicolon to separate items in a series?

- Should I use a bar graph or a pie chart to illustrate my data?

- Should I use headings in a report that's only three pages long?

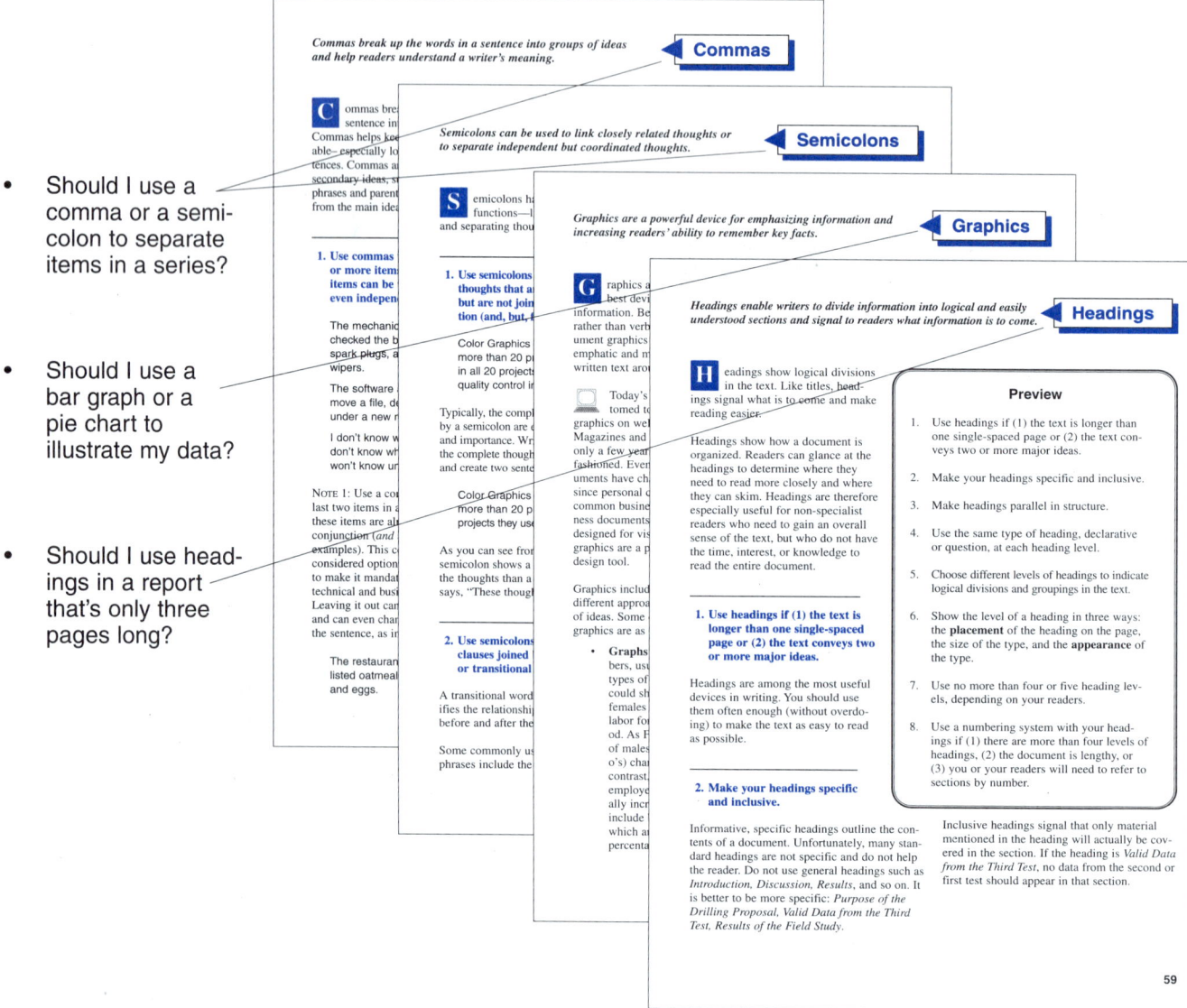

NOTE: You may need to refer to more than one topic entry in the *Style Guide* to answer a specific question. Look for cross-references within each section to guide you to more information.

How to Use the *Style Guide*

Using the Rules and Examples

Step 1:
Scan the topic for the pertinent rule. (Rules are numbered and printed in blue.)

Step 2:
Look through the examples for one that matches your sentence or paragraph.

Step 3:
Check the notes for exceptions or additional examples that might be helpful.

Step 4:
Look up the cross-references (in small capital letters) if you need further information.

Step 5:
Pay close attention to information indicated by the computer icon for special instructions on how to use your computer more effectively.

Résumés

When using verb phrases, lists, and headings, choose one form and use it throughout your résumé. Be consistent. Follow the rules of parallelism to ensure your résumé maintains consistency. See PARALLELISM.

Do This

Dependable

Managed food bank hotline over 12-month period

Delivered food to 20 recipients

Team Player

Participated on varsity basketball team

Worked successfully with six other food bank volunteers

NOTE: *Dependable* and *Team Player* might be required job applicant characteristics listed in a work-for-hire newspaper ad. See the résumé model in the back of the *Style Guide* which emphasizes the applicant's qualifications in those required areas. Note that the verb phrases below the headings are parallel—*Managed, Delivered, Participated, Worked.*

Not This

Hard Worker

Worked 12-hour shifts for summer job

Lifting heavy objects was part of my job

Worked in hot manufacturing environment

Flexible

Can do many office tasks efficiently

New tasks and skills **are welcomed**

NOTE: *Worked, Lifting, Can do,* and *are welcomed* are not parallel verb phrases.

7. Prepare (publish) your résumé so it has a clean, professional look.

Choose a format and appearance that is appropriate and professional. Choose high-quality white or cream paper (at least 20-pound paper). Avoid unusually colored papers.

Use a variety of fonts to help emphasize the important points, but avoid unusual fonts. Also, do not use too many fonts (i.e., not more than three fonts). See PAGE LAYOUT.

Proofread your résumé to ensure there are **absolutely no grammatical or typographical errors.** Grammatical and typographical errors give the impression you are sloppy or careless.

We recommend you take your completed résumé to a résumé service shop or photocopying shop where they can publish your résumé using the latest desktop publishing and high-quality photocopying machines. This step, while optional, will cost you little and will help set your résumé apart from the majority of résumés a company will receive.

Résumé Format

Whichever type of résumé you decide to prepare, you will have to decide how to record your information.

The following subsections suggest ways for you to gather information for your résumé, and they illustrate how to write different sections of a résumé. Remember, however, that the seven rules in the preceding discussion of résumés apply to any résumé you write, regardless of the sections you choose to include or the format you use.

How to Use the *Style Guide*

Using the Model Documents in the *Style Guide*

Step 1:
Read the model document, noting its organization, format, style, and tone.

Step 2:
Study the marginal comments for important notes, suggestions, and options.

Step 3:
Read the bottom comment for general guidance on writing the letter, memo, or document.

Step 4:
For further information or clarification, check one or more of the cross references, usually to entries in this *Style Guide*.

Letter, Proposal

▶ See LETTERS, pp. 75-91

Omit *Ms.* or *Mrs.* unless you know Linda Alvarez's preference. And in the salutation, if you don't want to use only the first name, either use *Dear Linda Alvarez* or omit the salutation. See LETTERS.

The content follows the 4-Box organization. The specific subject line and Paragraph 1 establish the purpose of the letter and introduce the three topics for discussion.

Use displayed lists to emphasize major points. No periods are necessary when listed items are not sentences. See LISTS.

Paragraphs 2, 3, and 4 each expand on one of these topics. Paragraph 5 closes the letter with an offer of more information.

Andromeda
7483 Esteles Court
Crescent Valley, CA 94057
714-555-9248

November 2, 1997

Linda Alvarez
Technical Support
TSX Inc.
234 Palo Verde Way
Dallas, TX 70647-3429

Dear Linda Alvarez:

Proposal to Andromeda for the Omega System

Gain greater speed, efficiency, and reliability with your computer system. The Omega System from Andromeda will give TSX Inc. the technical advantage needed to lead the engineering industry. During our phone conversation October 27, we determined the Omega System benefits your company in the following areas:

- Speed
- 3D modeling capability
- Reliability

Speed up your computer-aided design with the Omega System.

Reduce processing delays and ensure your graphics move smoothly. The 90 MHz processor gives you the speed required for computer-aided design. The system's access time is 16 milliseconds.

Support your 3D modeling software efficiently using the Omega System.

Develop complex graphics with clear detail when you use the power of a four gigabyte hard drive—installed by Andromeda professionals. Software for three-dimensional rendering works especially well on the system. Apollo and other applications, such as Intact and Move, are often used on the Omega System.

Rely on the Omega System backed by Andromeda experts.

Ensure your satisfaction with the Omega System because it includes a 9-month warranty. Receive all the benefits Andromeda offers when you purchase a system from us. Andromeda has invested 7 years of dedication in this superior product—approximately 35 percent of engineering CAD applications use an Andromeda system to ensure success.

For more information, please call me at 714-555-9248. I am anxious to help.

Sincerely,

John Rowski

John Rowski
Vice President, Marketing

JR:kn
Enc.

205

Proposal letters are essentially sales letters. They present details about a product or work to be done. Some proposal letters also give the cost for the service or product.

Highlight the benefits the customer receives from the product or service. In the above letter, faster design capabilities is the first benefit mentioned. The technical information about the 90 MHz processor is the product feature that provides the benefit. Benefits, not features, convince a customer to buy. See PERSUASION.

Reference Glossary

Table of Contents

Abbreviations	1–9
Active/Passive Voice	10–13
Agreement	14–17
Apostrophes	18–19
Bias-Free Language	20–24
Bibliography/Works Cited	25–28
Capitals	29–34
Citations	35–36
Colons	37–38
Commas	39–42
Conjunctions	43–46
Dashes	47–48
Ellipses	49–50
Emphasis	51–54
Graphics	55–60
Headings	61–63
Hyphens	64–67
Intellectual Property	68–70
Interviews	71–74
Letters	75–91
Lists	92–96
Memos	97–103
Numbers	104–107
Organization	108–114
Page Layout	115–125
Parallelism	126–127
Parentheses and Brackets	128–131
Persuasion	132–135
Plurals	136–138
Possessives	139–141
Quotation Marks	142–144
Résumés	145–160
Semicolons	161–162
Spelling	163–165
Titles	166–167
Tone	168–172
Transitions	173–174
Writing	175–184

English and Current Style

Like all languages, English is a set of conventions: sounds and ways to spell these sounds, words and ways to combine them, sentence structures, punctuation symbols, and word meanings that range from concrete to abstract.

These conventions change over time. Words are born, grow, and change in meaning; they evolve through usage and die from disuse when writers and speakers no longer need them. Similarly, punctuation, spelling, and stylistic conventions change. They evolve as the language adapts to printing presses, computers, space shuttles, television, new industries, changing social and political issues—in short, to everything in a constantly changing world.

English has changed dramatically since eighth-century *Beowulf*, one of the earliest English texts. Today, the original text of *Beowulf* looks as if it were written in a foreign language. English has even changed since Shakespeare was writing—only 400 years ago. The original language in Shakespeare's plays is often difficult for modern readers. And 400 years from now, readers of English will likely consider today's English just as challenging.

Living languages such as English constantly change. (Dead languages such as Latin do not.) If English were static, we could give precise rules for style and usage. We could ensure these rules were logical and consistent and had no unruly exceptions. But English conventions have evolved—often in unpredictable and seemingly nonsensical ways. The rules of English are not always logical; they are rarely consistent; and they have many exceptions.

However, with a little diligence and the right tools, you can use English effectively. This *Style Guide* is one of the right tools. **You** have to supply the diligence.

This *Style Guide* is written specifically to meet the needs of technical and business writers and readers. We have recorded the *currently* accepted stylistic conventions of English. We have labeled those conventions *rules,* but these rules merely describe the way language is now used in business and technical documents. The rules are not laws, and over time they will surely change. If you compare this *Style Guide* to other style guides or handbooks, you may find some disagreements.

We have simplified some discussions and descriptions to make them more useful to writers who are not experts in grammar and punctuation. Our simplifications do not misrepresent the current conventions of English grammar, but they may overlook certain exceptions and complexities (often of value only to university scholars).

Abbreviations are a form of shorthand used to make technical or repetitive information more accessible.

Abbreviations

Abbreviations are a form of shorthand appropriate in technical and business writing, particularly in lists, tables, charts, graphs, and other visual aids where space is limited.

The proper **use of abbreviations** allows writers to avoid cumbersome repetition of lengthy words and phrases. Following the rules, we have provided a **list of abbreviations** common for words and measurements.

Use of Abbreviations

1. Use periods in and after many standard abbreviations; however, punctuation is often eliminated in and after such abbreviations as acronyms and most units of measure.

Formerly, most abbreviations required periods. Today, the trend is to eliminate periods in and after abbreviations, especially in the abbreviated names of governmental agencies, companies, private organizations, and other groups:

AFL-CIO	AMA	CBS	DOE
FTC	IOOF	NFL	NLRB
OPEC	TVA	TWA	YWCA

NOTE 1: The abbreviations covered by this rule do not include informal ones such as *Dept.* and *Mgt.,* which use a final period but no periods between letters.

Preview

1. Use periods in and after many standard abbreviations; however, punctuation is often eliminated in and after such abbreviations as acronyms and most units of measure.

2. Use the same abbreviation for both singular and plural units of measurement.

3. Clarify an unfamiliar abbreviation by enclosing its unabbreviated form within parentheses following its first use in a document.

4. Do not abbreviate a unit of measurement unless it is used in conjunction with a number.

5. Do not abbreviate a title unless it precedes a name.

6. Spell out abbreviations that begin a sentence (except for abbreviated words that, by convention, are never spelled out, such as *Mr.* and *Mrs.*).

7. Spell out units of measurement connected to numbers by hyphens.

8. Do not abbreviate the names of months and days within normal text. Use the abbreviations in chronologies, notes, tables, and charts.

9. Avoid the symbol form of abbreviations within normal text. Use the symbol form in charts, graphs, illustrations, and other visual aids.

10. Use a single period when an abbreviation ends a sentence.

Abbreviations

NOTE 2: By convention some abbreviations still require periods:

A.D.	A.M.	B.C.	Dr.
e.g.	etc.	i.e.	Mr.
Mrs.	Ms.	P.M.	pp.
U.K.	U.S.A.		

NOTE 3: Notice A.M. and P.M. are presented in small capital letters. If your word processor cannot provide small capital letters, present these abbreviations in lowercase letters (*a.m., p.m.*). A.D. and B.C. are also presented in small capital letters. However, in this case, if your word processor cannot provide small capital letters, use uppercase letters to present these abbreviations: *A.D., B.C.*

Retain the period in abbreviations that spell normal words.

Do This

    in., inches

    no., number

Not This

    in

    no

A recent dictionary, such as the *Merriam-Webster Concise School and Office Dictionary*, is the best resource for determining if an abbreviation requires periods.

NOTE 4: Abbreviations with periods should be typed with no space between a period and a following letter.

Do This

    e.g.

    U.K.

Not This

    e. g.

    U. K.

---

2. Use the same abbreviation for both singular and plural units of measurement.

When you abbreviate a unit of measurement, use the same symbol for both the singular and the plural forms.

    6 lb and 1 lb

    3 m and 1 m

    20 ft and 1 ft

    23.5 cm and 1.0 cm

If you spell out the abbreviated word, use the plural form when the number is greater than one.

    15 kilometers and 1 kilometer

    6.8 meters and 1 meter

---

3. Clarify an unfamiliar abbreviation by enclosing its unabbreviated form within parentheses following its first use in a document.

    The applicant had insurance through CHAMPUS (Civilian Health and Medical Program of the Uniformed Services).

    All employees must identify their PINs (personal identification numbers) on the fitness surveys. Adding the PINs will speed processing time.

NOTE 1: Some authorities prefer to cite the unabbreviated form of the word before its

Abbreviations

abbreviation. We believe this practice slows the reader's comprehension of the abbreviation:

> The applicant had insurance through the Civilian Health and Medical Program of the Uniformed Services (CHAMPUS).

> All employees must identify their personal identification numbers (PINs) on the fitness surveys. Adding the PINs will speed processing time.

NOTE 2: Do not use an unfamiliar abbreviation unless you plan to use it more than once in the same document.

---

4. Do not abbreviate a unit of measurement unless it is used in conjunction with a number.

> Pipe diameters will be measured in inches.

> Standard pipe diameter is 3 in.

> The dimensions of the property were recorded in both meters and feet.

> The property is 88 ft by 130 ft.

> The southern property line is 45.3 m.

---

5. Do not abbreviate a title unless it precedes a name.

> The cardiac research unit comprises five experienced doctors.

> Our program director is Dr. Royce Smith.

---

6. Spell out abbreviations that begin a sentence (except for abbreviated words that, by convention, are never spelled out, such as *Mr.* and *Mrs.*).

Do This

> Oxygen extraction will be accomplished at high temperatures.

> Ms. Jean MacIntyre is responsible for preparing and presenting the report on athletic clothing sales.

Not This

> O_2 extraction will be accomplished at high temperatures.

---

7. Spell out units of measurement connected to numbers by hyphens.

Do This

> 6-foot gap

> 12-meter cargo bay

> 3.25-inch pipe

Not This

> 6-ft gap

> 12-m cargo bay

> 3.25-in. pipe

NOTE: The spelled-out form is preferred in text. The abbreviated form (as in *6-ft*) is common in some engineering documents, especially those with many numerical values. The hyphen is retained in the abbreviated form. See HYPHENS.

---

8. Do not abbreviate the names of months and days within normal text. Use the abbreviations in chronologies, notes, tables, and charts.

Abbreviations

Do This

The facilities modernization plan is due January 1997.

Not This

The facilities modernization plan is due Jan 1997.

The facilities modernization plan is due 1/97.

---

9. Avoid the symbol form of abbreviations within normal text. Use the symbol form in charts, graphs, illustrations, and other visual aids.

Do This

The company owns 55 percent of the existing computers.

You ordered an additional 15 ft of sprinkler pipe.

The width of the wallpaper needed is only 32.73 in.

Not This

The company owns 55% of the existing computers.

You ordered an additional 15' of sprinkler pipe.

The width of the wallpaper needed is only 32.73".

---

10. Use a single period when an abbreviation ends a sentence.

Do This

To head our laser redesign effort, we have hired the 1990 Nobel Prize winner from the U.S.A.

Not This

To head our laser redesign effort, we have hired the 1990 Nobel Prize winner from the U.S.A..

NOTE: If the clause or sentence ends with something other than a period (e.g., commas, semicolons, colons, question marks, exclamation points), the other mark of punctuation follows the period at the end of the abbreviation:

Have we hired the 1990 Nobel Prize winner from the U.S.A.?

If you plan to arrive by 6 P.M., you will not need to guarantee your reservation.

List of Abbreviations

Following is a list of many common abbreviations. Some abbreviations appear with periods, although the trend is to eliminate the periods (see Rule 1). For example, *Ph.D.* appears with periods to assist writers and typists who wish to retain the periods, although many writers today prefer the increasingly more common *PhD* without periods.

In this list, abbreviations printed without periods are ones that customarily appear without periods, e.g., *HF* or *PAC*.

Refer to *The Chicago Manual of Style,* 14th edition, and to the *Merriam-Webster Concise School and Office Dictionary.*

A

A	ampere
a	are
a	atto *(prefix, one-quintillionth)*
A.B. or **B.A.**	bachelor of arts
abbr.	abbreviation

Abbreviations

abs	absolute *(temperature and gravity)*
abs.	abstract
ac	alternating current
acct.	account
A.D. *(anno Domini)*	in the year of the Lord
ADP	automated data processing
AF	audio-frequency
Ah	ampere-hour
a.k.a.	also known as
A/m	ampere per meter
A.M. *(anno mundi)*	in the year of the world
A.M. or M.A.	master of arts
A.M. *(ante meridiem)*	before noon
approx.	approximately
at	atmosphere
atm	atmosphere *(infrequently,* As)
at wt	atomic weight
au	astronomical units
Ave.	avenue

B

b	barn
b	bit
bbl	barrel
bbl/d	barrel per day
B.C.	before Christ
Bd	baud
bd. ft.	board foot *(obsolete)*; use fbm
bf.	boldface
bhp	horsepower
Bldg.	building
B.Lit(t). or Lit(t).B.	bachelor of literature
Blvd.	boulevard
bm	board measure
b.o.	buyer's option
bp	boiling point
B.S. or B.Sc.	bachelor of science
Btu	British thermal unit
bu	bushel

C

c. and s.c.	caps and small caps
c, ¢, ct	cent(s)
c	centi *(prefix, one-hundredth)*
c	cycle *(radio)*
°C	degree Celsius
ca. *(circa)*	about
cal	calorie
c.b.d.	cash before delivery
cf. *(confer)*	compare or see
cg	centigram
c·h	candela-hour
cL	centiliter
cm	centimeter
c/m	cycles per minute
cm^2	square centimeter
cm^3	cubic centimeter
Co.	company
c.o.d.	cash on delivery
COLA	cost of living adjustment
con.	continued
Conus.	continental United States
corp.	corporation
cp	candlepower
cP	centipoise
C.P.A.	certified public accountant
cr.	credit; creditor
cSt	centistokes
Ct.	court
cu ft *(obsolete)*	use ft^3
cu in *(obsolete)*	use in^3
cwt	hundredweight

Abbreviations

D

d	day
d	deci (*prefix, one-tenth*)
dB	decibel
d.b.a.	doing business as
dc	direct current
D.D.	doctor of divinity
D.D.S.	doctor of dental surgery
Dist. Ct.	District Court
D.Lit(t). or Lit(t).D.	doctor of literature
do (ditto)	the same
dol	dollar
doz	dozen
DP	displaced person
D.P.H.	doctor of public health
D.P.Hy.	doctor of public hygiene
dr.	debit; debtor
Dr.	doctor; drive
D.V.M.	doctor of veterinary medicine

E

E.	east
e.g. (*exempli gratia*)	for example
emcee	master of ceremony
emu	electromagnetic unit
e.o.m.	end of month
et al. (*et alii*)	and others
et seq. (*et sequentia*)	and the following
etc. (*et cetera*)	and others

F

f., ff.	and following page (pages)
°F	degree Fahrenheit
fbm	board foot; board foot measure
f.o.b.	free on board
ft	foot
ft^2	square foot
ft^3	cubic foot
ft/min	foot per minute

G

g	gram; acceleration of gravity
gal	gallon
gal/min	gallons per minute
gal/s	gallons per second
GI	general issue; government issue
G.M.&S.	general, medical, and surgical
GNP	gross national product
Gov.	governor
Govt.	government
gr	grain; gross
gr. wt.	gross weight

H

h	hour
HE	high explosive
HF	high frequency
hp	horsepower
Hz	hertz (cycles per second)

I

ibid. (*ibidem*)	in the same place
id	inside diameter
id. (*idem*)	the same
i.e. (*id est*)	that is
ihp	indicated horsepower
in.	inch
in^2	square inch
in^3	cubic inch
Insp. Gen.	Inspector General
IOU	I owe you
IQ	intelligence quotient

Abbreviations

J

J.D. *(jurum doctor)*	doctor of laws
Jr.	junior

K

k	kilo *(prefix, 1,000)*
k	thousand (7k = 7,000)
kc	kilocycle
kg	kilogram
kHz	kilohertz
km	kilometer
kn	knot *(speed)*
kW	kilowatt
kWh	kilowatt-hour

L

L	liter *(also l)*
lat.	latitude
lb	pound
lb/ft	pound per foot
lb/ft^2	pound per square foot
lb/ft^3	pound per cubic foot
LC	Library of Congress
lc.	lowercase
liq.	liquid
lf.	lightface
LF	low frequency
LL.B.	bachelor of laws
LL.D.	doctor of laws
l/m	lines per minute
loc. cit. *(loco citato)*	in the place cited
long.	longitude
l/s	lines per second
L/s	liter per second
Ltd.	limited
Lt. Gov.	lieutenant governor

M

M	mega *(prefix, 1 million)*
m	meter
m	milli *(prefix, one-thousandth)*
M	million (3M = 3 million)
M	money supply: M_1; M_{1B}; M_2
M.	monsieur *(plural, MM., messieurs)*
m. *(meridies)*	noon
M.D.	doctor of medicine
memo	memorandum
mg	milligram
MHz	megahertz
mHz	millihertz
mi	mile *(statute)*
mi^2	square mile
MIA	missing in action *(plural, MIAs)*
mi/h	mile per hour
min	minute *(time)*
mL	milliliter
Mlle.	mademoiselle
mm	millimeter
Mme.	madam *(plural, Mmes., mesdames)*
mo.	month
mol wt	molecular weight
mp	melting point
Mr.	mister *(plural, Messrs.)*
Mrs.	mistress
Ms.	coined feminine title *(plural, Mses.)*
M.S.	master of science
MS., MSS.	manuscript, manuscripts
ms	millisecond
Msgr.	monsignor
m.s.l.	mean sea level
MW	megawatt
mW	milliwatt

N

n	nano *(prefix, one-billionth)*
N.	north

Abbreviations

NA.	not available; not applicable
NE.	northeast
n.e.c.	not elsewhere classified
n.e.s.	not elsewhere specified
net wt.	net weight
No., Nos.	number, numbers
n.o.i.b.n.	not otherwise indexed by name
n.o.p.	not otherwise provided (for)
n.o.s.	not otherwise specified
n.s.k.	not specified by kind
n.s.p.f.	not specifically provided for
NW.	northwest

O

od	outside diameter
OK	OK'd, OK'ing, OK's
op. cit. *(opere citato)*	in the work cited
oz	ounce *(avoirdupois)*

P

p	pico *(prefix, one-trillionth)*
PA	public address system
PAC	political action committee *(plural, PACs)*
pct	percent
Ph.B. or B.Ph.	bachelor of philosophy
Ph.D. or D.Ph.	doctor of philosophy
Ph.G.	graduate in pharmacy
PIN	personal identification number
Pl.	place
P.M. *(post meridiem)*	afternoon
p/m	parts per million
P.O. Box *(w/ number)*	but post office box *(in general sense)*
POW	prisoner of war *(plural, POWs)*
Prof.	professor
pro tem *(pro tempore)*	temporarily
P.S. *(post scriptum)*	postscript; public school *(with number)*
pt	pint

Q

QT	on the quiet
qt	quart

R

RAM	random access memory
R&D	research and development
Rd.	road
RDT&E	research, development, testing, and evaluation
Rev.	reverend
RF	radio frequency
R.F.D.	rural free delivery
r/min	revolutions per minute
R.N.	registered nurse
RR.	railroad
r/s	revolutions per second
Ry.	railway

S

s	second *(time)*
S.	south; Senate bill *(with number)*
S&L(s)	savings and loan(s)
sc. *(scilicet)*	namely *(see also ss)*
s.c.	small caps
s.d. *(sine die)*	without date

Abbreviations

SE.	southeast	**V**	
2d, 3d	second, third	**v. or vs.** *(versus)*	against
sic	thus	**V**	volt
SOP	standard operating procedure	**VA**	voltampere
		VAT	value added tax
SOS	wireless distress signal	**VCR**	videocassette recorder
sp. gr.	specific gravity	**VHF**	very high frequency
Sq.	square *(street)*	**VIP**	very important person
Sr.	senior	**viz** *(videlicet)*	namely
SS	steamship	**VTR**	videotape recording
ss *(scilicet)*	namely *(in law)* *(see also* sc.)		
St., Ste., SS.	Saint, Sainte, Saints	**W**	
St.	street	**W**	watt
STP	standard temperature and pressure	**W.**	west
		w.a.e.	when actually employed
Supt.	superintendent	**wf**	wrong font
Surg.	surgeon	**Wh**	watt-hour
SW.	southwest	**w.o.p.**	without pay
T		**X**	
T., Tps.	township, townships	**x**	unknown quantity
tbsp	tablespoonful		
Ter.	terrace	**Y**	
t.m.	true mean		
ton	ton	**yd**	yard
tsp	teaspoonful	**y**	year
TV	television		
		Z	
U		**ZIP Code**	Zone Improvement Plan Code *(Postal Service)*
uc.	uppercase		
UHF	ultrahigh frequency	**ZIP+4**	9-digit ZIP Code
U.S.A.	United States of America		
USA	U.S. Army		
U.S. 40, U.S. No. 40	U.S. Highway No. 40		

Active/Passive Voice

Business writing is more effective when written in the active voice, except in rare situations.

Active- and passive-voice sentences usually have three basic elements:

- The actor—the person or thing performing the action
- The action—the verb
- The receiver—the person or thing receiving the action

When the subject of the sentence is the one doing the action, the sentence is in the active voice:

> Australian companies manufacture millions of machine tools.

Companies is the actor; *manufacture* is the action; and *tools* receives the action. Because the subject of the sentence performs the action, the sentence is active.

When the subject of the sentence is the receiver of the action, the sentence is in the passive voice:

> Millions of machine tools are manufactured by Australian companies.

In this sentence, the subject (*tools*) is not doing the manufacturing. The tools are being manufactured. They are being acted upon; they are receiving the action. Therefore, the verb—and the sentence—is passive.

---

1. Prefer active sentences.

Active sentences are usually shorter and more dynamic than passive sentences. They generally have more impact and seem more natural because readers expect the actor-action-receiver pattern. Active writing is more forceful and more self-confident.

Passive writing, on the other hand, can seem weak-willed, indecisive, or evasive. In passive sentences, the reader encounters the action before learning who performed it. In some passive sentences, the reader never discovers who performed the action. Whenever your writing requires your readers to do or know something, the active voice is more effective.

Preview

1. Prefer active sentences.

2. Use passive voice when you don't know or don't want to mention the person responsible.

3. Use a passive sentence when the receiver is more important than the actor.

4. Use a passive sentence when you need to form a smooth transition from one sentence to the next.

5. Do not use passive sentences to avoid using first-person pronouns.

6. Make sentences active by turning the clause or sentence around.

7. Make sentences active by changing the verb.

8. Make sentences active by rethinking the sentence.

Active/Passive Voice

Most business writing requires action, so avoid passive sentences.

---

2. Use passive voice when you don't know or don't want to mention the person responsible.

> The failure occurred when the pressure dropped below the minimum level.
>
> The site had been inspected, but we found no report.

In the first example above, a passive sentence is acceptable because we don't know why the pressure dropped. In the second example, we might know who inspected the site but don't want to mention names because the situation could be sensitive or politically charged.

---

3. Use a passive sentence when the receiver is more important than the actor.

The strongest part of most sentences is the opening. Therefore, the sentence element appearing first will receive greater emphasis than those elements appearing later in the sentence. For this reason, a passive sentence is useful when you wish to emphasize the receiver of the action:

> Bonding techniques—the most important of our innovations—are currently being tested in our Latin American laboratory.
>
> Material size or thickness requirements will be established to ensure quality standards.

In both examples, we wish to emphasize the receiver of the action. Note how emphasis changes if we restructure the first example:

> The most important of our innovations (bonding techniques) is currently being tested in our Latin American laboratory.
>
> Our Latin American laboratory is currently testing the most important of our innovations—bonding techniques.
>
> Our Latin American laboratory is currently testing bonding techniques—the most important of our innovations.

The emphasis in each sentence differs, depending on sentence structure. The first revision emphasizes *innovations* and is still a passive sentence. The last two revisions are active, and both stress our *Latin American laboratory*.

The ending of a sentence is also emphatic (although not as emphatic as the beginning), so the sentence ending with *techniques* does place secondary emphasis on techniques. However, the best way to emphasize bonding techniques is by opening the sentence with that phrase.

---

4. Use a passive sentence when you need to form a smooth transition from one sentence to the next.

Occasionally, writers must arrange sentence elements so key words appearing in both sentences are near enough to each other for readers to grasp the connection between the sentences immediately. In the example below, for instance, the writer needs to form a smooth transition between sentences by repeating the key words *work packages:*

Do This

> We will develop a simplified list of tasks that will include all budget and work packages. These work packages will be scheduled and monitored by individual program managers.

11

Active/Passive Voice

The second sentence is passive. Although it would be shorter and stronger as an active sentence, it would not connect as well with the previous sentence:

Not This

> We will develop a simplified list of tasks that will include all budget and work packages. Individual program managers will schedule and monitor these work packages.

For a brief moment, the second sentence seems to have changed the subject. Not until readers reach the end of the second sentence will they realize that both sentences concern work packages. Therefore, making the second sentence passive creates a smoother transition and actually improves the passage.

---

5. Do not use passive sentences to avoid using first-person pronouns.

Some writers use passives to avoid using first person pronouns (*I, me, we,* or *us*). These writers wrongly believe first person pronouns are inappropriate in business writing. In fact, first person is preferable to awkward or ambiguous passive sentences like the example below:

> It is recommended that a state-of-the-art survey be added to the study.

Who is recommending it? You? The customer? Someone else? And who is supposed to add the survey?

In the following sentences, things seem to be happening, but no one seems to be doing them:

> Cost data will be collected and maintained to provide a detailed history of the employee hours worked during the program. This tracking effort will be accomplished by the use of a tracking system.

Writers who overuse the passive to avoid first-person pronouns convey the impression that they don't want to accept the responsibility for their actions. This implication is why passive sentences can seem evasive even when the writer doesn't intend them to be.

Passives allow you to eliminate the actor. In some cases, eliminating the actor is appropriate and desirable. In other cases (as in the previous examples), eliminating the actor creates confusion and doubt. Active versions of these examples, using first-person pronouns, are much better:

> We recommend that the study include a state-of-the-art survey.

> Using our tracking system, we will collect and maintain cost data to provide a detailed history of the employee hours worked during the program.

How to Convert Passives

Technical and scientific writers generally use too many passives. They use them unnecessarily, often more from habit than choice. Converting unneeded passives to actives will strengthen the style of the document, making it appear crisper and more confident. The following rules present three techniques for converting passives to actives.

---

6. Make sentences active by turning the clause or sentence around.

Passive

> These methods are described in more detail in Section 6.

Active

> Section 6 describes these methods in more detail.

Active/Passive Voice

Passive

Antilock brakes on both front wheels are activated by an on-board computer chip.

Active

An on-board computer chip activates antilock brakes on both front wheels.

Passive

After the project requirements are identified, we will develop a comprehensive list of available resource materials.

Active

After identifying the project requirements, we will develop a comprehensive list of available resource materials.

---

7. Make sentences active by changing the verb.

Passive

Inventory shortages were prevented by the development of new supply channels.

Active

Inventory shortages stopped after the development of new supply channels.

Passive

The in-line skate can be thought of as an ice skate "converted" to have wheels instead of a blade.

Active

The in-line skate is an ice skate "converted" to have wheels instead of a blade.

Passive

The job promotion requirements are expected to bring added emphasis to customer service.

Active

The job promotion requirements will probably emphasize customer service.

---

8. Make sentences active by rethinking the sentence.

Passive

Special consideration must be given to season ticket holders and owners of box seats.

Active

Season ticket holders and owners of box seats are especially important.

Passive

To ensure a good alternate stadium location is not overlooked, a comparison between urban and suburban sites will be made during the study.

Active

Comparing urban and suburban sites during the study will ensure that we consider alternate stadium locations.

Passive

This study will show what can be done to eliminate on-the-job injuries by shortening employee work shifts.

Active

This study will show how shortening employee work shifts can eliminate on-the-job injuries.

Agreement

Agreement is a basic grammatical rule that stipulates subjects and verbs must agree in number.

Agreement is a basic grammatical rule of English. According to this rule, subjects of sentences must agree in number with their verbs. This means that a subject that is a single person, place, or thing (noun or pronoun) must have a singular verb. A subject that is more than one person, place, or thing (noun or pronoun) must have a plural verb.

Singular and Plural Subjects and Verbs	Do This
Singular Noun + Singular Verb	The **proposal was** finished.
Plural Noun + Plural Verb	The **proposals were** finished.
Singular Pronoun + Singular Verb	**She is** our competitor on most major sales.
Plural Pronoun + Plural Verb	**They are** our competitors on most major sales.

Agreement also refers to the singular/plural agreement between pronouns and their antecedents (the words the pronouns stand for).

Jane Swenson submitted **her** report. (The pronoun her agrees with its antecedent Jane Swenson.)

Preview

1. The subject of a sentence (nouns or pronouns) should agree in number with the sentence verb.

2. Subjects connected by *and* require a plural verb.

3. Singular subjects connected by *either . . . or*, *neither . . . nor*, and *not only . . . but also* require a singular verb.

4. When used as a subject or as the modifier of the subject, *each, every, either, neither, one, another, much, anybody, anyone, everybody, everyone, somebody, someone, nobody*, and *no one* require singular verbs.

5. When used as a subject or as the modifier of a subject, *both, few, several, many*, and *others* require plural verbs.

6. *All, any, more, most, none, some, one-half of, two-thirds of, a part of,* and *a percentage of* require either a singular or a plural verb, depending upon the noun to which they refer.

7. Collective nouns and expressions with time, money, and quantities take a singular or a plural verb, depending upon their intended meaning.

---

1. The subject of a sentence (nouns or pronouns) should agree in number with the sentence verb.

Agreement

The **geologist is** examining rock samples. (singular noun and singular verb)

The **employees are** discussing the promotion policies. (plural noun and plural verb)

I am going to attend the student business conference in June.

We are designing a student government handbook.

Elements of Literature **is** the basic textbook.

Our **textbooks are** usually translated into Spanish, French, and German.

A **list** of Midwest states normally **includes** Kentucky and Missouri.

NOTE 1: Notice that a noun ending with an –*s* or –*es* is usually plural. A verb ending with an –*s* or –*es* is usually singular. *Employees* is plural. The verbs *is* and *includes* are both singular. Some verbs do not change their form to reflect singular and plural: *will include, included, had included, will have included,* etc.

Agreement problems sometimes occur because the subject of the sentence is not clearly singular or plural:

None of the **crew is** going to take leave.

OR

None of the **crew are** going to take leave.

NOTE 2: Both versions of the preceding are correct because *crew* is a collective noun and thus is either singular or plural. See Rule 7.

Don't become confused when the subject is separated from the verb by words or phrases that do not agree in number with the subject:

Only **one** of the issues we discussed **is** on the agenda for tomorrow's meeting.

One aspect of the problem we are now facing **is** not clear.

The **availability** of rice, as well as of medical supplies, **determines** the life expectancy of a typical adult in Hong Kong.

The verb agrees with its subject even if the subject follows the verb:

What **are** your **reasons** for suggesting a tax increase?

There **are** five new **pumps** in the warehouse.

Discussed are the basic design **flaws** in the preliminary specifications and the lack of adequate detail in the drawings.

Some noun subjects may look plural because they end in –*s* or –*ics*, but they are still singular:

Politics has changed drastically with the invention of television.

The **news** from Algeria **continues** to be discouraging.

Measles rarely **occurs** in adults.

---

2. Subjects connected by *and* require a plural verb.

Note: In the examples that follow, the subject and verb are boldfaced; the connecting word is shown in blue.

The **ceiling panels** and the **fasteners have been fabricated**.

The regional **engineer** and the field **geologist agree** that we should plug and abandon the well.

Agreement

A personal **computer** and a **photocopier are** essential business tools today.

EXCEPTION: Sometimes words connected by *and* become so closely linked that they become singular in meaning. In these cases, use a singular verb:

Bacon and **eggs is** my favorite breakfast.

Law and **order was** his major campaign issue in November.

---

3. Singular subjects connected by *or, either . . . or, neither . . . nor*, and *not only . . . but also* require a singular verb.

John or **Mary is** responsible for completing the report.

Either the tail **assembly** or the wing **design** of the airplane **is causing** excessive fuel consumption.

Neither the district **engineer** nor the **superintendent has approved** the plans.

Not only the **cost** but also the **design is** a problem.

NOTE: When one of a pair of subjects is plural, make the verb agree with the subject closest to it. (In the following examples the subject closest to the verb is underlined.)

Either the tail **assembly** or the wing <u>**struts**</u> **are causing** excessive fuel consumption.

Either the wing **struts** or the tail <u>**assembly**</u> **is causing** excessive fuel consumption.

The **company** or the company's <u>**lawyers**</u> **are sending** the forms.

---

4. When used as a subject or as the modifier of the subject, *each, every, either, neither,* *one, another, much, anybody, anyone, everybody, everyone, somebody, someone, nobody,* and *no one* require singular verbs.

Every **proposal has been evaluated**.

Each **engineer is** responsible for the final proofing of engineering proposals.

Everyone **has received** the pension information.

Somebody **was** responsible for the drop in production.

No one but the design engineer **knows** the load factors used in the calculations.

NOTE: Although words ending with *–one* and *–body* require a singular verb, sentences with such words often become awkward when a pronoun refers to the words:

Everyone **turns** in his report on Monday.

Use the singular pronoun *his* to maintain the agreement with the subject, but if the *everyone* mentioned includes women, the expression is sexist if you use *his*. Writers and editors who avoid sexist pronouns prefer to include both men and women in their sentences:

Everyone **turns** in his or her report on Monday.

Finally, some editors argue that *everyone* implies a plurality, so the plural *their* becomes the acceptable pronoun:

Everyone **turns** in their reports on Monday.

The sexism problem is avoidable in most sentences simply by making the subject plural and eliminating such troublesome words as *everyone*:

Agreement

All engineers **turn** in their reports on Monday.

You can choose which convention to use as long as you avoid sexist language. See BIAS-FREE LANGUAGE.

---

5. **When used as a subject or as the modifier of a subject, *both, few, several, many,* and *others* require plural verbs.**

   Both **proposals were** unsatisfactory.

   Several **were** available earlier this month.

   Few **pipes were** still in service.

---

6. ***All, any, more, most, none, some, one-half (of), two-thirds (of), a part (of),* and *a percentage (of)* require either a singular or a plural verb, depending upon the noun to which they refer.**

   All of the ***work has been assigned***. (singular)

   All of the **trucks have left.** (plural)

   Most **sugar is** now **made** from sugar beets.

   Most **errors were caused** by carelessness.

   Some of the **report was written** in an overly ornate style.

   Some design **features were** mandatory.

One-half of the **project is ready for mailing.**

One-half of the **pages have been edited.**

A percentage of the **room is** for storage.

A percentage of the **employees belong** to the company credit union.

---

7. **Collective nouns and expressions with time, money, and quantities take a singular or a plural verb, depending upon their intended meaning.**

   The committee **votes** on pension policy when disputes occur. (Committee, a collective noun, is considered singular.)

   The committee **do** not **agree** on the interpretation of the mandatory retirement clause. (Committee, a collective noun, is considered plural.)

   Two years **is** the usual waiting period. (Two years is an expression of time considered as a single unit.)

   The two years **were** each divided into quarters for accounting purposes. (Two years is an expression of time considered as a plural of year.)

   Six dollars **is** the fee.

   Six dollars **were** spread out on the counter.

   Five liters **is** all the tank can hold.

   Five liters of spring water **were sold** before noon.

17

Apostrophes indicate omitted letters, possession, time passage in certain phrases, and the plural of letters and symbols.

Apostrophes signal omitted letters, possession, and the plural of letters and symbols. An apostrophe (') can appear with or without a following –s.

Preview

1. Apostrophes indicate omitted letters, words, or numbers in a contraction.

2. Apostrophes indicate possession.

3. Apostrophes indicate the passage of time in certain commonly used phrases.

4. Apostrophes may come before the –s in the plural of letters, signs, symbols, figures, acronyms, and abbreviations. (The trend in business writing is to omit the apostrophe unless this would be confusing.)

1. Apostrophes indicate omitted letters, words, or numbers in a contraction.

It's not going to be easy. (It is not going . . .)

It **won't** be easy. (It will not be . . .)

We will coordinate with the manufacturer **who's** chosen to supply the belts. (. . . who is chosen . . .)

He was the acting director in **'95**. (. . . in 1995.)

NOTE: Use contractions in letters and memos to help establish an informal tone. Avoid contractions in more formal, edited documents. See TONE.

2. Apostrophes indicate possession.

DeKar's manufacturing capabilities are world renowned.

The **unit's** most unique feature is its double-screen filter.

- When the possessive word is plural and ends in –s, the apostrophe follows the –s:

The **suppliers'** requests are not unreasonable.

The **states'** concern for the environment is growing.

- Irregular plurals that do not end in –s require an –'s to show possession:

The report on **women's** status in the work force is due next Friday.

Materials for **children's** toys must comply with federal safety standards.

- When the possessive word is singular, the apostrophe comes before the –s:

Bellmont International's process for budgeting is very progressive.

The **circuit's** most unique feature is its durability.

- When the possessive word is singular and already ends with an –s, the apostrophe follows the –s and may itself be followed by another –s (although most writers prefer the apostrophe alone):

International Computers' (or **Computers's**) proposal includes specific suggestions for employee wages and benefits.

Apostrophes

Dr. Jones' experience has made him a leader in the field.

NOTE: The possessive form of the pronoun *it* is *its*, not *it's* (*it's* is the contraction of *it is* or *it has*):

Possessive: **Its** products have over 10,000 hours of testing behind them.

Contraction: **It's** (It is) in the company's interest that we carry out the safety program now.

Similarly, the possessive form of *who* is *whose*, not *who's*. *Who's* is a contraction for *who is* or *who has*.

See POSSESSIVES.

---

3. **Apostrophes indicate the passage of time in certain commonly used phrases.**

   a **month's** pay

   an **hour's** time

   4 **days'** work

   3 **years'** study

4. **Apostrophes may come before the –s in the plural of letters, signs, symbols, figures, acronyms, and abbreviations. (The trend is to omit the apostrophe unless this would be confusing.)**

   The **Xs** indicate added material. (or X's or x's but not xs)

   Our management process eliminates the **if's** and **but's**.

   All our senior staff have **Ph.D.s** (or Ph.D.'s)

   Put **#'s** in any of the last three positions in the transportation code.

   The code will include the **A's** and **I's**. (not As or Is nor as or is)

   The corporation began its strict safety program in the early **1990s.** (or 1990's)

   The research staff have prepared three **EAs** (Employee Assessments) for your review. (or EA's)

Cultural awareness is increasingly important for business and technical writers and speakers.

Bias-Free Language

Bias-free language is increasingly an important issue for business and technical writers and speakers. Bias-free language does not slant or influence the reader's opinion before the facts are known. Careful use of **nonprejudicial** and **gender-neutral language** removes unnecessary and objectionable distinctions in communication.

Nonprejudicial Language

Language must be unbiased, free of stereotypes, and fair in its treatment of all people. For example, unjustified references to a person's age, race, or gender may be interpreted as a subtle message about the person's ability to perform a job adequately. Your choice of words or representations should not show partiality or discrimination.

1. Do not use words that unnecessarily identify a person's race, religion, physical status, social status, age, national origin, or gender.

In most instances, write documents giving a person's name and, if appropriate, their job title. Do not include, for example, references indicating that the person is a Native American, a Methodist, a woman, the user of a wheelchair, a vegetarian, nearly 65, or born in Puerto Rico. These categorizations are irrelevant to any serious discussion of business topics.

Preview

1. Do not use words that unnecessarily identify a person's race, religion, physical status, social status, age, national origin, or gender.

2. When appropriate, choose terms and designations that are neutral and acceptable to the group you are discussing.

3. Be sure to choose graphics—especially photographs—that fairly represent all groups and types of people within society.

4. Do not use words that unnecessarily distinguish between male and female.

5. Avoid unnecessary uses of *he, him,* or *his* to refer back to such indefinite pronouns as *everyone, everybody, someone,* and *somebody*.

6. Avoid unnecessary uses of *he, him, his* or *she, her, hers* when the word refers to both males and females.

7. Avoid the traditional salutation *Gentlemen* if the organization receiving the letter includes males and females.

8. Do not substitute *s/he, he/she, hisorher,* or other such hybrid forms for standard personal pronouns.

9. Do not call adult females *girls,* especially in a business or technical situation.

United States federal and many state laws mandate that an employee may not be discriminated against based on race, creed, sex, age,

Bias-Free Language

disability, or national origin. These laws have various provisions, but penalties for violations apply both to individual employees and to their company.

NOTE 1: In some contexts, such personal categories are appropriate for discussion and documentation. Census surveys routinely ask for such information. The personnel department for a company may develop survey information about employees to comply with federal guidelines relating to Equal Employment Opportunity or Affirmative Action programs.

NOTE 2: In a résumé do not include information about your race, creed, sex, age, disability, or national origin. Also, in a job interview employers should not ask you about these personal features. See RÉSUMÉS.

Usually personal information about any of these categories should be kept confidential.

Do This

person who uses crutches

person without sight (or with partial sight)

person mentally disabled (or mentally impaired)

person unable to speak

person with multiple sclerosis

person who doesn't speak clearly

Not This

crippled

blind

mentally defective

dumb

afflicted with MS

unfortunately has a speech problem

---

2. When appropriate, choose terms and designations that are neutral and acceptable to the group you are discussing.

News articles, research reports, and other serious documents properly and legally analyze and discuss data for various groups. Such discussions, which would not be based on stereotypes, include terms for a group or category of person.

When you use racial or ethnic terms to identify a group of people, be careful to choose the one most current and acceptable. If in doubt, don't assume your choice makes no difference. Your choice may be insulting and even a legal issue.

When dealing with people who have disabilities, choose terms and phrases that do not emphasize the negative features of the disabilities.

3. Be sure to choose graphics—especially photographs—that fairly represent all groups and types of people within society.

All photographs, illustrations, cartoons, etc., need to be balanced as to their representations of typical people. The graphics should not rely on either an obvious or a subtle use of stereotyping.

A recent court case dealt with a realty firm that consistently advertised using pictures of middle-aged Caucasians who appeared wealthy. In court, the firm was challenged as sending a signal that first-time black buyers would not be welcome. The realty firm lost.

The same sort of problem exists in training materials or procedures that present women in secretarial roles and men in managerial roles. Again, this is a subtle reliance on stereotypes.

Bias-Free Language

Gender-Neutral Language

Gender signals are an integral part of our language. From its earliest history, English has often marked words as either male or female (and even sometimes neuter). Pronouns are the most common surviving examples: *he, him, his* vs. *she, her, hers.*

A number of nouns also have had different male and female forms: *waiter/waitress, steward/stewardess, heir/heiress, count/countess, host/hostess, actor/actress, usher/usherette.* And some words used for everyone seem to include only males: *mankind, layman, manpower,* and so on.

Many such distinctions, called gender distinctions, have become objectionable, especially in recent years. Many publishing firms and most writers now routinely remove unnecessary and objectionable gender distinctions from published writing.

---

4. Do not use words that unnecessarily distinguish between male and female.

Do This

    flight attendant

    people, humans

    work force

    layperson (amateur)

    employee

    heir

    chair (moderator)

    serving person

Not This

    stewardess

    mankind

    manpower

    layman

    workman

    heiress

    chairman

    waitress

NOTE 1: The use of female forms such as *waitress* and *heiress* has declined. *Heir* now includes both male and female; *waiter* still has male echoes, but these may fade soon. The best advice is to be sensitive to this issue and avoid female forms.

NOTE 2: Historically the word *man* (especially used in compound words like *chairman* or *layman*) could include both males and females; its closest modern equivalent would be, for instance, the indefinite pronoun *one* or *person*. Where possible, use the more neutral term. Often a number of replacement words exist.

---

5. Avoid unnecessary uses of *he, him,* or *his* to refer back to such indefinite pronouns as *everyone, everybody, someone,* and *somebody.*

The problem sentences are often ones in which the indefinite pronouns introduce a single person and then a later pronoun refers to that person:

Everyone should take (his? her?) coat.

Someone left (his? her?) report.

Bias-Free Language

Unless we clearly know who *everyone* and *someone* refer to, we cannot pick the proper singular pronoun. We thus have to choose among several options:

- Make the sentences plural, if possible:

All **employees** should take **their** coats.

- Remove the pronoun entirely:

Someone left a (*or* this) report.

- Use both the male and female pronouns:

Each **employee** should take **his** or **her** coat.

Someone left **his** or **her** report.

See AGREEMENT.

---

6. Avoid unnecessary uses of *he, him, his* or *she, her, hers* when the word refers to both males and females.

As with Rule 5, writers have several options:

- Change the sentences to plurals:

Secretaries should set **their** priorities daily.

Writers should begin **their** outlines with the main point.

- Remove the pronouns:

Do This

The **engineer** began the presentation with an overhead transparency.

A **secretary** should set firm priorities daily.

Not This

A **secretary** should set **her** (his?) priorities each day.

The **engineer** opened **her** (his?) presentation with an overhead transparency.

A **writer** should begin **his** (her?) outline with the main point.

NOTE: The third option (offered in Rule 5) of using the phrase *his or her* becomes clumsy in a text of any length, so it is better to use one of the first two options given.

---

7. Avoid the traditional salutation *Gentlemen* if the organization receiving the letter includes males and females.

Omit the salutation if your letter is to an organization, not to an individual. Your letter would then have an inside address, a subject line, followed by your text. This format is called a simplified block letter. See LETTERS.

If you are writing to individuals, but you don't know their gender, use the title or the name without a title:

Dear Personnel Manager:

Dear Amy Smithers:

Dear G. L. Branson:

Dear Volunteers:

NOTE 1: We do not recommend *Ladies and Gentlemen* or *Gentlemen and Ladies*. The term *Ladies* (and maybe *Gentlemen*) seems old-fashioned. Similarly, *Dear Sir or Madam* is old-fashioned and overly formal.

Bias-Free Language

NOTE 2: In recent years a number of unusual salutations have appeared. Avoid them.

Not This

    Dear Gentlepersons:

    Dear Gentlepeople:

    Dear People:

    Dear Folks:

---

8. Do not substitute *s/he, he/she, hisorher*, or other such hybrid forms for standard personal pronouns.

These hybrid forms are unpronounceable and are not universally accepted by English users, so avoid them. Instead, either remove pronouns or change the sentences to plurals, as suggested under Rule 6.

Where you must use singular personal pronouns, use *she and he, his or her*, or *her and him*.

---

9. Do not call adult females *girls*, especially in a business or technical situation.

Referring to adult females as *girls* is not acceptable to most people except in contexts (typically humorous) in which it would also be appropriate to refer to adult males as *boys*. Labeling women as *girls* in serious (or even casual) conversation indicates a bias (intentional or otherwise) that is inappropriate in the business and technical community.

Bibliographic entries provide complete source references for cited information.

Bibliography/Works Cited

Bibliographic forms appear in standard bibliographies at the end of chapters, articles, and books. Whatever the exact form, complete bibliographic entries include the name of the author, the title, and the full publication history (including the edition, the publisher or press, the city of publication, and the date of publication).

The bibliographic form we illustrate is the format used by the Modern Language Association (MLA).

The title "Works Cited" is increasingly the preferred title or heading for a list of references in a report (i.e., a list of books, magazine articles, newspaper articles, personal letters, videotapes, audiotapes, or any other sources). The items listed usually include only those actually cited in the body of the report. See CITATIONS.

NOTE: In the following rules, the titles of publications in bibliographic entries are italicized. Underlining replaces italics when documents are typed or when italic type is not available.

Preview

1. For a book, give the name of the author or authors, the full title, the volume number, the edition, the city of publication, the publisher, and the date of publication.

2. For a journal or a magazine article, give the name of the author or authors, the full title of the article (in quotation marks), the name of the journal or magazine, the volume, the month or quarter of publication, the year of publication, and the page numbers.

3. For unpublished material, give the author or authors, the title (in quotation marks), and as much of its history as available.

4. For public documents, give the country, state, county, or other government division; the full title; and complete publication information.

5. Alphabetize bibliographic entries by the author's last name.

---

1. For a book, give the name of the author or authors, the full title, the volume number, the edition, the city of publication, the publisher, and the date of publication.

Book by one author

Dempster, Jacob B. *The Art of Fine Book Publishing.* New Haven: The Cottage Press, Inc., 1982.

Book by two authors

Gallo, George, and L. J. Lane. *Paper and Paper-Making.* Baltimore: The Freedom Press & Co., 1978.

Book by three authors

Green, H. J., Ellen Jacoby, and James Reed. *The Art of Graphic Illustration.* New Orleans: The Creole Community Press, 1976.

Bibliography/Works Cited

Book by more than three authors

Grundvik, K., et al. *The Evolution of the Printing Press.* Los Angeles: The Hispanic Press, 1971.

Book by one editor

Hough, R. William, ed. *Fine Lettering.* New York: Simon and Schuster, 1968.

Book by two editors

Millman, Howie J., and Fred Stein, eds. *Preparing Leather Book Covers.* Boston: J. L. Cabot and Sons Publishing, 1974.

Two volumes by an organization

Modern Language Association of America. *Scholarly Publishing in North America.* 2 vols. New Haven: The Classical Press, 1974.

Chapter of a book

Williams, Clive. "The Opacity of Ink." In *The Art of Printing,* edited by Jason Farnsworth. New York: Holt, Rinehart & Winston, 1979.

NOTE 1: Beginning each bibliographic entry with the author's last name allows the entries to be alphabetized. The author's last name appears in parentheses in the report text, along with the page number of the source. This citation style is the MLA preference.

> A 1981 study revealed that fleas transmit the virus (Babcock 43). This study relied on two earlier studies (Duerdun 201 and Abbott 78–79).

NOTE 2: Publications in the social sciences and natural sciences usually cite the publication date in parentheses following the name of the author, according to the preferred style of the American Psychological Association (APA):

Smithson, Arthur J. (1976). *The History of Modern China.* New York: Simon and Schuster.

NOTE 3: Bibliographic entries in the physical and biological sciences often capitalize only the first word of the title:

Smithson, Arthur J. (1976). *The history of modern China.* New York: Simon and Schuster. [*China* is capitalized because it is a proper noun.]

---

2. **For a journal or a magazine article, give the name of the author or authors, the full title of the article (in quotation marks), the name of the journal or magazine, the volume, the month or quarter of publication, the year of publication, and the page numbers.**

Article by one author

Broward, Charles Evans. "Traveling the Southern California Desert." *UCLA Chronicle* 15 (Spring 1981): 45–54.

Article by two authors

Calleston, Dwight R., and James Buchanan. "The Desert Tortoise: Its Vanishing Habitat." *The Californian 7* (April 1976): 23–28: [Follow the book format in Rule 1 for articles with more than two authors.]

Article appearing in more than one issue

Stevens, Harold, and Jason Drew. "The Family of Bighorn Sheep." *The Bighorn Sheep Newsletter 8* (1976): 34–35, 28–31.

Bibliography/Works Cited

Article from a popular magazine

Trump, Josiah. "The Desert Indians." *Time,* 12 December, 1969: 45–49.

Review of a published book

Williams, Ellen. Review of *Prospecting in the Southern Desert* by Amy Van Pol and James Freeman. *The Californian* (July 1980): 24–31.

See QUOTATION MARKS.

NOTE 1: As with books, these entries follow the MLA format by citing the year of publication immediately after the name of the publication. In publications for the social sciences, the date appears after the name of the author:

Stillman, Wendy. (1981). "Photographing Desert Sunsets." *UCLA Chronicle* 15 (Spring): 4–8.

NOTE 2: Some editors, especially in the biological and physical sciences, prefer to omit the quotation marks around the title of the article and to capitalize only the first word of the title:

Stillman, Wendy. (1981). Photographing desert sunsets. *UCLA Chronicle* 15 (Spring): 4–8.

---

3. For unpublished material, give the author or authors, the title (in quotation marks), and as much of its history as available.

Dissertation or thesis

Johnson, Dugdale. "The Habitat of the Desert Tortoise: Its Inter-Relationship with Man." D.Sc. diss., University of Southern California, 1983.

Professional paper

Rusk, Joan, and Elaine Yardley. "The Diseases of the Bighorn Sheep." Paper presented at the annual meeting of the Bighorn Sheep Society, Los Angeles, 24–26 May, 1980.

Personal communication

Turgott, Edward. Letter to the author, 31 May, 1983.

NOTE: The formats for other unpublished documents (television shows, radio shows, interviews, duplicated material, diaries, etc.) should supply as much bibliographic information as possible. The bibliographic form should allow readers to locate the document easily.

---

4. For public documents, give the country, state, county, or other government division; the full title; and complete publication information.

Iowa State Assembly. Committee on Farm Commodities. *Report to the Farm Bureau on Corn Subsidies.* 45th Assembly, 2nd. sess., 1974.

U.S. Congress. House Committee on Ways and Means. *Hearings on Import Duties on Shellfish.* 79th Cong., 1st sess., 1945.

U.S. Bureau of the Census. *Gross and Net Fishing Revenues, 1980.* Prepared by the Commerce Division in cooperation with the Commodities Division. Washington, DC: United States Government Printing Office, 1984.

Bibliography/Works Cited

5. Alphabetize bibliographic entries by the author's last name.

>Adam
>
>Adams
>
>Berg
>
>Berger
>
>Bergerson
>
>Michael
>
>Michaels
>
>Michaelsen
>
>Michaelson
>
>Mickael
>
>Zucker

If two or more authors have the same last name, alphabetize according to first names or initials. A set of initials always precedes a first name beginning with the same letter:

>Brown, A. W.
>
>Brown, Andrew
>
>Brown, J. B.
>
>Brown, Jane
>
>Brown, John

If single- and multiple-author entries begin with the same last name, list the single authors first:

>Davis, Jeanne
>
>Davis, Jeanne, and Kristen Cooper
>
>Davis, Jeanne, Kristen Cooper, and Ellen James

Treat all names beginning with *Mc* and *Mac* as though they begin with *Mac*. Alphabetize them letter by letter, as you would with other words:

>Mabrey
>
>McDonald
>
>MacDougal
>
>McHenry
>
>MacMillian

If you attribute the document or item to an institution or agency, the first word in the institution's or agency's name becomes the key word for alphabetizing:

>Atomic Energy Commission
>
>Boston Globe
>
>MacMillian Institute
>
>Manchester Chronicle
>
>Merrimack Morning News
>
>U.S. Department of Commerce (not Department of Commerce)
>
>U.S. Geological Survey
>
>Water Resources Division, U.S. Geological Survey

NOTE: In names beginning with articles (*a, an,* and *the*), alphabetize by the second word in the name, but list the article if the article is part of the legal name:

>Albany State College
>
>The American University
>
>Antioch College
>
>Brown University
>
>The Johns Hopkins University

Capitalization follows two basic rules, but writers must also follow many subordinate rules for specific situations.

Preview

1. Capitalize the first letter of proper nouns—specific, one-of-a-kind names for a person, animal, place, university or school, organization, religion, race, month or holiday, historic event, trade name, or titles of a person or of a document.

2. Do not capitalize the first letter of common nouns—nouns that are general.

3. Capitalize the first letter of the first word of sentences, quotations, and listed items (either phrases or sentences).

4. Capitalize the first letter of the names of directions when they indicate specific geographical areas. Do not capitalize the first letter of the names when they merely indicate a direction or a general or unspecified portion of a larger geographical area.

5. Capitalize the first letter of names for specific deities, names of sacred writings, names of religious bodies and their adherents, and names of holy days.

6. Capitalize the first letter of the first word and all main words of headings and subheadings and of titles of books, articles, and other documents. Do not capitalize the first letter of the articles (*a, an,* and *the*), the coordinate conjunctions (*and, but, or, nor, for, so, yet*), or the short prepositions (*to, of,* etc.) unless they appear as the first word.

7. In titles and headings, capitalize the first letters of the initial word and of all later words in a hyphenated compound except for articles, short prepositions, and short conjunctions.

8. Capitalize the first letter of the geological names of eras, periods, systems, series, epochs, and ages.

9. Capitalize the first letter of a common noun used with a date, number, or letter.

10. Capitalize the first letter of proper nouns combined with common nouns, as in the names of plants, animals, diseases, and scientific laws or principles.

Capitalization follows two basic rules—the first two rules in the preview list. Unfortunately, these two rules cannot begin to account for the number of exceptions and options facing writers who have to decide whether or not a word should be capitalized. Because of the number of exceptions and options, this section includes many minor rules that supplement the two basic rules. Together, the basic and supplementary rules provide guidance, but you should also check an up-to-date dictionary for additional guidance if the proper choice is still not clear.

Capitals

1. **Capitalize the first letter of proper names—that is, those specific, one-of-a-kind names for a person, animal, place, university or school, organization, religion, race, month or holiday, historic event, trade name, or titles of a person or of a document.**

Person
- John F. Kennedy
- Babe Ruth
- Janet Reno
- Newt Gingrich
- Secretariat
- Morris
- Lassie

Place
- the Far East
- China
- the Eastern Shore (Maryland)
- Massachusetts
- Grove County
- Baltimore City (or Baltimore)
- United States of America
- Lake Michigan
- the Missouri River

University or school
- the University of Utah
- Western High School
- the Golden Daycare Center

Organization
- Jurassic Oil Company
- the American Legion
- the United Mine Workers
- the Republican Party

Religion
- Baptists
- Judaism

Race
- Japanese
- Hindus

Month or holiday
- May
- Fourth of July
- New Year's Day

Historic event
- the Reformation
- World War I
- Battle of Bull Run

Trade name
- Chuck's Crunchy Chicken™
- MicroDot Write®

Title of a person or of a document
- Mrs. Louise Brantly
- Dr. Georgia Burke
- Professor Robert Borson
- Lieutenant Jeb Stuart

Capitals

Handbook of Chemical Terms

"Time-Sharing" in *Training* magazine

NOTE 1: Do not capitalize *the* unless it has become part of the official name.

> The Hague
>
> *The New York Times*
>
> The University of Texas

NOTE 2: When proper names are several words, do not capitalize conjunctions, short prepositions, and articles (*a, an,* and *the*).

> the Federal Republic of Germany
>
> Johnson and Sons, Inc.
>
> "Recovery of Oil in Plugged and Abandoned Wells"

See Rule 6.

NOTE 3: Capitalize the first letter of an individual's title only when it precedes the individual's proper name.

> Professor George Stevens
>
> George Stevens, a college professor
>
> President Ellen Dobbs
>
> Ellen Dobbs, the president of our company

NOTE 4: Capitalize the names of languages and course names if they are followed by a number. Do not capitalize names of school subjects.

> Spanish
>
> French
>
> Algebra II

> algebra
>
> mathematics
>
> physical education

2. Do not capitalize the first letter of common nouns—nouns that are general.

> a geologist
>
> the engineers
>
> your secretary
>
> a country
>
> a river
>
> north
>
> the city
>
> a trade school
>
> college
>
> high school
>
> a holiday
>
> the swing shift
>
> a copier
>
> the facial tissue
>
> a foreman
>
> my supervisor
>
> the doctor
>
> spring
>
> summer
>
> fall
>
> winter

NOTE 1: To determine if a noun is common, ask yourself if *a* or *an* does or can precede the noun. If *a* or *an* makes sense before the noun,

Capitals

the noun is common and should not be capitalized.

Do This

    a pope

    an attorney

    a U.S. senator

Not This

    a Pope

    an Attorney

    a U.S. Senator

Because of special deference, the word *President* is usually capitalized when it refers to any or all of the Presidents of the United States. This is an exception to Rule 2 above.

NOTE 2: You can capitalize nouns separated from their proper nouns (or names) as follows:

- Titles of high company officials when the titles take the place of the officials' names

    We spoke to the President about the new labor policy.

    The State Director has to sign before the plan goes into effect.

- Names of departments when they replace the whole name of the department

    We sent the letter to Accounting.

    According to Maintenance, the pump had been replaced just last month.

- Names of countries, national divisions, or governmental groups when the common noun replaces the full name

    From the beginning of the Republic, a balance of powers was necessary.

    The State submitted a brief as a friend of the court.

    The Department has a policy against overtime for employees at professional levels.

    The House sent a bill to the Conference Committee.

- Names of close family members used in place of their proper names, especially in direct address

    Please understand, Mother, I will pay my share of the purchase price.

    Before leaving I spoke to Mother, Father, and Uncle George.

NOTE 3: Capitalize plural common nouns following two or more proper nouns unless the common nouns represent topographical features (such as lakes, rivers, mountains, oceans, and so on).

Do This

    West and South High Schools

    the Korean and Vietnam Wars

    the Mississippi and Missouri rivers

    the Wasatch and Uinta mountains

Not This

    West and South high schools

    the Korean and Vietnam wars

    the Mississippi and Missouri Rivers

    the Wasatch and Uinta Mountains

Capitals

3. Capitalize the first letter of the first word of sentences, quotations, and listed items (either phrases or sentences).

Astronomers study satellite photographs.

The software manual stated: "Make sure the printer is turned on."

The principal discussed the following issues:

- Tardiness rules
- Student fees
- Grading guidelines

NOTE 1: Capitalize displayed lists to make them more visually emphatic. See LISTS.

NOTE 2: Capitalize the first letter of a word following a colon or a dash within a sentence if the part following the colon or dash could be a complete sentence.

The Clean Water Act, Section 309(c)(1) states the rule: "Negligent violations are subject to criminal penalties. . . ."

We followed one principle: Short-term investments must be consistent with long-term goals.

OR

We followed one principle—Short-term investments must be consistent with long-term goals.

4. Capitalize the first letter of the names of directions when they indicate specific geographical areas. Do not capitalize the first letter of the names when they merely indicate a direction or a general or unspecified portion of a larger geographical area.

the Deep South

the Midwest

the Near East

the North

the Northwest

blowing from the southeast

eastern Missouri

southern Italy

the northern Midwest

toward the south

traveling north

NOTE: Sometimes titles are not clearly a geographical area—for instance, *East Texas*. If local custom identifies *East Texas* as including a particular number of counties, then the capital *E* is correct. If, however, *east Texas* means merely the general eastern portion of the state, then the lowercase *e* is correct. Of course, *eastern Texas* (rather than *east Texas*) would be a clearer means of indicating a general rather than a specific geographical area.

5. Capitalize the first letter of names for specific deities, names of sacred writings, names of religious bodies and their adherents, and names of holy days.

God

the Torah

a Muslim

Episcopal Church

Easter

33

Capitals

6. **Capitalize the first letter of the first word and all main words of headings and subheadings and of titles of books, articles, and other documents. Do not capitalize the first letter of the articles (*a, an,* and *the*), the coordinate conjunctions (*and, but, or, nor, for, so, yet*), or the short prepositions (*to, of,* etc.) unless they appear as the first word.**

   Moby Dick

   Declaration of Independence

   "The Gift of the Magi"

   A Tale of Two Cities

7. **In titles and headings, capitalize the first letters of the initial word and of all later words in a hyphenated compound except for articles, short prepositions, and short conjunctions.**

   See Rule 6 above.

   State-of-the-Art Technology

   Technology-Based Emission Standards

   Seventy-Five World Leaders as Voting Representatives

8. **Capitalize the first letter of the geological names of eras, periods, systems, series, epochs, and ages.**

   Jurassic Period

   Late Cretaceous

   Little Willow

   Paleozoic Era

   Upper Triassic

9. **Capitalize the first letter of a common noun used with a date, number, or letter.**

   Appendix A

   Collection 3

   Drawing 8

   Figure 5

   Plate VI

   Section C

   Volume III

   NOTE: In the following cases, *no., #,* or *No.* (for *Number*) is unnecessary.

   ### Do This

   Appendix A

   Page 45

   Site 5

   ### Not This

   Appendix No. A

   Page no. 45

   Site #5

10. **Capitalize the first letter of proper nouns combined with common nouns, as in the names of plants, animals, diseases, and scientific laws or principles.**

    Boyle's law

    Brittany spaniel

    Cooper's hawk

    Down's syndrome

    Fremont silktassel

Citations enable writers to identify the source of information within the body of the text. A citation refers readers to the bibliography.

Citations

Citations (short bibliographic entries) enable writers to identify sources of information. The methods of citation vary, depending on the technical field and its traditions, the type of publication, and the publisher. Many professional societies and journals also have their own methods of citation.

The method of citation we illustrate represents the conventions of the Modern Language Association (MLA). However, if you are writing for a particular professional society or technical journal, you should follow its method of citation. See BIBLIOGRAPHY/WORKS CITED.

Preview

1. Enclose the author's name with the page number in parentheses following the material quoted or the ideas referred to. Attach at the end of the text an alphabetical list of the cited works.

2. Use a consistent format for citing the name of the author and the page.

3. Include a full alphabetized list of cited sources (titled "Works Cited") following the article or chapter.

1. Enclose the author's name with the page number in parentheses following the material quoted or the ideas referred to. Attach at the end of the text an alphabetical list of the cited works.

> One critic called the whole dispute a "galaxy of confusion" (Jameson 47). In reply, the spokesman for the conservative wing rebutted Jameson point by point (S. Clarke 202–204).

The information in this MLA style of citations is so brief that it does not interrupt the text, and the author's name indicates the source. A variation of this citation style is to use the author's name in the text while retaining the page number in parentheses:

> Jameson called the whole dispute a "galaxy of confusion" (47). In reply, Clarke, who is the spokesperson for the conservative wing, rebutted Jameson point by point (202–204).

NOTE 1: Scholars in social sciences and in some of the natural sciences use a citation style recommended by the American Psychological Association (APA). The APA style cites the year of publication following the name of the author(s). The APA style uses a page number only when the material cited is a direct quote.

> (Jameson 1992, p. 47)
>
> (Clarke 1991, pp. 202–204)

NOTE 2: An alternative method uses only numbers in the text, not the author's last name and date:

> One critic called the whole dispute a "galaxy of confusion" (1). In reply, the spokesman for the conservative wing rebutted Jameson point by point (2).
>
> One critic called the whole dispute a "galaxy of confusion" [1]. In reply, the spokesman for the conservative wing rebutted Jameson point by point [2].

Citations

The numbers appearing within parentheses or brackets are keyed to a list of sources that appears at the end of the text. The list is not alphabetized because it follows the order in which the sources were cited in the text.

2. Use a consistent format for citing the name of the author and the page.

(Jakobson 401)

(Bains and Eveslong 209–210)

(Federal Science Committee 33)

(Smithson, Haarke, and Bruppe 107–110)

(U.S. Department of Agriculture 18–19)

The abbreviations *p.* and *pp.* (for *page* and *pages*) are unnecessary in the MLA style but are used in the APA style, along with the date.

MLA style

(Bains and Eveslong 156)

(Federal Science Committee 2:33–36)

APA style

(Bains & Eveslong 1964, p. 156)

(Federal Science Committee 1979, pp. 33–36)

NOTE: In the last MLA example, *2* is the volume number.

Whatever the format used, authors should be consistent in their method of citation within the same document.

3. Include a full alphabetized list of cited sources (titled "Works Cited") following the article or chapter.

Book by one author

Bricke, Larry N. *Canadian Political Parties.* Toronto: New Country Press, 1984.

Book by two authors

Campbell, Josiah, and Wallace Daughterly. *Conflict in the Provinces.* Edmonton, Alberta: The Royal Penny Press, 1976.

Journal or magazine article

Mahoney, Edward G. "A Dissident's View of Canadian Politics." *The Political Review* 2 (1978):56–59.

NOTE 1: In standard bibliographic reference format, the first line is set at the left margin, while the second, third, and so on are indented.

NOTE 2: In these bibliographic entries, the date of publication comes near the end of the reference. In the APA bibliographic form, the date appears after the name of the author:

Bricke, Larry N. (1984). *Canadian Political Parties.* Toronto: New Country Press.

See BIBLIOGRAPHY.

NOTE 3: The titles may be underlined rather than italicized if handwritten or typed.

Colons connect ideas and signal readers to keep reading for more information, explanation, or a list.

Colons signal readers to keep reading because related thoughts or a list follows. In this role, colons differ from periods, semicolons, and even commas, all of which signal a pause or even a full stop.

Preview

1. Colons link related thoughts, one of which must be capable of standing alone as a sentence.

2. Colons introduce lists or examples.

3. Colons separate hours from minutes, volumes from pages, and the first part of a ratio from the second.

4. Colons follow the salutation in a formal letter.

5. Colons separate titles from subtitles.

---

1. Colons link related thoughts, one of which must be capable of standing alone as a sentence.

Colons shift emphasis forward. They tend to make the second thought the most important part of the sentence. By contrast, semicolons emphasize both thoughts equally, and dashes emphasize the break in the sentence and can emphasize the first thought. The use of a colon indicates that explanation or elaboration follows:

> The shipyard needed one thing to remain solvent: to win the oil tanker's contract.
>
> The shipyard needed one thing to remain solvent: It had to win the oil tanker's contract.

NOTE: Full sentences begin with a capital letter after a colon. See CAPITALS.

The two complete thoughts in the second example could also appear as two sentences:

> The shipyard needed one thing to remain solvent. It had to win the oil tanker's contract.

However, linking these thoughts with a colon emphasizes their close connection. Writing them as two sentences is less emphatic if the writer wishes to stress that the one thing the shipyard needs is to win the contract.

2. Colons introduce lists or examples.

Our management development study revealed the need for greater monitoring during these crucial phases:

1. Initial organization
2. Design and development
3. Construction and quality control

The Mars Division's audit of field service centers found the following general deficiencies:

1. Service personnel do not fully understand the new rebate policy.
2. Parts inventories are inadequate.
3. The centralized customer records cannot be operated even though the computer terminals are all installed.

NOTE 1: The items listed do not require periods unless they are complete sentences. See LISTS.

Colons

NOTE 2: Do not use a colon if the list follows a preposition or a verb. For both paragraph lists and displayed lists, add an anticipatory word like *following* or *follows* to the lead-in sentence. See LISTS.

Do This

The 1103 camera has the following key features: (1) automated flash, (2) automated exposure, and (3) low battery alarm.

Not This

The key features of the 1103 camera are: (1) automated flash, (2) automated . . .

The 1103 camera includes built-in features to: (1) automate the flash, (2) automate . . .

---

3. Colons separate hours from minutes, volumes from pages, and the first part of a ratio from the second.

The deadline is 3:30 P.M. on Friday.

See *Government Architecture* 15:233.

The ratio of direct to indirect costs is 1:1.45.

---

4. Colons follow the salutation in a formal letter.

See LETTERS

Dear Ms. Labordean:

Dear Account Manager:

Dear Harold:

---

5. Colons separate titles from subtitles.

Government Architecture: Managing Interface Specifications

Swedish Pancakes: Easy Recipes for All Ages

NOTE 1: In published titles, use italics as in the example above. When writing unpublished titles, frame the titles with quotation marks

Commas break up the words in a sentence into groups of ideas and help readers understand a writer's meaning.

Commas break up the words in a sentence into groups of ideas. Commas help keep sentences readable—especially long, complicated sentences. Commas are also used to set off secondary ideas, such as introductory phrases and parenthetical expressions, from the main idea of the sentence.

---

1. Use commas to separate three or more items in a series. These items can be words, phrases, or even independent clauses.

The mechanic should have checked the brakes, oil, filters, spark plugs, and windshield wipers.

The software allows the user to move a file, delete it, or save it under a new name.

I don't know where I'm going, I don't know why I'm going, and I won't know until I get there.

NOTE 1: Use a comma to separate the last two items in a series, even though these items are already separated by a conjunction (*and* and *or* in the above examples). This comma was once considered optional, but the trend is to make it mandatory, especially in technical and business English. Leaving it out can confuse readers and can even change the meaning of the sentence, as in this example:

The restaurant's breakfast menu listed oatmeal, French toast, ham and eggs.

Preview

1. Use commas to separate three or more items in a series. These items can be words, phrases, or even independent clauses.

2. Use commas to separate two or more adjectives that modify the same noun.

3. Use a comma to separate two complete thoughts joined by the conjunctions *and, but, or, for, nor, so,* or *yet.*

4. Use a comma to separate an introductory phrase or clause from the main body of a sentence.

5. Use commas to set off parenthetical expressions.

6. Use commas to set off nonessential clauses and phrases.

7. Use commas to set off names or words used as a direct address.

8. Use commas to separate people's names from their titles and degrees.

9. Use a comma after the salutation in an informal letter and the complimentary closing in any letter.

10. Use commas to separate items in dates and addresses.

11. Put commas inside closing quotation marks but outside parentheses and brackets.

Commas

In this example, it's not clear whether *ham and eggs* are one item or two. With a comma before the *and*, *ham* would be separate from *eggs*.

NOTE 2: If all the items in the series are already linked by conjunctions, do not use commas.

> Lisa **and** Basil **and** Raul will write the report about our department's third-quarter performance.

NOTE 3: If a sentence contains phrases or clauses that already have commas, use semicolons to separate each phrase or clause.

> The Human Resources department is preparing policies on equal employment opportunity; on job reviews, which are scheduled for next month; and on vacations, holidays, and sick leave.

See CONJUNCTIONS and SEMICOLONS.

---

2. Use commas to separate two or more adjectives that modify the same noun.

> We want the **fastest, cheapest, most reliable** delivery system money can buy.

> Sarah pried the door open with an **old, rusty** steam pipe.

EXCEPTION: Don't use a comma after the last adjective in a series if the adjective can be considered part of the noun. If you aren't sure where to put a comma, try using the word *and* instead. If the word *and* makes sense in a certain place, a comma would make sense there also.

> old rusty steam pipe (This is the original phrase.)

> old **and** rusty **and** steam pipe (This phrase doesn't make sense.)

> old **and** rusty steam pipe (This phrase does make sense; replace the word *and* with a comma to get *old, rusty steam pipe*.)

---

3. Use a comma to separate two complete thoughts joined by the conjunctions *and, but, or, for, nor, so,* or *yet*.

> Gustav has applied for a student loan, **and** Maria has just received her college application.

> We are known for our superior customer service, **but** we have also won several quality awards.

EXCEPTION: You can leave the comma out if both complete thoughts are short.

> The product must sell or the company will fail.

NOTE: The simple conjunctions *and, but, or, for, nor, so,* and *yet* are called coordinate conjunctions. When they link two complete thoughts, the resulting sentence is called a compound sentence. See CONJUNCTIONS.

If you use any other transitional or connecting word (such as *however, furthermore,* or *consequently*) to link two complete thoughts, use a semicolon. See SEMICOLONS.

> These standards are common in our industry; **however,** we consistently meet or exceed them.

Commas

4. Use a comma to separate an introductory phrase or clause from the main body of a sentence.

Consequently, we cannot finish the project before next week.

Although we are new to this technology, we have worked with high-power lasers for years.

Once you have reviewed the account, forward a copy of the statement to my secretary.

EXCEPTION: You may leave the comma out if the introductory phrase or clause is short and the reader will not be confused.

In either case you should make an appointment with the doctor today.

5. Use commas to set off parenthetical expressions.

A parenthetical expression is a phrase that is inserted into a sentence but is not part of the main thought of the sentence. Parenthetical expressions describe, explain, or comment on something in the sentence, often the word or phrase before the parenthetical expression.

This new airplane, **though designed for smaller airports,** requires over 10,000 feet of runway for takeoff and landing.

Our only option, **therefore,** is to find another consultant.

The test results, **though not what I expected,** show that the glue will hold.

Your term paper, **on the other hand,** could use a little more work.

NOTE: You can also use parentheses or dashes around parenthetical expressions. Commas are fine most of the time, but when you want to make a parenthetical expression stand out, enclose it with parentheses (which are more powerful than commas) or dashes—like these—which are more powerful than parentheses. See PARENTHESES AND BRACKETS and DASHES.

6. Use commas to set off nonessential clauses and phrases.

A nonessential (or nonrestrictive) clause or phrase contains information that is not necessary to the meaning of the sentence.

Your last memo, **which I didn't read,** has been posted on the bulletin board.

Marcus, **following the instructions in the manual,** finally managed to fix the computer glitch.

The nonessential clauses or phrases in the examples above can be left out of the sentence without changing the main idea expressed in the rest of the sentence.

Your last memo has been posted on the bulletin board.

Marcus finally managed to fix the computer glitch.

An essential (or restrictive) clause or phrase is not set off by commas because it contains information that is necessary to the meaning of the sentence.

He is the architect **who designed our corporate headquarters**.

Every employee **meeting our quality standards** should be rewarded.

Commas

If the essential clause or phrase in each of the examples above is left out of the sentence, the meaning changes.

>He is the architect.

>Every employee should be rewarded.

7. Use commas to set off names or words used as a direct address.

>If you return the book tomorrow, **Louis**, we won't charge you a fine.

>Would you give me a ride home, **my friend**?

8. Use commas to separate people's names from their titles and degrees.

>The man holding the microphone is John Ferrero, Vice President of Operations.

>Ann Nakamura, Ph.D., will chair the new Quality Control Committee.

NOTE: When the degree or title appears in the middle of a sentence, use commas before and after it. See CAPITALS.

9. Use a comma after the salutation in an informal letter and the complimentary closing in any letter.

>Dear Joan,

>Sincerely,

See COLONS and LETTERS.

10. Use commas to separate items in dates and addresses.

>The final report is due January 15, 1995, just a month before the board meeting.

>Contact Benson Aerodynamics of Lindsay, Indiana, for further information.

Use a comma to separate the day from the year *(January 15, 1995)* and the city from the state *(Lindsay, Indiana)*. Also, use a comma to separate the final item in a date or an address from the rest of the sentence.

EXCEPTIONS: Don't use a comma to separate the month from the day *(January 15)*, the month from the year *(January 1995)*, or the day from the month in day-month-year format (15 January 1995).

11. Put commas inside closing quotation marks but outside parentheses and brackets.

>The graduation speaker said we were "standing on the threshold," and I seem to be there still.

>Thanks to months of hard work (and a large, last-minute donation), we were able to meet our fundraising goal.

Conjunctions connect words and ideas and establish relationships between them.

Conjunctions

Preview

1. Use the coordinating conjunctions *and* and *or* to connect the last two items in a series.

2. Use a coordinating conjunction to connect two complete thoughts (independent clauses) in a compound sentence.

3. You may begin a sentence with a coordinating conjunction, but this should not be a common practice.

4. When you use a correlating conjunction, put words that are the same parts of speech after each coordinating conjunction.

5. Put a comma after a subordinate phrase or clause that begins a sentence.

6. Don't use a comma if the subordinate phrase or clause follows the independent clause or main thought of a sentence.

7. Use commas to set off a subordinate phrase or clause that interrupts the main thought of a sentence.

8. You may begin a sentence with a subordinating conjunction.

9. If you use a conjunctive adverb to join two complete thoughts, put a semicolon before the adverb and a comma after it.

10. If you begin a sentence with a conjunctive adverb, put a comma between the adverb and the rest of the sentence.

Conjunctions connect words or groups of words and establish relationships between them. The four types of conjunctions are **coordinating conjunctions, correlating conjunctions, subordinating conjunctions,** and **conjunctive adverbs**.

Coordinating Conjunctions	Correlating Conjunctions	Subordinating Conjunctions	Conjunctive Adverbs
and, but, or, for, nor, so, yet	both . . . and either . . . or neither . . . nor not only . . . but also whether . . . or	after, although, as, because, before, if, once, since, that, though, until, when, where, while in that, so that, such that, except that, in order that, now (that), provided (that), supposing (that), considering (that), as far as, as long as, so long as, sooner than, rather than, as if, as though, in case if . . . then, although . . . nevertheless, as . . . so, so . . . that, such . . . as, such . . . that, no sooner . . . than, whether . . . or not	accordingly, also, besides, consequently, further, furthermore, hence, however, moreover, nevertheless, otherwise, then, therefore, thus, too

43

Conjunctions

Coordinating Conjunctions

Coordinating conjunctions connect words, phrases, or clauses that have the same purpose in the sentence. Coordinating conjunctions are the following:

and, but, or, for, nor, so, yet

These words establish a relationship between the thoughts they connect.

- *And* shows addition or similarity.
- *Or* and *nor* show alternatives.
- *But* and *yet* show contrast.
- *For* and *so* show cause and effect.

---

1. **Use the coordinating conjunctions *and* and *or* to connect the last two items in a series.**

   The mechanic should have checked the brakes, oil, filters, spark plugs, **and** windshield wipers.

   The software allows the user to move a file, delete it, **or** save it under a new name.

NOTE: When you use *and* or *or* to connect the last two items in a series, put a comma before the conjunction. The two previous sentences illustrate this rule. See COMMAS.

---

2. **Use a coordinating conjunction to connect two complete thoughts (independent clauses) in a compound sentence.**

   Gustav has applied for a student loan, **and** Maria has just received her college application.

   We are known for our superior customer service, **but** we have also won several quality awards.

NOTE: You can use a semicolon in place of both the comma and the conjunction. See SEMICOLONS.

   We are known for our superior customer service; we have also won several quality awards.

---

3. **You may begin a sentence with a coordinating conjunction, but this should not be a common practice.**

Many students and writers have been told, "Never begin a sentence with *and*." This rule was intended to prevent fragmented sentences and choppy-sounding sentences such as these:

   Make sure you back up your document files onto a disk. **And** your system files.

   We went to the park. **And** we visited my aunt. **And** we saw the baby giraffe at the zoo.

In the first example, the phrase *your system files* is a sentence fragment, not a complete thought. In the second example, the *and*s don't make a necessary connection with the previous sentence, and the example could be rewritten as a single sentence:

   We went to the park, visited my aunt, **and** saw the baby giraffe at the zoo.

You may begin a sentence with *and* or another coordinating conjunction as long as the second sentence is a complete thought (an independent clause) and the conjunction makes a logical

Conjunctions

connection with the previous sentence. This is usually done to add emphasis to the conjunction.

> We have sent them several letters to remind them of our deadlines. **But** the shipments still have not arrived.

In this example, the second sentence is a complete thought, and the conjunction *but* shows the contrast between the two sentences.

Correlating Conjunctions

Correlating conjunctions are pairs of coordinating conjunctions that connect words, phrases, or clauses that have the same purpose in the sentence.

> both . . . and, either . . . or, neither . . . nor, not only . . . but also, whether . . . or

---

4. When you use a correlating conjunction, put words that are the same parts of speech after each coordinating conjunction.

Do This

> The committee was interested in **both** real estate **and** stock investments.
>
> The company is successful with **both** its new ventures **and** its old products.

Not This

> The committee was interested **both** in real estate **and** the stock investments.
>
> The company is successful **both** with its new ventures **and** its old products.

See PARALLELISM.

Subordinating Conjunctions

There are many more subordinating conjunctions than coordinating conjunctions. The more common subordinating conjunctions are as follows:

> after, although, as, because, before, if, once, since, that, though, until, when, where, while

> in that, so that, such that, except that, in order that, now (that), provided (that), supposing (that), considering (that), as far as, as long as, so long as, sooner than, rather than, as if, as though, in case

> if . . . then, although . . . nevertheless, as . . . so, so . . . that, such . . . as, such . . . that, no sooner . . . than, whether . . . or not

Subordinating conjunctions introduce subordinate (or dependent) phrases and clauses—phrases and clauses that are not complete thoughts.

> **After** the engineer gave her talk
>
> **Since** you are clearly qualified for the job

These subordinate phrases and clauses must be attached to independent clauses (complete thoughts) to form sentences.

> **After** the engineer gave her talk, several people had questions.
>
> **Since** you are clearly qualified for the job, we have decided to omit the formal interview.

---

5. Put a comma after a subordinate phrase or clause that begins a sentence.

The two examples above illustrate this rule. See COMMAS.

Conjunctions

6. Don't use a comma if the subordinate phrase or clause follows the independent clause or main thought of a sentence.

Several people had questions **after** the engineer gave her talk.

We have decided to omit the formal interview **since** you are clearly qualified for the job.

7. Use commas to set off a subordinate phrase or clause that interrupts the main thought of a sentence.

Occasionally, a subordinate phrase or clause will interrupt the main thought of the sentence. If this happens, use commas to set off the subordinate phrase or clause.

The company president, **after** seeing the last financial report, decided to cut our department's budget.

Frederico's hard work, **rather than** my suggestion, was the reason for our team's success.

8. You may begin a sentence with a subordinating conjunction.

When the test results come in, we'll have to check them carefully.

Because I didn't make a backup file, I'll have to retype the proposal.

Many students and writers have been told, "Never begin a sentence with *because*." However, you may begin a sentence with *because* or another subordinating conjunction as long as the subordinate phrase or clause it introduces is followed by a complete thought (an independent clause). See Rule 3.

Conjunctive Adverbs

Conjunctive adverbs are adverbs that act as conjunctions, usually by connecting complete thoughts (independent clauses). The most common conjunctive adverbs are as follows:

accordingly, also, besides, consequently, further, furthermore, hence, however, moreover, nevertheless, otherwise, then, therefore, thus, too

See TRANSITIONS.

9. If you use a conjunctive adverb to join two complete thoughts, put a semicolon before the adverb and a comma after it.

Assembling an airplane is a long process; **however,** the individual steps must still be carefully monitored.

Increasing the pressure in the pipe could be dangerous; **nevertheless,** we will begin tests tomorrow.

See COMMAS and SEMICOLONS.

10. If you begin a sentence with a conjunctive adverb, put a comma between the adverb and the rest of the sentence.

However, a new production process might not be the answer either.

Therefore, we should look at all our options before we make a decision.

NOTE: If the sentence is short, you can leave out the comma.

Furthermore the plan failed.

Dashes link introductory or closing thoughts to the rest of a sentence and may also be used to add emphasis.

Dashes are excellent devices for emphasizing key material and for setting off explanatory information in a sentence. They can also be used to indicate where each item in a list begins and to separate paragraph headings from the text that follows. See LISTS and HEADINGS.

Dashes are roughly twice as long as hyphens. You can create dashes on a typewriter by typing two unspaced hyphens. Most word processing software has a special code for a dash so it appears as a solid line, not two separate hyphens. Using this code makes your text appear to be typeset, not typed on a typewriter.

When you use a dash between two words, leave no space on either side of the dash.

> ### Preview
> 1. Dashes link introductory or concluding thoughts to the rest of the sentence.
> 2. Dashes interrupt a sentence for insertion of thoughts related to, but not part of, the main idea of the sentence.
> 3. Dashes emphasize explanatory information enclosed in a sentence.
> 4. Dashes link particulars to a following summary statement.

1. Dashes link introductory or concluding thoughts to the rest of the sentence.

Using dashes to link thoughts emphasizes the break in the sentence. Dashes often make the first thought the most important part of the sentence:

> Winning the oil tanker's contract—that's what the shipyard needed to remain solvent.
>
> Signing the business agreement by October 1—this was the only goal of the meeting with our lawyer.

Dashes can act like colons, however, and throw emphasis to the last part of the sentence:

> We subjected the design to rigorous testing—but we discovered that stress was not the problem.

Often, the information following the dash clarifies, explains, or reinforces what came before the dash:

> We consider our plan bold and unusual—bold because no one has tried to approach the problem from this angle, unusual because it's a unique use of laser technology.

Dashes can also link otherwise complete sentences:

> The problem was not the design of the filter—the problem was quality assurance.

NOTE: In this example, the two complete sentences could also be linked with a semicolon or they could be separate sentences.

> The problem was not the design of the filter; the problem was quality assurance.

Dashes

OR

The problem was not the design of the filter. The problem was quality assurance.

As in this example, choosing a dash instead of a semicolon or a period is stylistic choice. The dash is visually emphatic and even unusual in most texts. The semicolon or the period says the ideas are ordinary, even expected. See SEMICOLONS.

2. Dashes interrupt a sentence for insertion of thoughts related to, but not part of, the main idea of the sentence.

The Airstream 7 had been in the design phase—airfoil studies were being done by Bartlett Industries—for 6 years before the government canceled its contract.

In this case parentheses could replace the dashes. With parentheses, the sentence becomes slightly less emphatic. See PARENTHESES AND BRACKETS.

3. Dashes emphasize explanatory information enclosed in a sentence.

Two of Bartlett's primary field divisions—Industrial Manufacturing and Product Field Testing—will supervise the construction and performance testing of the model.

In this case, commas or parentheses could replace the dashes. Dashes, however, provide the most emphatic break in a sentence. Parentheses are less emphatic, and commas are the least emphatic. See PARENTHESES AND BRACKETS and COMMAS.

Sometimes the explanatory information may interrupt the stylistic flow of the sentence:

Our plan for updating the facilities—rebuilding the storage shed, installing new valve assembly equipment, and upgrading the existing sprinkler system—would require over $2 million and nearly 2 years.

If a sentence like this one seems stylistically abrupt or awkward, rephrase the sentence and perhaps even replace the dashes:

Our plan for updating the facilities included rebuilding the storage shed, installing new valve assembly equipment, and upgrading the existing sprinkler system. The plan would cost $2 million and would take nearly 2 years.

See LISTS and PARALLELISM.

4. Dashes link particulars to a following summary statement.

Reliability and trust—this is what Bartlett Industries has to offer.

Developing products that become an example for the industry, minimizing the risk of failure, and controlling costs—these characteristics form the basis of our reputation.

Ellipses, which consist of three spaced periods, indicate omissions of words, sentences, or paragraphs, primarily in quoted material.

Ellipses

Ellipses, which consist of three spaced periods (. . .), indicate omissions, primarily in quoted material. Some word processing systems have a function that produces ellipses with unspaced periods (…); this option is rare in printed texts, possibly because it makes the text look jammed together.

Ellipses are the opposite of brackets, which indicate insertions in quoted material. See PARENTHESES AND BRACKETS.

Preview

1. Use ellipses within quoted material to indicate omissions of words, sentences, or paragraphs.

2. Do not use ellipses to omit words if such omissions change the meaning or intent of the original quotation.

3. Do not use ellipses to open or close a quotation if the quotation is clearly only part of an original sentence.

4. Use a line of spaced periods to indicate that one or more entire lines of text are omitted.

5. Use ellipses to indicate faltering speech.

---

1. Use ellipses within quoted material to indicate omissions of words, sentences, or paragraphs.

"Labor costs . . . caused an operating loss for January of nearly $10,000."

The original text for this example was as follows:

Labor costs, which our executive committee has been studying, caused an operating loss for January of nearly $10,000.

"No tax increases . . . for 1997 will occur."

The original text for this example was as follows:

No tax increases in personal withholding for 1997 will occur.

NOTE 1: If omitted material comes at the beginning of a sentence, the quoted material opens with ellipses, especially if the material appears to be a complete sentence:

". . . the printed budget will remain unchanged."

The original text for this example was as follows:

Despite a few inconsistencies, the printed budget will remain unchanged.

NOTE 2: If the omitted material comes at the end of a sentence, the quoted material ends with ellipses following the ending punctuation of the sentence, in this case, a period.

"The Department of Energy denied our request for an energy subsidy. . . ."

The original text for this example was as follows:

The Department of Energy denied our request for an energy subsidy even though we felt our request would be cost effective.

49

Ellipses

2. Do not use ellipses to omit words if such omissions change the meaning or intent of the original quotation.

"Chairman James Aubrey indicated that financing the debts would . . . seriously undermine efforts to recover overdue loans."

The original text for this example was as follows:

Chairman James Aubrey indicated that financing the debts would not detract from or seriously undermine efforts to recover overdue loans.

3. Do not use ellipses to open or close a quotation if the quotation is clearly only part of an original sentence.

Do This

We discussed the "three legal loopholes" mentioned in the last Supreme Court decision on school busing.

Not This

We discussed the ". . . three legal loopholes . . ." mentioned in the last Supreme Court decision on school busing.

4. Use a line of spaced periods to indicate that one or more entire lines of text are omitted.

Friends, Romans, countrymen, lend me your ears;

I come to bury Caesar, not to praise him.

. . . .

He was my friend, faithful and just to me:

NOTE 1: The line of periods does not tell a reader how much was omitted. The writer is responsible for retaining the intent and meaning of the original material.

NOTE 2: Poems and other long quotations do not require quotation marks. Instead, indentation and extra lines above and below the quoted material indicate that it is a quotation. See QUOTATION MARKS.

5. Use ellipses to indicate faltering speech.

I protest . . . or maybe I should only suggest that you have made a mistake.

I wonder . . . perhaps . . . if . . . that is a wise choice.

50

Emphasis techniques make documents more readable and enable writers to direct readers to specific information within a document.

Emphasis

Emphasis includes any techniques writers use to make their messages both readable and obvious. Readers must immediately see and understand your major point or points.

Every misleading sentence or disputed fact represents a waste of time and money in today's technical society. Organizations cannot afford vague procedures, unclear memos, and inconclusive reports.

A well-designed, emphasis-driven document forces every reader to come away with the same message. A simple example would be the instructions for assembling an exercise bike.

Every customer assembling the bike should be 100 percent successful. No calls to the bike company's customer service center should be necessary, and the final bike should have no unfastened parts or other unsafe features.

Successful world-of-work documents are 100 percent useful. Use the following format and emphasis principles to help you create your first draft. Your intended format should guide your content. You will be writing to fit the format, not forcing a format on content that is already created. See WRITING.

NOTE: The Garbage-In-Garbage-Out (GIGO) principle applies to emphasis techniques. If you fail to set content priorities, you may wind up with well-designed and attractive garbage! The GIGO principle is most evident when emphasis techniques are applied as a cosmetic step late in the writing process.

Preview

1. Control your readers' eyes by controlling the position and appearance of your ideas.

2. Open with important ideas.

3. Subordinate minor ideas.

4. Repeat important ideas.

5. (Optional) Close with repetition of important points.

6. Use space and page design to highlight important ideas.

7. Use headings and lists to highlight important ideas.

8. Use graphics to emphasize important ideas.

9. Use single-sentence paragraphs to emphasize important ideas.

10. Use typographical features and color to emphasize words and ideas.

1. Control your readers' eyes by controlling the position and appearance of your ideas.

Effective writing is document design, not spinning out words and phrases. Proper emphasis techniques help guarantee readers take one and only one meaning from a passage.

Writers achieve emphasis in documents by working with the position and appearance of words on the page.

Emphasis

Position refers to the placement of words within a sentence, paragraph, or section. Language, both written and oral, moves from word to word, so the order and sequence of language is important even if it is not always speedy or efficient.

Appearance refers to the visual presentation of ideas and to the physical character of the words or ideas—for example, page layout, spacing, indentation, boldface type, underlining, type size, type style, color, and production quality. See PAGE LAYOUT.

2. Open with important ideas.

The beginnings of documents, sections, paragraphs, and sentences are the most visible and memorable parts of any document. Make the first page, the first line, and the major subheading count by using them to record and convey important ideas. Lead away from important ideas, not up to them. See ORGANIZATION.

If the opening page, the opening paragraph, the opening sentence, and the opening words fail to capture the most important ideas, you may mislead your reader. Or at the very least, you force your reader to read and reread for information.

Emphasize your most important ideas by placing them in opening positions.

3. Subordinate minor ideas.

Arrange your document so minor ideas receive less emphasis than major ideas. Minor ideas should receive less time and less space than major ideas. Minor ideas should not appear in headings, in graphics, or in boldface.

Place minor ideas in the middle of documents, paragraphs, and sentences. This placement will happen automatically if you have followed Rule 2, which tells you to open with major ideas. See ORGANIZATION.

In some cases, minor ideas should not appear in a document except as reference. These referenced ideas become part of the legal record or organizational documentation.

4. Repeat important ideas.

Repetition is important because readers (and listeners) may tend to forget earlier messages as new words and ideas appear. Repetition of ideas signals that the ideas are important and guarantees that readers will remember them.

Effective repetition occurs when the design of a document repeats important ideas. The title, subject line, and major headings introduce major ideas. Graphics and accompanying captions further illustrate these ideas. And if an executive summary is included, it presents the highlights of these same ideas.

Each mention of a major idea should use the same wording and the same technical data. This type of deliberate repetition means that the most important ideas should be 100 percent consistent each time they appear.

Effective repetition is one indication a document has been carefully designed and well edited.

5. (Optional) Close with repetition of important points.

This rule is optional because the visual nature of documents has decreased the role of the

Emphasis

closing section, the closing paragraph, or the closing sentence. See ORGANIZATION.

Some documents still may require closings that repeat important points. Letters and memos quite often should end with a repetition of the requested meeting, the follow-up action, or other activity.

Of course, oral language still relies on the final statement, the final word. In oral presentations, speakers must lead up to their clincher idea, their major point, their most memorable phrase. In writing, however, this emphasis technique may be unnecessary in a well-designed document.

6. Use space and page design to highlight important ideas.

Make your page design, especially its open spaces, support and reinforce your important ideas. See PAGE LAYOUT.

Initially, readers see the overall appearance, not the details. They have a general impression of your intent and your content before they ever begin reading sentence by sentence.

If readers scan your first page, what should they see? If you've designed the page well, the title and major headings convey the important ideas, and these are always set off by surrounding space. Perhaps the page has a graphic on it, with an interpretative caption; this graphic should also present important ideas.

Make sure, however, that your pages are not so cluttered and busy that the important ideas are lost. For more details about the use of space, see PAGE LAYOUT.

7. Use headings and lists to highlight important ideas.

Business writing today is designed to be read quickly and efficiently. The use of headings and lists means that a reader can easily skip and scan your document for crucial content. People often will not read the entire document unless they need to. See HEADINGS and LISTS.

8. Use graphics to emphasize important ideas.

Graphics are increasingly important. Today's readers expect, even demand, that well-designed documents use graphics. See GRAPHICS.

The availability of graphics software has revolutionized routine reports and other everyday documents. Readers are now accustomed to seeing bar graphs, illustrations, and other common graphics. What was innovative some years ago in *USA Today* is now commonplace in many world-of-work documents and business presentations.

9. Use single-sentence paragraphs to emphasize important ideas.

A document with a sequence of long paragraphs is not very readable, even if the paragraphs are well written and the language interesting.

The single-sentence paragraph is a valuable emphasis tool when it breaks the sequence of medium and long paragraphs.

Readers can quickly scan a document to find and read a single-sentence paragraph. Of course, too many short paragraphs are not

Emphasis

effective because they make a document choppy. Reserve single-sentence paragraphs for important ideas.

10. Use typographical features and color to emphasize words and ideas.

CAPITALS, underlining, **boldface**, *italics*, and different type styles stand out when used within ordinary text. Don't overuse such typographical techniques, but design your pages to draw on these tools when appropriate. See PAGE LAYOUT.

Color is also a valuable tool, especially if used in graphics. It is probably the most visually effective of the document design tools available to writers.

Unfortunately, color is still a costly and time-consuming option, given the need for many copies. As with typeface styles, don't overuse color or mix too many colors into a single page or graphic.

Graphics are a powerful device for emphasizing information and increasing readers' ability to remember key facts.

Graphics are one of the writer's best devices for emphasizing information. Because they are visual rather than verbal (as writing is), document graphics are often more emphatic and memorable than the written text around them.

Today's readers are accustomed to seeing sophisticated graphics on well-designed pages. Magazines and newspapers published only a few years ago now look old-fashioned. Even routine business documents have changed in the years since personal computers became a common business tool. Today's business documents are increasingly designed for visual accessibility, and graphics are a primary document design tool.

Preview

1. Choose appropriate graphics to emphasize your important ideas and data.

2. Create your graphics before you write the text.

3. Introduce graphics in the text before they appear.

4. Number graphics in the order of appearance.

5. Use clear, active-voice interpretive captions and cite the source for any information borrowed.

Graphics include a wide variety of types and different approaches to the visual presentation of ideas. Some of the most common types of graphics are the following:

- **Graphs** present information in numbers, usually reflecting two or more types of change. A simple graph or plot could show the percentage of males and females employed in the U.S. civilian labor force during a 35-year time period. As Figure 1 shows, the percentage of males employed (the line with the *o*'s) changes little over the 35 years. In contrast, the percentage of females employed (the line with the *x*'s) gradually increases. Other types of graphs include bar graphs and pie graphs, which are often used to show different percentages or parts of a whole.

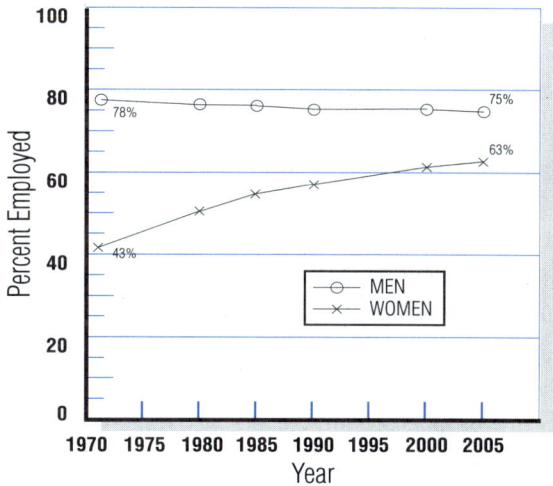

Figure 1. Percentage of U.S. Males and Females Employed. *The percentage of working-age males employed has remained nearly constant for the last 25 years and is projected to remain so through 2005. The similar figures for females show an increasing percentage, growing from 43 percent in 1970 to a projected 63 percent in 2005. (From* Statistical Abstract of the United States 1993, *Table No. 622.)*

Graphics

- **Charts** show relationships, not numerical values. Common charts include organizational charts, which show how a company is organized and who works for whom, as shown in Figure 2. A chart can also show the steps in a process, as in a manufacturing process such as printing a book.

- **Illustrations, photographs, and diagrams** make complex processes or equipment more understandable. Illustrations of some kind are essential, for instance, when you need to assemble a piece of equipment or when you need to design something (such as a coat or a piece of furniture).

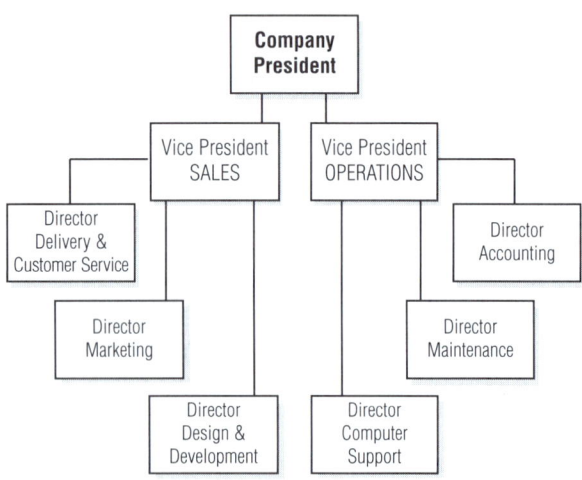

Figure 2. A Typical Organizational Chart. *The structure or responsibilities in many companies begin at the top and work down. The company president's box is at the top because this person is responsible for all activities within the company. Lower boxes in the chart represent individuals with different levels of responsibility for specific company functions. For example, the director of design and development is responsible for that specific activity and answers, in order, to the vice president of sales and the company president. A more detailed chart would outline managers, supervisors, and employees in descending order below each director's box.*

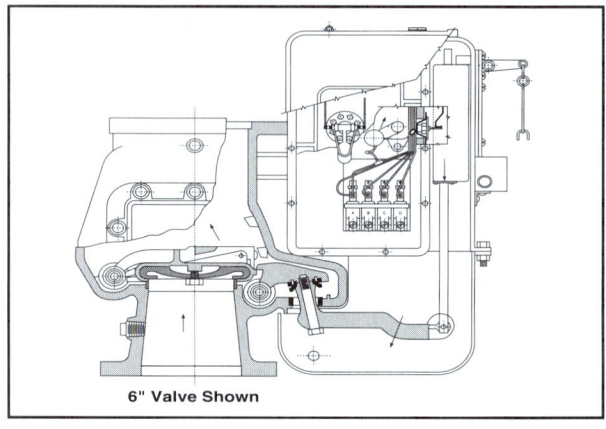

Figure 3. An Injection Matrix Oil Separation Pump. *The detailed internal structure of this pump used in a typical oil refinery is clearly represented in this illustration. Using a computer-aided drafting package, illustrations can show very complex graphical information.*

- **Maps** show geographic relationships and suggest relative distance.

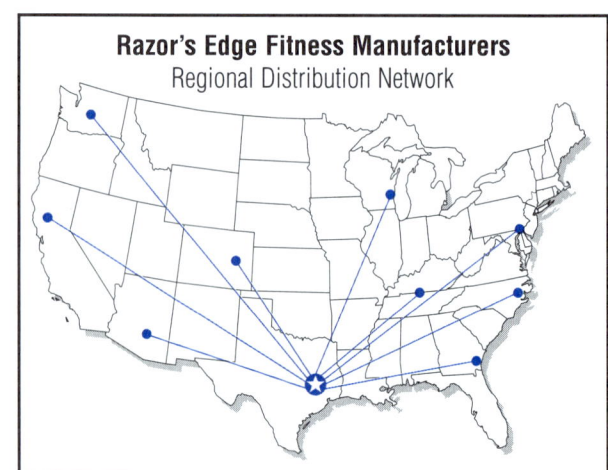

Graphics

- **Tables** are graphics, although they are perhaps the least readable of all. Tables present detailed numerical and text data using rows and columns. As in Figure 4, dense data in a table make reading difficult and are not as visually powerful as some of the preceding graphic types.

OCCUPATION Largest Job Growth	EMPLOYMENT				REAL CHANGE		
	1990	2005			Low	Moderate	High
		Low	Moderate	High			
Salespersons, retail	3,619	4,180	4,506	4,728	561	887	1,109
Registered nurses	1,727	2,318	2,494	2,648	591	767	921
Cashiers	2,633	3,094	3,318	3,474	461	685	841
General office clerks	2,737	3,149	3,407	3,587	412	670	860
Truck drivers light and heavy	2,362	2,767	2,979	3,125	405	617	763
General managers and top executives	3,086	3,409	3,684	3,871	323	598	785
Janitors and cleaners	3,007	3,332	3,562	3,728	325	555	721
Nursing aides, orderlies, and attendants	1,274	1,700	1,826	1,934	426	552	660
Food counter, fountain, and related workers	1,607	2,067	2,158	2,229	460	551	622
Waiters and waitresses	1,747	2,110	2,196	2,262	363	449	515
Secretaries, except legal and medical	3,064	3,065	3,312	3,488	1	248	424

Note 1: All numbers are shown in thousands; e.g., 3,619 = 3,619,000.
Note 2: Jobs are arranged in descending order according to the real number of new jobs projected, as shown in the shaded *"Real Change: Moderate"* column.

Figure 4. Civilian Jobs with Largest Growth by 2005. *The 1990 data reflect actual jobs for that year. The data for 2005 are based on projected growth by that year. Because projections can be inaccurate, the table presents three options (low, moderate, and high growth), which depend on how energetic the U.S. economy is for the next decade. (From* Statistical Abstract of the United States 1993, *Table No. 845.)*

---

1. **Choose appropriate graphics to emphasize your important ideas and data.**

Graphics should capture the key recommendation, the surprising trend, the unexpected financial problem, and the most convincing facts. Choose graphics to clarify and highlight your message.

First, determine what point (or points) you most want to emphasize, or which is the most difficult to make using words alone. These points are what you should capture in graphics.

Second, choose an appropriate graphic from the various types of graphics listed above.

Some graphics work well for some topics, but not for others.

As an example, consider that you have researched job opportunities in the future. As part of your research, you found the previous table of occupations with the largest potential growth (Figure 4) with current employment and projections for the year 2005. The projections include a low, moderate, and high profile, which vary based on economic conditions. If the economy performs better than expected, the high projection will apply; if the economy performs worse, the low projection will apply.

If your report dealt only with the numbers of office clerk positions available in 2005, you could use the table depicted in Figure 4. However, a bar graph might be more effective, since you have a single main point to illustrate. Compare Figure 4 (the table) with Figure 5, which shows how you might use the information you need from the table in a bar graph.

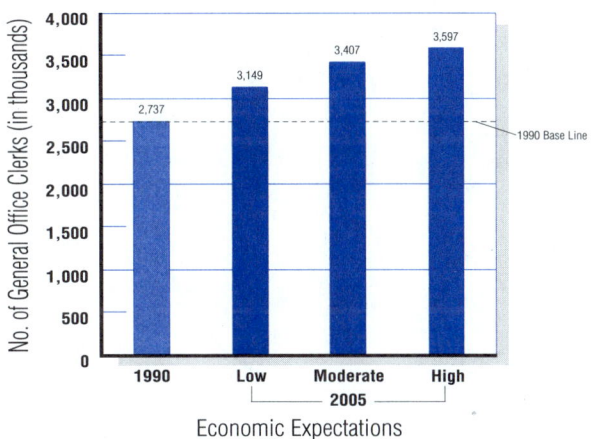

Figure 5. Projected Job Growth for General Office Clerks: 1990 to 2005. *The number of general office clerks in 1990 was 2,737,000. The number of clerks will grow during the next 15 years, but the rate may be low, moderate, or high. The dotted line represents the number of jobs in 1990. The distance each bar rises above the dotted line represents the number of new clerk jobs projected for 2005 in different economic conditions. (From* Freeman's Economic Forecast 1996, *p. 42.)*

Graphics

If you were asked to report on how the average wage earner under 25 years of age spends his or her money, you might write something like the following:

> According to the *Statistical Abstract of the United States 1993*, Table No. 708, the total annual expenses in 1991 for the average wage earner under 25 years of age were $16,745. Of this figure, the percentage breakdowns for the various items were as follows: $912 for food (at home), $1,118 for food (away from home), $4,886 for housing (shelter and utilities), $3,868 for transportation (vehicle plus expenses), $5,162 for miscellaneous (health care, insurance, apparel, etc.), and $799 for personal taxes.

Or, you might choose to use a graphic similar to this pie chart (Figure 6). Which do you think is more effective?

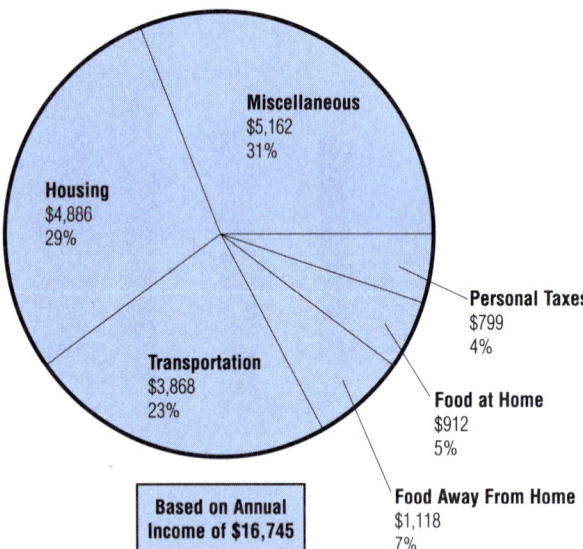

Figure 6. Average Annual Expenditures for Wage Earners Under 25. *The typical U.S. wage earner under the age of 25 spends his or her money in 6 general areas. The largest amount is spent on miscellaneous expenses, including clothing, entertainment, school, and savings. (From* Statistical Abstract of the United States 1993, *Table No. 708.)*

2. Create your graphics before you write the text.

Graphics should never be an afterthought. Visuals drive text. Create visuals first; write text last.

Graphics are more emphatic than text and should therefore receive greater attention early in the writing process.

As you generate ideas and begin to focus your message, list the important ideas you want to convey to your readers. Then ask yourself how you can visualize these ideas.

Do some rough sketches or a prototype. For longer documents, a prototype is simply a collection of proposed pages, with potential graphics and related text sketched in. See WRITING. Also, prepare a style sheet that gives your page format. See PAGE LAYOUT.

Later, as you write the draft, return to your notes or the mock-up to assist you in refining or changing your graphics.

3. Introduce graphics in the text before they appear.

Always precede graphics with a clear introduction in the text. A graphic appearing suddenly, without introduction or explanation, generally confuses the reader.

The introduction should be informative and specific:

Do This

> As Figure 5 shows, the average hourly wages for computer technicians are

Graphics

increasing at a rate that exceeds the annual rate of inflation. Their wages in constant (1982) dollars are increasing.

This project is estimated to cost $34,500. The cost breakdown in Table 15 shows that hardware costs account for nearly 65 percent of the total costs, while labor costs constitute only 12 percent of the total.

Not This

See Figure 5.

The total cost of this project is $34,500. Table 15 provides a cost breakdown.

A good introduction indicates not only what the graphic is about but also explains how the reader should interpret it.

4. Number graphics in the order of appearance.

The caption of each graphic—graphs, charts, tables, diagrams, illustrations, photographs, and maps—should begin with a figure number.

In a short document, or a document with few figures, number the figures sequentially through the entire text. In a document with chapters or numbered sections, give figures hyphenated numbers, such as *Figure 3-2*. The first number is the chapter or section, and the second number denotes the number of the graphic (figure) within a chapter or section.

In longer documents, especially formal reports and publications (pamphlets, books, research studies, etc.), include a list of figures. Place the list immediately after the table of contents (usually on a separate page).

A list of figures should provide, in sequence, each figure number, a title, an interpretive caption, and page number for each graphic, such as the following:

Figure 1. Percentage of U.S. Males and Females Employed. The percentage of working-age males employed has remained nearly constant for the last 25 years. The similar figures for females show an increasing percentage. (2)

Figure 2. A Typical Organizational Chart. The structure or responsibilities in many companies begin at the top and work down. (4)

Figure 3. An Injection Matrix Oil Separation Pump. The detailed internal structure of this pump used in a typical oil refinery is clearly represented in this illustration. (4)

Figure 4. Civilian Jobs with Largest Growth by 2005. The 1990 data reflect actual (measured) jobs for that single year. The data for 2005 are based on projected growth by that year. (12)

Figure 5. Projected Job Growth for General Office Clerks: 1990 to 2005. The number of employed general office clerks in 1990 was 2,737,000. Based on the health of the U.S. economy during the next 15 years, the number of clerks will grow. (14)

5. Use clear, active-voice interpretive captions and cite the source for any information borrowed.

Interpretive captions are informative and specific without being lengthy.

Graphics

Do This

Figure 17. Pronghorn Population Trends in Montana. *The pronghorn antelope population in Montana has declined steadily since 1971.*

Table 2. Air Quality in Sonoma Valley, California. *From May to October 1984, air quality in Sonoma Valley, California, has remained well within EPA air quality standards.*

Not This

Figure 17. *Pronghorn Population Trends in Montana.*

Table 2. *Air Quality in Sonoma Valley, California.*

Interpretive captions should provide enough information so the graphic with caption could stand alone and still be understood. Captions tell what the graphics are about and also what the readers should learn from them.

Cite the sources for any information you borrow for use in graphics. See INTELLECTUAL PROPERTY. Place the information in parentheses. For instance, if the pronghorn data (and maybe even the graphic itself) come from a source, include the author's name and a page number in parentheses following the caption.

Figure 17. Pronghorn Population Trends in Montana. *The pronghorn antelope population in Montana has declined steadily since 1971. (Jefferson 336)*

As in this example, you would list full information about the Jefferson publication in the list of works cited. See BIBLIOGRAPHY and CITATIONS.

NOTE: In the figures in this Graphics *Style Guide* entry, the citations are more detailed, providing both the full title of the book and the name of the table. The reason for this detail is that this entry does not include a list of works cited, so the parenthetical information needs to provide enough detail so readers know the source of the data.

Headings enable writers to divide information into logical and easily understood sections and to signal readers what information is to come.

Headings show logical divisions in the text. Like titles, headings signal what is to come and make reading easier.

Headings show how a document is organized. Readers can glance at the headings to determine where they need to read more closely and where they can skim. Headings are therefore especially useful for nonspecialist readers who need to gain an overall sense of the text, but who do not have the time, interest, or knowledge to read the entire document.

1. Use headings if (1) the text is longer than one single-spaced page or (2) the text conveys two or more major ideas.

Headings are among the most useful devices in writing. You should use them often enough (without overdoing) to make the text as easy to read as possible.

2. Make your headings specific and inclusive.

Informative, specific headings outline the contents of a document. Unfortunately, many standard headings are not specific and do not help the reader. Do not use general headings such as *Introduction, Discussion, Results*, and so on. It is better to be more specific: *Purpose of the Drilling Proposal, Valid Data from the Third Test, Results of the Field Study*.

Preview

1. Use headings if (1) the text is longer than one single-spaced page or (2) the text conveys two or more major ideas.

2. Make your headings specific and inclusive.

3. Make headings parallel in structure.

4. Use the same type of heading, declarative or question, at each heading level.

5. Choose different levels of headings to indicate logical divisions and groupings in the text.

6. Show the level of a heading in three ways: the **placement** of the heading on the page, the **size** of the type, and the **appearance** of the type.

7. Use no more than four or five heading levels, depending on your readers.

8. Use a numbering system with your headings if (1) there are more than four levels of headings, (2) the document is lengthy, or (3) you or your readers will need to refer to sections by number.

Inclusive headings signal that only material mentioned in the heading will actually be covered in the section. If the heading is *Valid Data from the Third Test*, no data from the second or first test should appear in that section.

Headings

3. Make headings parallel in structure.

Parallel structure means that all headings at the same level have the same basic grammatical structure. For example, if one heading opens with an *–ing* word, then other headings should also begin the same way. See PARALLELISM.

Do This

    Develop**ing** the Appropriate Tests

    Send**ing** Out for Bids

    Select**ing** the Winner

    Agree**ing** on Preliminary Contract Talks

Not This

    Develop**ing** Appropriate Tests

    Send**ing** Out for Bids

    Select**ion** of the Winner

    Preliminary Contract Talks

4. Use the same type of heading, declarative or question, at each heading level.

Most headings are declarative. They state or announce a topic:

    Facilities in the Local Area

    Summerhill Treatment Plant

    The Basics of Computer Credit Memos

An alternative heading form is the question heading:

    How Great Is the Avalanche Danger?

    What Are the Alternatives?

    Will the Public Accept Our Position?

As long as you don't overdo them, question headings offer interesting possibilities and can be very effective. Question headings stimulate interest because they pose questions that curious readers will want to see answered.

Question headings are generally more engaging than declarative headings because they seem to speak directly to the reader. However, do not pose obvious or condescending questions:

    Doesn't Everyone Know About Credit Memos?

Be consistent. If you decide to use question headings, use them for all headings at that heading level. Mixing question and declarative headings at the same level is confusing. However, you can use question headings at a major level and then use declarative headings at subordinate levels, or vice versa.

5. Choose different levels of headings to indicate logical divisions and groupings in the text.

The level of a heading indicates its logical relation to other headings as well as to the whole. The levels are most apparent in an outline:

    3.3 Component Costs

    3.4 Component Descriptions
        3.4.1   Gearbox Assembly
        3.4.2   Brakes
        3.4.3   Hydraulic Motor
        3.4.4   Remote Signal Interface
            3.4.4.1   Controller
            3.4.4.2   Encoder
            3.4.4.3   Tachometer
        3.4.5   Antenna Connectors

Headings

In both text and outlines (such as a table of contents), the levels may be indicated by the placement, size, or appearance of the heading, or by a numbering system (like the one above).

---

6. Show the level of the heading in three ways: the placement of the heading on the page, the size of the type, and the appearance of the type.

PLACEMENT VARIATIONS
A heading may be centered on the page, placed flush left, indented, or run-in. A centered heading is strongest, and a run-in heading is weakest.

A Centered Heading

A Flush-Left Heading

   An Indented Heading

   A Run-in Heading. The text begins following the period and two spaces.

   A Run-in Heading   Sometimes, a run-in heading has only three spaces between it and the succeeding text. When you do not use punctuation, make the heading visually distinct from the text in the rest of the paragraph. You might use boldface type or a larger typeface.

SIZE VARIATIONS
If you are using a computer you can vary the point size of the lettering in the different heading levels. The larger the point size, the greater the level of the heading. For example, a 24-point heading is on a higher level than a 12-point heading. See PAGE LAYOUT.

A 24-point Heading
An 18-point Heading
A 14-point Heading
A 12-point Heading

APPEARANCE VARIATIONS
You can vary the appearance of a heading by using ALL CAPITAL LETTERS, underlining, **boldface type**, different typefaces, and *italics*. See EMPHASIS and PAGE LAYOUT.

The appearance variations may be added singly or in combination. Thus, a heading may be in all capital letters, or it may be boldfaced, or both. Appearance variations used in combination create higher level headings than headings with a single appearance feature. So a boldfaced, all-capital-letter heading is on a higher level than a heading featuring only all capital letters.

Appearance, size, and placement variations used together allow writers many heading types—and consequently many heading levels.

---

7. Use no more than four or five heading levels, depending on your readers.

Dozens of heading levels are possible, but readers can't comprehend the difference among too many levels. Use fewer heading levels for less educated or less technical readers.

Experienced and well-educated scientific readers are more used to reading text with multiple levels of headings. If you suspect that your readers will have trouble remembering the heading levels, use fewer levels.

---

8. Use a numbering system with your headings if (1) there are more than four levels of headings, (2) the document is lengthy, or (3) you or your readers will need to refer to sections by number.

Report writers normally construct their tables of contents by listing the headings and subheadings in their reports. If you use a numbering system with your headings, include the numbers in the table of contents.

Hyphens

Hyphens follow many rules to show connection between parts of words and among parts of phrases or compound modifiers.

Hyphenation is one of the trickier aspects of English. There are many rules of hyphenation—including some that apply only in limited circumstances—and all the rules have exceptions. For further discussions of hyphenation, refer to *The Chicago Manual of Style, The Gregg Reference Manual,* the *United States Government Printing Office Style Manual,* or the *Merriam-Webster Concise School and Office Dictionary.*

Hyphens as Connectors

Fundamentally, hyphens show a connection. Typically, the connection is between two words or between a prefix and a word. The connected words (known as compounds) can function as nouns, verbs, or adjectives:

Connected words as nouns

> brother-in-law
>
> ex-mayor
>
> follow-up
>
> know-how
>
> run-through
>
> self-consciousness
>
> two-thirds

Connected words as verbs

> to blue-pencil
>
> to double-space
>
> to spot-check
>
> to tape-record

Preview

1. Hyphenate two or more words that act together to create a new meaning.

2. Hyphenate two or more words that act together to modify another word.

3. Do **not** hyphenate connected words that function as adjectives if they occur **after** the word they modify. Do hyphenate connected words if they precede the word they modify.

4. Do **not** hyphenate connected words that act as adjectives if the first word ends in –*ly*.

5. Hyphenate compound numbers from twenty-one to ninety-nine and compound adjectives with a numerical first part.

6. Prefixes generally do not require hyphens.

7. Hyphenate words that must be divided at the end of a line.

Connected words as adjectives

> all-around person
>
> black-and-white print
>
> decision-making authority
>
> high-grade ore
>
> little-known program
>
> long-range plans
>
> matter-of-fact approach
>
> off-the-record comment
>
> old-fashioned system

Hyphens

part-time employees

three-fourths majority

twenty-odd inspections

up-to-date methods

well-known researcher

Unfortunately, not all connected (or compounded) nouns, verbs, and adjectives require hyphens. Here are a few of the exceptions:

Connected but unhyphenated nouns

ball of fire

breakdown

fellow employee

goodwill

problem solving

takeoff

trademark

trade name

Connected but unhyphenated verbs

to downgrade

to handpick

to highlight

to proofread

to waterproof

Connected but unhyphenated adjectives

barely known researcher

bright red building

crossbred plants

halfhearted attempts

highly complex task

10 percent increase

very well known leader

worldwide problem

As the above examples show, connected words have three possible forms. They can appear as two separate words *(highly motivated),* as one word formed by connecting the two original words with a hyphen *(high-pressure),* and as one word formed by joining the original two words *(highbrow).*

Tradition and current usage direct which form the connected words will take. If you are not sure which form is correct, refer to the *Merriam-Webster Concise School and Office Dictionary.*

Hyphenation Rules

1. Hyphenate two or more words that act together to create a new meaning.

the V-space between units

one-half of the annular ring

to double-check the tests

This rule indicates a possible use of the hyphen, not a required one. In some instances the two words become a single word, without a hyphen: *highlight, bumblebee, barrelhead.* In other instances, the two words remain separate: *base line, any one* (one item from a group). The words sometimes remain separate because combining them would produce strange-looking forms: *beautyshop, breakfastroom.* Because the presence or absence of a hyphen is often a matter of agreement, check a current dictionary if you are not sure how the compound word should be written.

Hyphens

See CAPITALS for the proper capitalization of hyphenated words in titles.

2. Hyphenate two or more words that act together to modify another word.

   squared-and-welded construction

   full-scale testing

   no-error edit process

   3-year, multimillion-dollar program

   12-foot-wide wall

   up-to-scale modeling

   U-tube arrangement

   well-documented success

This rule applies only when the connected or compound modifier occurs **before** the word it modifies. See Rule 3.

3. Do <u>not</u> hyphenate connected words that function as adjectives if they occur <u>after</u> the word they modify. Do hyphenate connected words if they precede the word they modify.

   The compartment is 32 feet wide.

   The program is well documented.

   The 32-foot-wide compartment

   The well-documented program

4. Do <u>not</u> hyphenate connected words that act as adjectives if the first word ends in –*ly*.

   highly motivated engineer

   poorly conceived design

   vastly different approach

   completely revised program

NOTE: The words ending in –*ly* are actually adverbs. The –*ly* form indicates the structure of the modifying phrase, so a hyphen is unnecessary.

5. Hyphenate compound numbers from twenty-one to ninety-nine and compound adjectives with a numerical first part.

See NUMBERS.

   thirty-four

   eighty-one

   five-volume proposal

   13-phase plan

   24-inch tape

   500-amp circuit

6. Prefixes generally do not require hyphens.

   illegal

   midpoint

   nonperson

   progovernment

   undesirable

NOTE 1: Hyphens are used when the prefix precedes a capitalized word.

   un-American

   mid-August

   non-Soviet

Hyphens

NOTE 2: Hyphens are sometimes necessary to prevent confusion: *re-treat* (to treat again) versus *retreat* or *un-ionized* versus *unionized*. If you are not sure whether a prefix requires a hyphen, refer to the *Merriam-Webster Concise School and Office Dictionary*.

7. Hyphenate words that must be divided at the end of a line.

Words are always divided between syllables, and hyphens should appear at the end of the line where the word division has occurred. Try not to end more than two consecutive lines with hyphens. Try not to divide at the end of the first line or at the end of the last full line in a paragraph. Do not divide the last word on a page.

Hyphens and Technical Terminology

The use of hyphens in technical expressions varies considerably. Some writers try to adhere strictly to the rules outlined above. But many, because of tradition, agreement, or local preference, violate the rules of hyphenation when they believe that the technical expression will be clear:

> We will need a high pressure hose.

In this sentence, *high* obviously modifies *pressure*. The sentence refers to a hose that is capable of withstanding high pressures. It is not a pressure hose that happens to be high (off the ground). Yet if we followed the rules of hyphenation strictly, the sentence should be:

> We will need a high-pressure hose.

Hyphens are often left out in technical expressions because the expressions without the hyphens are clear to technical readers. In many cases, however, missing hyphens can cause confusion or a complete lack of understanding, as in this sentence:

> Before removing the blade, refer to the steering gear bolt positioning release mechanism drawing.

Nontechnical (or technical but unknowledgeable) readers can only guess which words are associated with which other words. Does *bolt* link with *steering gear,* or does *bolt* link with *positioning?* Hyphens would help clarify the modifier relationships:

> steering-gear bolt-positioning release-mechanism drawing

If agreement or tradition allows you to do away with hyphens where they would normally appear in compound words, do so unless eliminating them will confuse some readers. If you are uncertain, use hyphens. Proper use of hyphens will not baffle knowledgeable technical readers, and it will help those readers who are not familiar with a technical expression.

Intellectual Property

Ideas and inventions are considered intellectual property and are protected by various laws.

Intellectual property includes a person's or company's ideas, inventions, or creative expressions (movies, music, graphics, etc.). A person or company may also own various types of *real property*—things such as buildings, land, airplanes, or machinery. The law protects both real and intellectual property from theft.

A person's or an organization's intellectual property may be protected by the registration of a patent, a trademark (™), a service mark (℠), or a copyright (©). The term *intellectual property* covers many kinds of media, including text, graphics, software, film, video, animation, and recordings.

The following discussion summarizes the highlights of current copyright rules. It also includes a brief mention of service marks and trademarks. It does not cover patents, which have special and very detailed legal requirements.

If you have questions about copyrights, service marks, trademarks, or patents, obtain legal advice from an attorney who specializes in copyright or patent law.

Preview

1. Accurately quote and credit proper sources for any information you use in your writing or speaking.

2. Identify the source for any photographs, graphics, charts, tables, pictures, drawings, or other media you use. Also, do not modify visual creations without considering the rights of the creator of a visual.

3. When using the intellectual properties of others, do not distort the original meaning.

1. Accurately quote and credit proper sources for any information you use in your writing or speaking.

Keeping this rule is both ethically and legally important.

Personal ethics require that you give others credit for their ideas, contributions, and originality. You expect no less when someone uses your ideas or words.

Legally, you must carefully quote and cite the source for any published information you choose to use. If you do not, you will violate U.S. copyright laws. See CITATIONS.

Copyrights (©) Anyone's original work is protected by a copyright, even if the person who creates a work has not chosen to apply formally for a copyright. The copyright exists when the writer makes the first original version, even if it is only a handwritten copy.

Copyright covers the expression of an idea, not the idea itself. You must always credit actual words and phrases that you borrow. Ideas may not be legally copyrightable, but ethically you should credit someone else's idea if it is distinctively theirs, not yours.

Copyright protection initially applied only to "writings," but protection now covers videos, paintings, photographs, cartoons, recordings, songs, sculptures, computer images, computer programs, or any other creative product when

Intellectual Property

it is physically recorded. Thus, the manuscript for a song may be copyrighted and the physical recording may also be copyrighted.

Under copyright law, you must obtain permission from the author(s) (or the holder of the copyright, if an author has signed the rights to someone else—for instance, a publisher). Often, you have to pay a fee to use copyrighted material in something you wish to publish.

If you obtain permission, keep the written permission (usually a brief form letter). In your own work, identify the author and the holder of the copyright (usually a full bibliographic citation) and include a note like the following:

> Reprinted by permission of Holt, Rinehart and Winston, Inc.
>
> OR
>
> Reproduced courtesy of the photographer's heirs (Susan Jameson and Dwight Jameson).

Fair Use In some instances, especially in academic studies, critical reviews, teaching, or research, you may reproduce without permission excerpts (written or visual) from a copyrighted work. In such cases, you do not need to obtain written permission before you publish. You must still identify the source for any quotations or excerpts you use.

Fair use applies if you are not using enough of the original work to affect its value. The number of words is not the sole measure of fair use. You may use a quotation of fifty words from a book and still be under fair use; but if you use a few key words from a short poem without permission, you may be violating fair use. A detail from a single painting might be fair use; the whole painting would not be fair use.

Don't rely on the fair use exemption if you are in doubt about the fair use status or if you are going to profit from quoting someone else's copyrighted material. In these cases, write for permission and pay any necessary fees.

Public Domain Works Works produced by the U.S. government are in the public domain. This includes works produced by individuals working under U.S. government contracts.

Some works also are in the public domain because their copyright has expired. The time limits for a copyright vary, based on different copyright laws. Under the 1976 law, which took effect on January 1, 1978, the copyright lasts for the life of the author, plus 50 years. In cases of joint authorship, the copyright lasts 50 years after the death of the last surviving author.

You can freely quote, without permission, from public domain works, but include full citations for any materials you are borrowing. Your readers need to know which are your words (and ideas) and which words you are borrowing. See CITATIONS.

Trademarks (™) Trademarks are names or symbols used to identify a particular product or service. Before registration, a trademark has an attached ™ to show it is a trademark. After registration, an ® replaces the ™.

Trademarks are registered with the U.S. government, and their use is prohibited without the accompanying ™ or ®. Trademarks are usually capitalized. See CAPITALS.

Some trademarks have become such familiar terms (for example, Kleenex®, Jell-O®, Coke®, and Xerox®) that people tend to use these trademarked names as general references. Avoid this practice unless you are making specific reference to the actual company product. Instead, use

Intellectual Property

more generic terms such as *tissue*, *gelatin*, *soft drink*, or *photocopy*.

When you use a trademarked name, be sure to follow the company's style and spelling. Also, include the ® or ™ the first time you use the name. Later in the same document, you do not need to repeat the trademark symbol.
See ABBREVIATIONS.

2. Identify the source for any photographs, graphics, charts, tables, pictures, drawings, or other media you use. Also, do not modify visual creations without considering the rights of the creator of a visual.

Photos and other graphics, including computer graphics, have copyright protection, just as any other publications do. Sometimes writers borrow a graphic without remembering that a reproducible image has the same copyright protection as words. This guidance applies, for example, to your favorite newspaper cartoon.

As with any copyrighted material, using a cartoon requires you to contact the cartoonist or a publisher (often a newspaper syndicate) for permission, which is usually granted after payment of a one-time fee or a royalty fee for each copy made.

Modifying a graphic does not make it yours! As with the cartoon example, some people provide their own captions or write in new balloon comments. Use of this modified cartoon is still a violation of the cartoon's copyright.

Similarly, you are not free to modify or adjust a copyrighted photograph, computer graphic, or illustration to suit your purposes. Even if you have obtained permission to use a photograph or illustration, this permission can include requirements as to how and when you will reproduce the photograph or illustration. For example, printing a small black-and-white version of a large color photograph might damage the original intent or artistic value. Sometimes the photographer might even refuse permission based on what you intend to say about the photograph.

3. When using the intellectual properties of others, do not distort the original meaning.

The authors or creators of intellectual property deserve to have the original meaning and intent of their work preserved. If, for example, an author has written a book condemning the destruction of the rain forest, isolated quotes that might support an opposing position should not be used without placing them in proper context. See QUOTATION MARKS.

Do This

> A reviewer of *The Last Waltz* noted an "outstanding lack of logic or sequence between the scenes in the movie." The reviewer continued: "The central character—Josephine Lane—was not equal to the range of emotional situations required by the script."

Not This

> According to a reviewer of *The Last Waltz* the movie contained "outstanding . . . scenes." The reviewer also commented about Josephine Lane's wide "range of emotional situations" as the central character.

The summaries use quotation marks and even, in the second version, an ellipsis, but the second summary is dishonest because it reverses the reviewer's message.

Interviews are a critical part of the job-search process and require careful attention to listening and presentation skills.

Interviews are one of the last requirements in a successful job search. Most companies ask an applicant back for an interview when the applicant is one of several finalists. The applicant's skill during the interview will determine whether or not the applicant gets the job.

Interview questions are unpredictable and harder to control than the content of a résumé and cover letter. You can design your written documents to express the image you wish to communicate. In an interview, however, you may be asked questions which you did not anticipate or which are difficult to answer.

Thorough preparation for an interview can often help you control how the interview goes. If you prepare, you will also decrease your own nervousness, build your confidence, and give yourself a psychological edge.

Preparation begins by learning about the interviewer and the interviewer's company. If you know someone who works at the company, ask them to tell you about the working conditions and about the job for which you have applied. Next, develop a list of sample questions you suspect the interviewer might ask. Practice answering these questions.

Your goal is to do what you can to avoid any major surprises during the interview.

Preview

1. Arrive on time and be appropriately dressed for the interview.

2. When you arrive at the interviewer's office, knock and then follow the interviewer's cues about where to sit and how formal or informal to be during your initial greetings and any associated small talk.

3. Let the interviewer set the agenda for the interview content and be alert to any cues as to what the interviewer expects.

4. Answer questions directly and honestly, and explain your answers with sound examples and references to your qualifications.

5. Reinforce your verbal content with good nonverbal signals (posture, facial expressions, and eye contact).

6. Practice ahead of time answering hard questions so you won't be surprised.

7. Prepare to ask the interviewer questions about the company, the job, and the working conditions.

8. Plan when and how you expect to end the interview.

9. Follow up on the interview with a call or a thank-you letter, whichever seems most appropriate.

Interviews

1. Arrive on time and be appropriately dressed for the interview.

Punctuality is a necessity. In some cultures, punctuality is not as important as it is in American business situations. American business etiquette mandates that you be on time, so always leave early enough to have plenty of time to find an unknown street.

If you are unavoidably late, be prepared to apologize. Failure to apologize is considered a sign of rudeness. If you will be very late (more than 15 minutes), call **before** your appointment and tell them when you will arrive.

Each job and each company has its own dress expectations. If you are applying to drive a truck or to be an electrician's apprentice, ordinary work clothes are appropriate. Be sure they are clean and neatly pressed. If you are applying for a retail sales job or for a job as a company receptionist, your clothing should be more dressy. For a man, dressy might mean a sport coat and slacks and possibly even a tie. For a woman, a dress would be appropriate, or perhaps a coordinated skirt and blouse.

Whatever clothes you decide to wear, stay away from faddish or outlandish styles.

If you have no idea about how to dress, call the company's main office number and ask about their dress code. Some companies, for example, require a shirt and tie for men and dresses for women.

---

2. When you arrive at the interviewer's office, knock and then follow the interviewer's cues about where to sit and how formal or informal to be during your initial greetings and any associated small talk.

Remember you are the interviewer's guest. As a guest, you need to abide by the interviewer's "house rules." These rules include whether or not to shake hands and when and where to sit. Most men who are interviewing will shake hands with another man and often with a woman. With a woman interviewer, follow the woman's lead; if she extends her hand, shake it, but if she doesn't, don't extend yours.

Unspoken rules also include how formal to be. For example the interviewer may ask you to use his or her first name. If the interviewer makes no such request, use the more formal option—for example, *Mr. Johnson, Mrs. Allen*, or *Ms. Halvorsen*.

---

3. Let the interviewer set the agenda for the interview content and be alert to any cues as to what the interviewer expects.

Sometimes an interviewer will begin with small talk—perhaps about where you went to school or even comments about the weather. You can still be businesslike and alert even if the small talk is trivial. Remember that small talk has a role because the interviewer will really be judging your ability to get along with people.

In other instances, an interviewer will move immediately into substantial questions or comments. Follow the interviewer's lead as the interview develops.

---

4. Answer questions directly and honestly, and explain your answers with sound examples and references to your qualifications.

Answers are direct when they address the issues raised by an interviewer's questions. You

Interviews

don't gain any credit if you seem to be evading a question.

Support your answers with appropriate examples and facts. Some of these facts may already be on your application or in your résumé. The interviewer may not have noticed them or may want you to go through them again.

Many questions will lead to information beyond the details you included in your resume. For example, the interviewer might ask how good your computer skills are. Your job application might have listed software you are familiar with, but you would need to explain your exact skill level with a specific software program. You may mention the kind of computing or documentation tasks you are comfortable performing using that software.

Expand on or explain any *yes* or *no* answers. The questions may be simple enough, but you want to show the interviewer you appreciate the importance of the questions. For example, the interviewer might ask if you know how to mix pesticides for spraying. Your simple answer might be *yes*, but don't stop there. Go on to mention how long you have known how to mix pesticides and, perhaps, the types of pesticides you have had experience mixing.

5. Reinforce your verbal content with good nonverbal signals (posture, facial expressions, and eye contact).

Communication research has repeatedly shown that the nonverbal message is overwhelmingly more powerful than the words and sentences from a speaker. As much as 70 or 80 percent of the success in an interview is determined by nonverbal cues.

One of the first nonverbal signals in most interviews is the handshake. Your handshake should be firm and positive. If your hand feels like a dead fish, you seem similarly lifeless.

Other poor nonverbal signals include a slouching posture, a negative or bored facial expression, and no eye contact. These all imply, rightly or wrongly, that you are low-energy, not very intelligent, and perhaps even evasive or dishonest.

Practice sample interviews with friends or a family member. If possible, make a video of your sample interview and review it for your nonverbal effectiveness.

6. Practice ahead of time answering hard questions so you won't be surprised.

Prepare a list of hard questions and practice (aloud) how you would answer them. Unless you practice, you won't remember what you intended to say and you will be more nervous than you need to be.

What are some of the harder questions to answer? Here are some common ones, but you will need to compile your own list:

- How did you get along with your last boss?
- What strengths would you bring to this company?
- What are your weaknesses?
- Why did you leave your last job?
- Why do you want to work for XYZ Company?
- Why have you been unemployed so long?
- Tell me about a time when you had to cope with one of your own mistakes. Did you handle it effectively?

Interviews

These are only a few of the many possible questions an interviewer might ask. As you make your list, look closely at the information on your job application form or your résumé. Are there any facts which will cause the interviewer to ask questions? For instance, how would you explain three or four jobs in a row, none lasting more than a month? Or, perhaps you have only two character references listed. What will you say if the interviewer wants a third one?

7. Prepare to ask the interviewer questions about the company, the job, and the working conditions.

Most interviewers leave some time for you to ask questions. Prepare ahead of time to ask thoughtful questions. You might even want to take a written list of questions to the interview.

Make your questions serious ones about the working conditions, the training you would receive, or the opportunities for advancement within the company. Be careful about asking questions that imply you are only interested in the salary and benefits of the job. You have a right to know this type of information, but no one wants to hire a person who is already planning to take a few days off.

A good source of questions is the job description or want ad. If the ad said "good with details," you can ask what job tasks require an attention to details.

8. Plan when and how you expect to end the interview.

Knowing when to end the interview is a valuable skill. Watch the interviewer for cues. Less obvious cues are when the interviewer summarizes the interview and is clearly not going to ask anything else. An obvious cue is when the interviewer stands up.

As soon as you perceive the interview to be over, thank the interviewer for taking time with you, offer to supply any additional information, shake hands (if appropriate), and leave.

9. Follow up on the interview with a call or a thank you letter, whichever seems most appropriate.

The follow-up call or letter is a good technique, especially if you are eager to get the job. Many people ignore this step to their loss.

The follow-up call shows you are still interested in the job and gives you a chance to ask how you did in the interview. Sometimes you can get valuable information for use in other interviews.

The thank you letter is a small courtesy. See the model thank you letter at the back of this book. Such a letter is usually brief, no longer than four or five sentences, and includes the following information:

- A thank you to the interviewer for seeing you

- A restatement of the two or three key reasons you would be a good choice for the job

- An offer of any additional information

Letters are an important business communication tool that can be adapted to a variety of purposes and audiences.

Letters are a form of written communication usually sent to people outside the writer's organization. Letters tend to be somewhat formal and are usually printed on company letterhead. While memos, electronic mail, and voice mail are becoming more popular, letters are still an important business communication tool.

There are many types of letters—commendation letters, complaint letters, proposal letters, application letters, and rejection letters, to name a few. **Letter content** and **letter format** vary depending on the purpose and intended audience of your letter.

Preview

1. Begin with a subject line that clearly expresses the purpose of your letter.

2. Include the main point(s) in the first lines of your text.

3. Design and organize your letters so key points are immediately visible.

4. Make your letters personal and convincing.

5. Choose direct and simple letter closings.

Letter Content

1. Begin with a subject line that clearly expresses the purpose of your letter.

A reader should be able to determine the purpose of your letter quickly. To accomplish this, begin your letter with a subject line. The subject line should capture both the purpose of the letter and the main idea, fact, or point. An effective subject line usually requires more than three or four words, and may even require two lines of text.

To test the effectiveness of your subject line, cover the text in the body of the letter. Does the subject line capture both the purpose of the letter and the main idea? Can the reader predict exactly what ideas will appear in the rest of the letter?

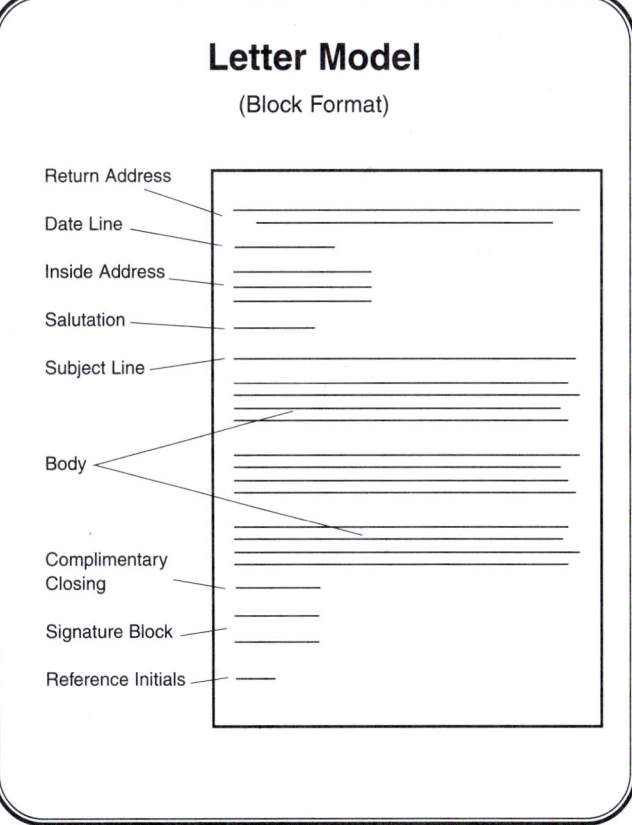

75

Letters

Use boldface, underlining, white space, or another emphasis technique to set off the subject line from the rest of the letter. See Figure 1 for a visual example of what an effective subject line looks like in a business letter.

NOTE 1: Sometimes the lead-in word *Subject* or the old-fashioned *Re (Regarding)* is omitted from the subject line.

Empire Electronics
1234 South Main Street, Centertown, MD 21131
301-555-7771   Fax: 301-555-7779

November 10, 1997

Alex Lofgreen
Anderson Laboratories
1834 Richmond Avenue
Centertown, MD 21131

Dear Alex Lofgreen:

Subject: Request to Resolve Unnecessary Shipping Delays

Please help us track down the cause or causes for the unnecessary shipping delays. Nearly 50 percent of the Anderson shipments . . .

Figure 1. An Example of an Effective Subject Line. *The subject line clearly expresses the purpose of your letter. Use boldface type to set the subject line off from the rest of the letter.*

NOTE 2: The following words are commonly used in a subject line to show the purpose of a letter: *proposal, request, update, application,* and *complaint.*

Do This

   Subject: Proposal to Provide Fast, Efficient Courier Service to Brown and Company

   Subject: Request for Replacement of the Purchasing Department's Defective Hard Drive

Not This

   Subject: Courier Service

   Re: Request for a Replacement

See EMPHASIS and HEADINGS.

2. Include the main point(s) in the first lines of your text.

If you begin a letter with the main points, your readers will immediately see and understand the most important information. If you begin with a long introduction, your readers will start skimming through the text to find the main points of your letter. If they don't find anything important in 15 or 20 seconds, they will probably toss your letter aside to read later (if they have time).

The opening lines of text should repeat words and phrases from the subject line. You can confuse your readers if your subject line goes in one direction and your opening sentence goes someplace else.

Do This

> **Subject: Request for Replacement of the Purchasing Department's Defective Hard Drive**
>
> Please **replace** our **defective hard drive**. Three weeks after we purchased the Medusa system, the hard drive went out. This put the Purchasing Department a day behind schedule. We need a system we can depend on to support our company and keep us in business.

Not This

> Subject: Request to Replace the Purchasing Department's Defective Hard Drive
>
> As you know, the Purchasing Department has been a day behind schedule. This is due to the hard drive on the Medusa system going out three weeks after we bought it. We need a system we can depend on to support our company and keep us in business. So we are asking you to **replace** the **defective hard drive**.

3. Design and organize your letters so key points are immediately visible.

The design and organization of your letter should grow naturally out of your opening sentences. A strong opening outlines main points that will appear in the rest of the letter. See Rule 2.

Letters, like all forms of written communication, must be concise and well organized. Use the principles of good organization in your letters: up and left, previews, headings, lists, and emphasis. See ORGANIZATION.

When a document is designed effectively, its visual impression mirrors the message conveyed by individual words and sentences. In other words, the main points in your letter should *look* important—they should be at the top of the letter, in boldface type, in a bulleted list, or set off in some other way from the rest of the text. See PAGE LAYOUT.

Design and organize your letters by answering the following questions:

- What are the key points I want to make?
- Which point should come first? Which points should come next and in what order?
- Where should I use headings and lists to organize information?
- Where should I use boldface, italics, etc., to emphasize information?
- What information does the reader not need to know?
- Should the letter be formal or informal?

4. Make your letters personal and convincing.

While design and organization are important, you must also pay attention to the language in your letters. Readers will hear your voice in the words and phrases you choose.

If you make your writing personal, you will also be convincing. A convincing style arises as much from your tone and your attention to your readers as it does from citing facts and figures. See TONE and PERSUASION.

Talk directly to your readers, using pronouns and contractions where appropriate. In an informal letter, you can use a conversational tone (as if you were speaking to your reader in person). However, in a formal letter, you should use a more businesslike tone.

Letters

Informal Letter

Dear **Bill,**

Last year, we quoted **you** a price on our RFS 6500 water treatment system. Recently, **we've** reduced the price for this system and added several new features. I hope **you'll** take a few minutes to review the enclosed information and find out why the RFS 6500 should be **your** next water treatment system.

Formal Letter

Dear **Mr. Williams**:

Last year, we quoted **Brown and Company** a price on our RFS 6500 water treatment system. Recently, **we have** reduced the price for this system and added several new features. I hope **you will** take a few minutes to review the enclosed information and find out why the RFS 6500 should be **Brown and Company's** next water treatment system.

Figure 2. Informal Tone Versus Formal Tone in a Letter. *When the writer is familiar with the reader, an informal tone can effectively remove barriers to communication. But if the writer does not know the reader, anything but a formal tone may be offensive.*

NOTE: If you haven't met your reader, you should use a formal tone.

Use simple, direct words and sentences. To keep your words simple, use common words and phrases instead of impressive-sounding ones. The sentences below wouldn't be any clearer if you replaced *met* with *convened* and *plant* with *manufacturing facility*, but it would be more formal.

The committee **met** and made its recommendation Monday. The committee urged a new stock issue by January 1997. This issue would finance an expansion of the Hong Kong **plant**, which now runs three shifts a day.

To keep sentences simple, avoid long sentences. Where possible, keep average sentence length to 13 words or fewer. See Figure 2 for an example of an informal versus a formal letter.

5. Choose direct and simple letter closings.

Make your closing as direct and simple as your opening lines. One option is to close your letter by restating your main point.

By reviewing the enclosed information, you can see for yourself the flexibility and value of the RFS 6500 water treatment system.

Another option is to give the name of a person (maybe yourself) whom the reader can contact with any questions or problems. If you choose this option, keep it short and be sure to include a telephone number.

If you'd like more information about the RFS 6500 water treatment system, please call me at 412-555-2245.

Letter Format

MARGINS
Your letter should have equal left and right margins. For a long letter, use one-inch left and right margins. For a short letter, use wider margins so the text takes up more of the page.

Top and bottom margins are usually determined by the layout of the company letterhead. A one-page letter should be centered on the page both vertically and horizontally.

SPACING
Most business letters are single-spaced with a blank line between paragraphs. However, for short letters, you can use one-and-a-half- or double-line spacing.

LETTER FORMAT STYLES
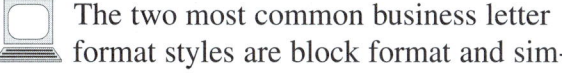
The two most common business letter format styles are block format and simplified block format. In block format, every line is even with the left margin, including the date and the complimentary closing. Paragraphs are separated by a blank line and are not indented. This format is preferred by many writers because it is easy to create on a word processor. The writer can simply press ENTER twice after every paragraph and continue typing. See Figure 3 for an example of a letter presented in the block format.

The simplified block format is similar to the block format except the salutation and complimentary closing are omitted. This format is becoming more popular because salutations (such as *Dear*) and complimentary closings (such as *Yours truly*) are not really appropriate for business letters. See Figure 4 for an example of a letter presented in the simplified block format.

A third letter format style is called the modified block format. This style is uncommon, but still may be seen and used in business letters. In the modified block format, the date, complimentary closing, and signature block are indented to the right of the center of the page. All paragraphs are indented five spaces. The remaining parts of the letter are even with the left margin. See Figure 5 for an example of a letter presented in the modified block format.

Letters

Block Format

FAMILY FRESH FARMLAND FOODS
511 Franklin Road • Lincoln, NB 68506 • 402–555–7070 • Fax 402–555–7079

March 15, 1997

Mr. Donald Allston
1465 Jackson Avenue
Jordan, MO 64833

Dear Mr. Allston:

Subject: Blackened Material in Package Is Burned Potato

Thank you for your letter about Potato Ripples. The black material you found was a harmless chunk of burned potato, although I appreciate your distaste at finding it.

We value the quality of our products and make every effort to prevent burned potato chunks from being packaged in our Potato Ripples. We continuously filter the frying oil, clean the fryers weekly, and visually check all Potato Ripples before packaging. Despite these precautions, we occasionally miss a chunk of blackened potato and it is packaged.

Please accept the enclosed coupons for free Potato Ripples. I hope you will try our product again. Call me directly at 800–555–3110 x324 if you experience any further problem with Family Fresh Farmland Foods.

Sincerely yours,

Melba Davidson

Melba Davidson
Customer Service Representative

MD: goj

cc: Mrs. Florence Lynch

Annotations:
- Block format means that all information lines up with the left margin.
- This letter shows standard punctuation—the salutation with a colon and the complimentary closing with a comma.

Figure 3. Block Letter Format. *Block style is the most commonly used format for business letters. This format can be created easily using a computer word processor or a standard typewriter. Company letterhead is optional, but if it is not used, be sure to include a return address.*

Letters

Simplified Block Format

FAMILY FRESH FARMLAND FOODS
511 Franklin Road • Lincoln, NB 68506 • 402–555–7070 • Fax 402–555–7079

March 15, 1997

D.L. Allston
1465 Jackson Avenue
Jordan, MO 64833

Subject: Blackened Material in Package Is Burned Potato

Thank you for your letter about Potato Ripples. The black material you found was a harmless chunk of burned potato, although I appreciate your distaste at finding it.

We value the quality of our products and make every effort to prevent burned potato chunks from being packaged in our Potato Ripples. We continuously filter the frying oil, clean the fryers weekly, and visually check all Potato Ripples before packaging. Despite these precautions, we occasionally miss a chunk of blackened potato and it is packaged.

Please accept the enclosed coupons for free Potato Ripples. I hope you will try our product again. Call me directly at 800–555–3110 x324 if you experience any further problem with Family Fresh Farmland Foods.

Melba Davidson

Melba Davidson
Customer Service Representative

MD: goj

cc: Mrs. Florence Lynch

> Simplified block format means that all information lines up with the left margin, but you do not include the salutation or the complimentary closing.

Figure 4. Simplified Block Letter Format. *Use a simplified format when you know the name of an organization but not the name of the person who will receive the letter. A simplified format allows you to avoid the old fashioned salutations of* Gentlemen *or* Ladies and Gentlemen. *Also, use a simplified format when you don't know the gender of the person who will receive the letter. In the above letter, the omission of* Dear D.L. Allston *makes the letter less formal sounding. Notice, however, that the simplified format always retains the subject line.*

Letters

Modified Block Format

FAMILY FRESH FARMLAND FOODS
511 Franklin Road • Lincoln, NB 68506 • 402–555–7070 • Fax 402–555–7079

                March 15, 1997

Mr. Donald Allston
1465 Jackson Avenue
Jordan, MO 64833

Dear Mr. Allston:

Subject: Blackened Material in Package Is Burned Potato

  Thank you for your letter about Potato Ripples. The black material you found was a harmless chunk of burned potato, although I appreciate your distaste at finding it.

  We value the quality of our products and make every effort to prevent burned potato chunks from being packaged in our Potato Ripples. We continuously filter the frying oil, clean the fryers weekly, and visually check all Potato Ripples before packaging. Despite these precautions, we occasionally miss a chunk of blackened potato and it is packaged.

  Please accept the enclosed coupons for free Potato Ripples. I hope you will try our product again. Call me directly at 800–555–3110 x324 if you experience any further problem with Family Fresh Farmland Foods.

                Sincerely yours,

                Melba Davidson

                Melba Davidson
                Customer Service Representative

MD: goj

cc: Mrs. Florence Lynch

Callouts:
- Modified block format means that the date, complimentary closing, and signature block are indented just to the right of the center of the page.
- The first line of all paragraphs is indented five spaces; the rest of the document is flush left.

Figure 5. Modified Block Letter Format. *Although common in the past, the modified block format has become obsolete for business letters and only appears occasionally. The previous letter formats displayed in Figure 3 and Figure 4 are preferred, depending on the purpose of the letter.*

Letters

PUNCTUATION STYLES

The two most common business letter punctuation styles are the standard style and the open style. In the **standard** style, the writer uses a colon (or comma) after the salutation and a comma after the complimentary closing.

In the **open** style, the writer omits all nonessential punctuation, including punctuation after the salutation and complimentary closing.

STANDARD LETTER COMPONENTS

While letter formats vary among companies, most have a combination of these components:

- Return address
- Date
- Special notations
- Inside address
- Attention line
- Salutation
- Subject line
- Body
- Heading for additional pages
- Complimentary closing
- Signature block
- Reference initials
- Enclosure notation
- Courtesy copy notation

Business letters are usually printed on company letterhead stationery that gives the company's **return address**, including company name, address, and telephone number. However, if your letter will not be printed on letterhead, type the return address information at the top of the page above the date.

The **date** appears on its own line, usually two or three lines below the letterhead, but it can appear further down if your letter is short. If your letter will not be printed on letterhead, place the date two lines below the typed return address.

In the United States, the standard date format is month-day-year: *March 15, 1997*. Do not use abbreviations in the date.

Special notations appear between the date and the inside address and indicate how the letter should be delivered or handled. Include any special notations on the envelope as well. (See the discussion regarding envelopes on p. 88.) Special notations include the following:

- SPECIAL DELIVERY
- REGISTERED MAIL
- CERTIFIED MAIL
- CONFIDENTIAL
- PERSONAL
- FAX COPY

The **inside address** includes the following:

- The recipient's courtesy title, such as *Dr., Mr.,* or *Ms.* (optional)
- The recipient's name
- The recipient's title (optional)
- The name of the organization
- The street address or post office box number
- The city, state abbreviation, and ZIP code

Ms. Esmeralda Alvarez
Director of Admissions
St. Ambrose College
100 Edgewater Street
Albany, NY 11401

Letters

The inside address usually appears two lines below the date, but this spacing can vary depending on the length of the letter.

Courtesy titles are a complicated issue, since some women prefer to be addressed as *Ms.* while others do not. And, in some cases, you may not know the recipient's gender (for example, if the recipient's name appears as *C. J. Saxon*). If you aren't sure what courtesy title to use, don't use one at all. See the discussion regarding salutations on p. 85 and BIAS-FREE LANGUAGE.

Make sure you spell the recipient's name and organization correctly. The information in the inside address should match the information on the recipient's own letterhead or business card.

Do not use abbreviations in the inside address except for the standard U.S. Postal Service abbreviations. See NOTE 4 in the discussion regarding envelopes on p. 90. Use the following two-character state abbreviations both in the inside address and on envelopes:

Alabama	AL
Alaska	AK
Arizona	AZ
Arkansas	AR
California	CA
Canal Zone	CZ
Colorado	CO
Connecticut	CT
Delaware	DE
District of Columbia	DC
Florida	FL
Georgia	GA
Guam	GU
Hawaii	HI
Idaho	ID
Illinois	IL
Indiana	IN
Iowa	IA
Kansas	KS
Kentucky	KY
Louisiana	LA
Maine	ME
Maryland	MD
Massachusetts	MA
Michigan	MI
Minnesota	MN
Mississippi	MS
Missouri	MO
Montana	MT
Nebraska	NE
Nevada	NV
New Hampshire	NH
New Jersey	NJ
New Mexico	NM
New York	NY
North Carolina	NC
North Dakota	ND
Ohio	OH
Oklahoma	OK
Oregon	OR
Pennsylvania	PA
Puerto Rico	PR
Rhode Island	RI
South Carolina	SC
South Dakota	SD
Tennessee	TN
Texas	TX
Utah	UT
Vermont	VT
Virgin Islands	VI
Virginia	VA
Washington	WA
West Virginia	WV
Wisconsin	WI
Wyoming	WY

NOTE: Some companies use the same format for the inside address as is used for the mailing address on the envelope (typed in capital letters and all punctuation removed). See the discussion regarding envelopes on p. 88.

Letters

Use an **attention line** if the inside address does not contain either the name of an individual or the name of a department. The attention line appears two lines below the inside address.

> Attention Personnel Department

NOTE: An attention line is not the same as a subject line.

The **salutation** has traditionally begun with the greeting *Dear* followed by the recipient's courtesy title and name.

> Dear Ms. Alvarez:
>
> Dear Mr. Saxon:

However, courtesy titles are a complicated issue. See the discussion regarding the inside address beginning on p. 83. If you aren't sure what courtesy title to use, don't use one at all. Simply use the recipient's name.

> Dear Esmeralda Alvarez:
>
> Dear C. J. Saxon:

NOTE 1: If you are using standard punctuation style, put a colon after the recipient's name. If you are using open punctuation style, don't use any punctuation after the recipient's name.

NOTE 2: If you are writing an informal business letter to someone you are well acquainted with, you can use the person's first name followed by a comma.

> Dear Esmeralda,

NOTE 3: In simplified letter format, the salutation is omitted.

Include a **subject line** that clearly expresses the purpose of your letter. Place the subject line either before or after the salutation. See Rule 1.

The **body** of the letter begins two lines below the salutation (or subject line, if it follows the salutation). The body of most business letters is single-spaced with a blank line between paragraphs. However, for short letters, you can use one-and-a-half- or double-line spacing with a blank line between paragraphs.

If your letter is more than one page, make sure at least three lines of text appear on the last page.

If your letter is more than one page, include a **heading on additional pages.** The additional pages should begin with a heading that contains the recipient's name, the page number, and the date. Put at least two blank lines between the heading and the body text. See Figure 6 for examples of second-page headings.

The **complimentary closing** appears two lines below the last line of body text. Capitalize only the first word of the closing and use a comma after the closing.

> Sincerely,
>
> Best regards,

NOTE: In the simplified block format, the complimentary closing is omitted.

The **signature block** follows the complimentary closing and includes your signature, your typed name, and your title. Allow four or five blank lines between the complimentary closing and your typed name for your signature.

> Sincerely,
>
> *Chris L. Peterson*
>
> Chris L. Peterson
> Sales Associate

Letters

Heading for Additional Pages

Ms. Esmeralda Alvarez   - 2-   March 15, 1997

We value the quality of our products and make every effort to prevent burned potato chunks from being packaged in our Potato Ripples. We continuously filter the frying oil, clean the fryers weekly, and visually check all Potato Ripples before packaging. Despite these precautions, we occasionally miss a chunk of blackened potato and it is packaged.

Please accept the enclosed coupons for free Potato Ripples. I hope you will try our product again...

Ms. Esmeralda Alvarez
March 15, 1997
Page 2

We value the quality of our products and make every effort to prevent burned potato chunks from being packaged in our Potato Ripples. We continuously filter the frying oil, clean the fryers weekly, and visually check all Potato Ripples before packaging. Despite these precautions, we occasionally miss a chunk of blackened potato and it is packaged.

Please accept the enclosed coupons for free Potato Ripples. I hope you will try our

Figure 6. Heading on an Additional Page. *Most business letters, particularly sales or proposal letters, should not run longer than one page. However, be certain to use as much space as needed to completely communicate the message of the letter. When a letter does require additional pages, follow one of these examples to indicate the order of pages.*

NOTE: If you are using open punctuation style, do not put a comma after the complimentary closing.

Reference initials are used to indicate who typed the letter, if the typist is different from the writer. The reference initials appear two lines below the signature block and can indicate either the writer and the typist or just the typist. See Figure 7 for examples of how to present reference initials.

An **enclosure notation** reminds readers that one or more documents were sent with the letter. The enclosure notation appears directly under the reference initials and can either indicate the number of enclosures or list the enclosures separately. See Figure 8 for examples of how to present an enclosure notation.

A **courtesy copy notation** shows that people other than the person listed in the inside address have been sent copies of the letter. The courtesy copy notation appears at the bottom of the letter after the enclosure notation. See Figure 9 for an example of a courtesy copy notation.

Letters

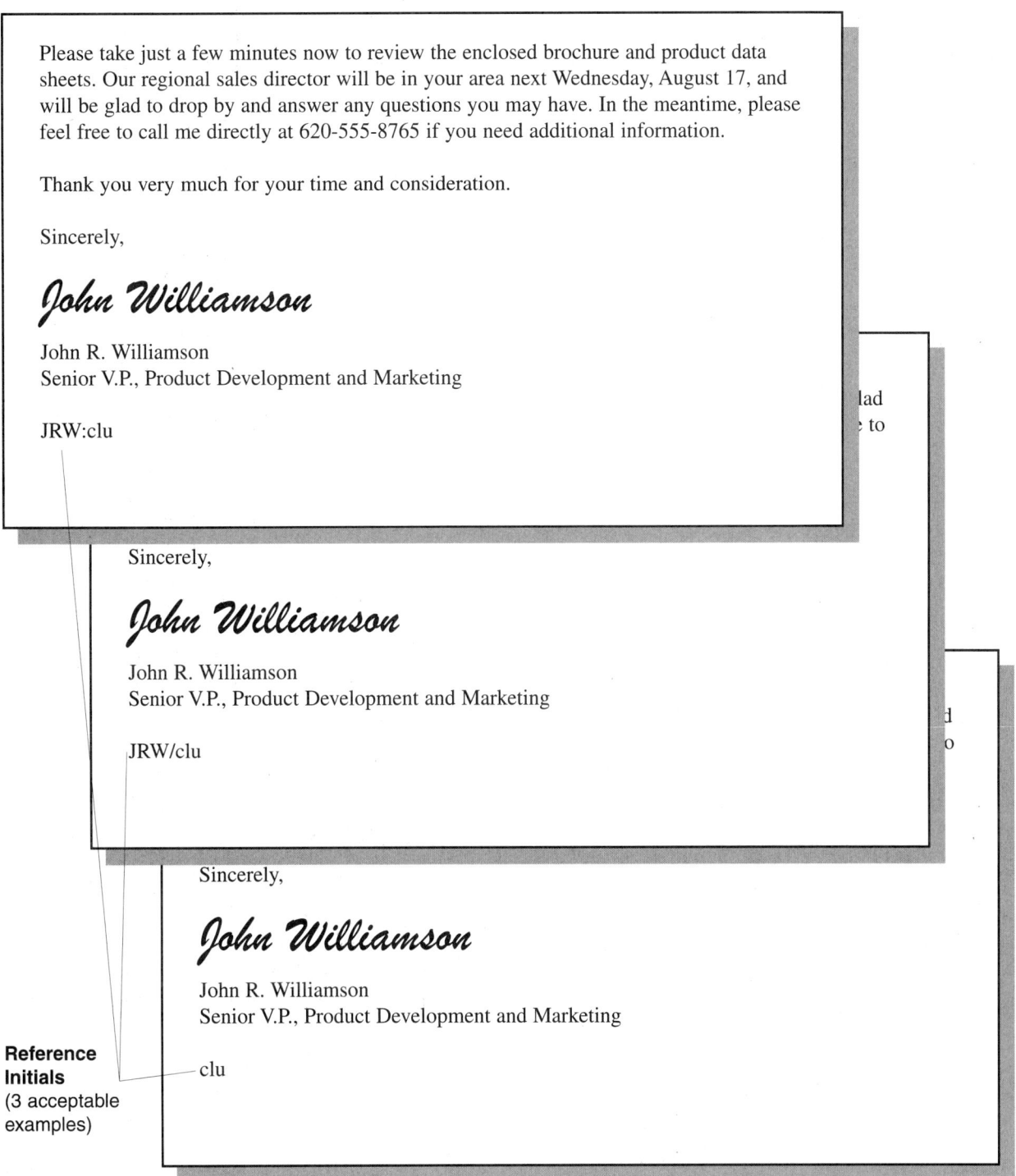

Figure 7. Reference Initials at the Close of a Letter. *Reference initials are a convention unique to business communication. The initials indicate the person who typed the letter, if different from the person sending or writing the letter. Often businesspeople will have an administrative assistant type a letter they have written. The reference initials are designed to keep track of the person who actually types and sends the letter.*

Letters

> to drop by and answer any questions you may have. In the meantime, please feel free to call me directly at 620–555–8765 if you need additional information.
>
> Thank you very much for your time and consideration.
>
> Sincerely,
>
> *John Williamson*
>
> John R. Williamson
> Senior V.P., Product Development and Marketing
>
> JRW/clu
>
> Enclosures (3)

Enclosure Notation (2 acceptable examples)

> *John Williamson*
>
> John R. Williamson
> Senior V.P., Product Development and Marketing
>
> JRW/clu
>
> Enclosures:
> 1. Invoice 599868
> 2. Minutes of August 14 meeting
> 3. Brochure on the RFS 6500 water treatment system

Figure 8. Enclosure Notation at the Close of a Letter. *A cover letter is a letter written to accompany and introduce other materials. Enclosure notations direct readers' attention to additional materials within the letter package. In addition, enclosure notations may indicate reference or support materials used as background information for the contents of the letter.*

ENVELOPES

The U.S. Postal Service gives these guidelines for addressing your envelope. Following these guidelines will help ensure your letter can be processed by the Postal Service's optical scanning equipment.

- Include the recipient's complete address, including name, organization, street address, city, state abbreviation, and ZIP code.

- Center the recipient's address horizontally and vertically on the envelope.

- Type all address information in capital letters.

- Do not use punctuation in the address information.

- Type the address in block format (an even left margin).

Letters

> Thank you very much for your time and consideration.
>
> Sincerely,
>
> *John Williamson*
>
> John R. Williamson
> Senior V.P., Product Development and Marketing
>
> JRW/clu
>
> Enclosures (3)
>
> cc: Huang Wei
>   Ulric Schmidt
>   Florence Halley

Courtesy Copy Notation — points to the cc line.

Figure 9. Courtesy Copy Notation at the End of a Letter. *The courtesy copy reference in a business letter serves much the same purpose as the distribution list in a memo. While the letter is written to one specific individual, it may be distributed to several additional people as indicated in the courtesy copy reference.*

- Type any special notations above and slightly to the right of the address (beneath the postage area). See the discussion regarding special notations on p. 83.

- If your company's return address is not already printed on the envelope, type it in the upper left corner. Follow the guidelines above regarding block format, capital letters, and no punctuation.

For a visual example of how to correctly address a business envelope, see Figure 10.

NOTE 1: The address on the envelope may not exactly match the inside address on the letter, since the address on the envelope will be typed in capital letters and will have all punctuation removed. Compare the examples in Figure 10 to the example given in the discussion regarding the inside address on p. 83.

NOTE 2: The Postal Service's optical scanning equipment reads the envelope from the bottom up. If you have a post office box number and a street address, and you want the letter delivered to the post office box, enter the post office box number on the line just above the city and state.

NOTE 3: Use a sans-serif typeface on all envelope address information. This increases readability and ensures that post office machinery will correctly route the letter.

Letters

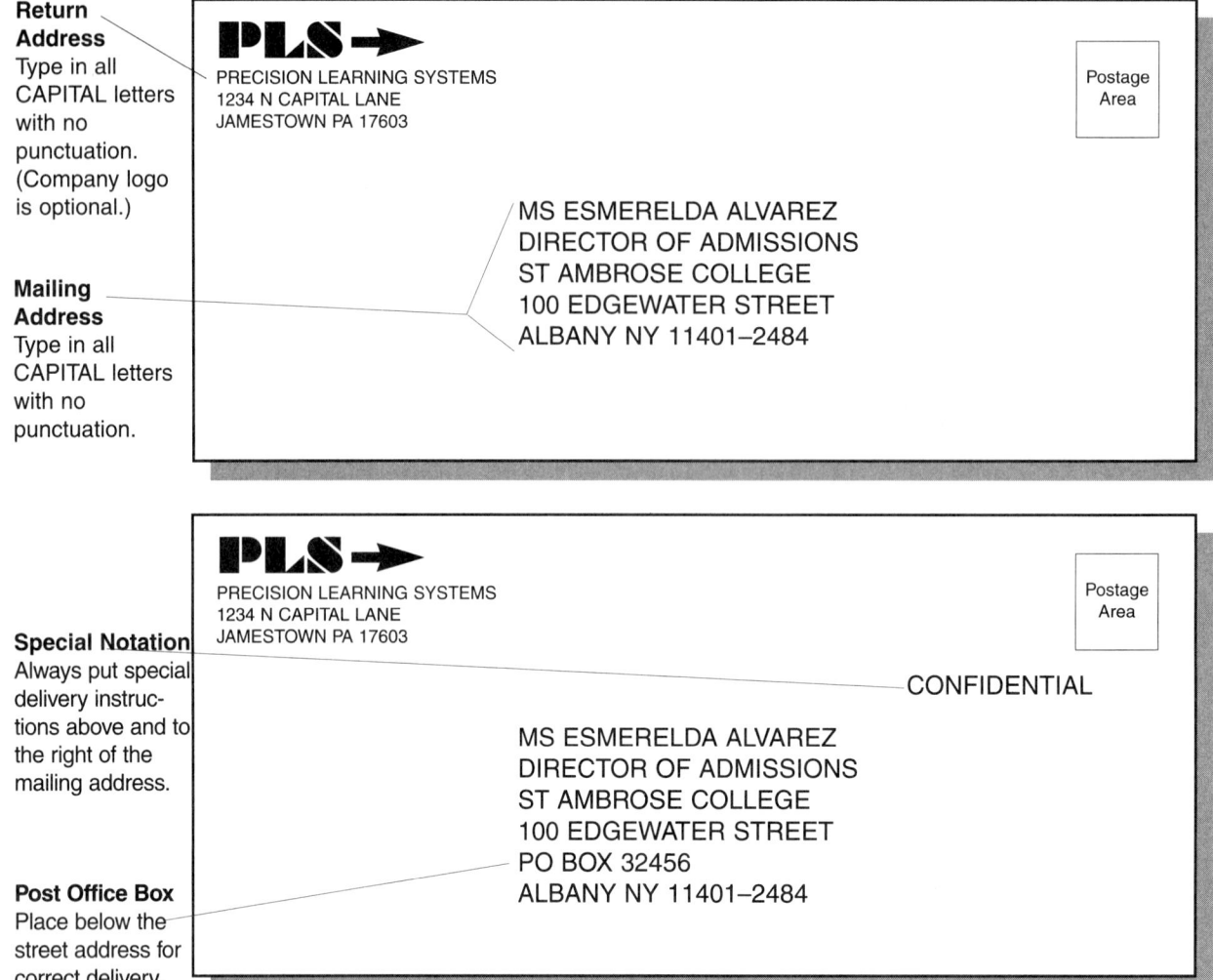

Figure 10. A Correctly Addressed Business Envelope. *Addressing a business envelope requires careful attention to several specific conventions for two reasons: first, to ensure correct reading by routing machinery at the post office; second, to make the information as clear as possible for the person receiving the letter. This annotated figure illustrates the correct way to complete each element of a business envelope.*

NOTE 4: Postal Service standard abbreviations for commonly used address elements are as follows:

- APT (Apartment)
- AVE (Avenue)
- CIR (Circle)
- DR (Drive)
- LN (Lane)
- RD (Road)
- ST (Street)
- STE (Suite)
- HWY (Highway)

See the discussion regarding the inside address on p. 84 for state abbreviations.

Letters

Fold your letter as follows for mailing in a long business envelope (No. 10):

1. Fold the bottom third of the letter up and crease it.
2. Fold the top third of the letter down and crease it.

NOTE: Make sure the top fold does not bend or crease the bottom third of the letter.

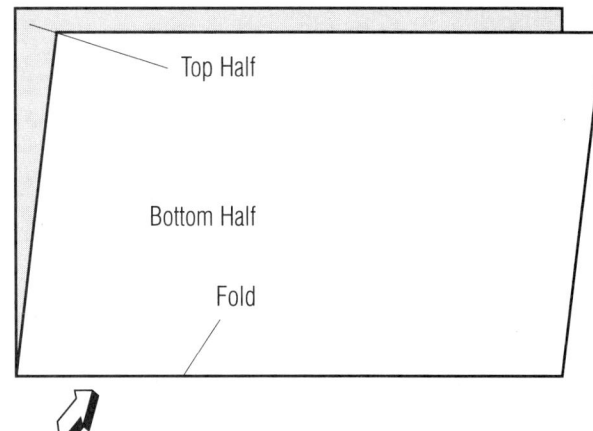

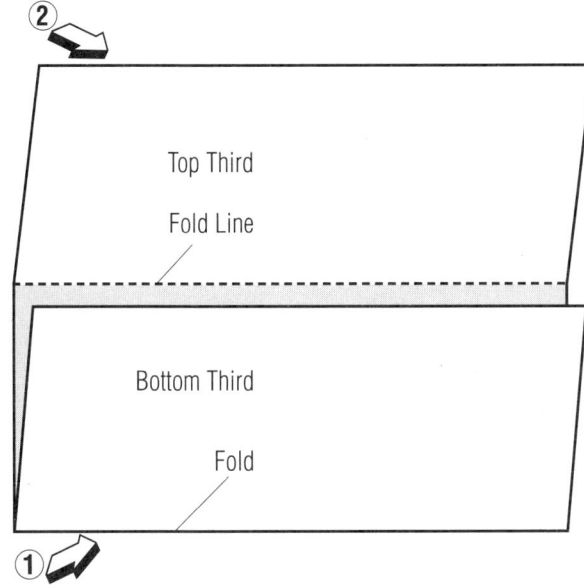

Most businesses use the No. 10 business envelope; however, you may be in a situation where a regular envelope (No. 6¾) is used. In that case, fold your letter as follows:

1. Fold the bottom half of the letter up (with about one-half inch of the top of the paper visible above the folded position) and crease it.

2. Fold the letter in thirds, starting with the right third over the middle third.

3. Fold the left third over the other thirds. (If folded properly, the upper left corner of the letter is on the top of all of the folds.)

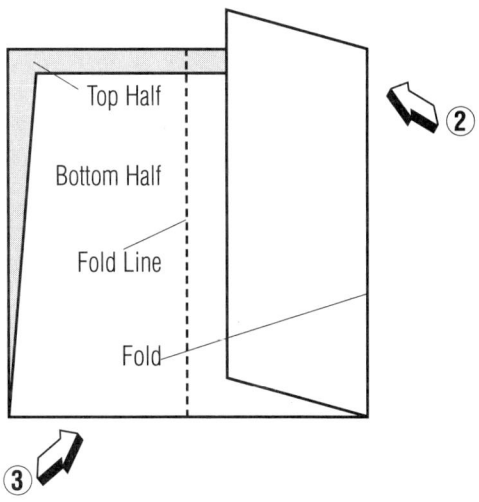

Lists

Lists include a series of items within a paragraph or a series displayed vertically that a writer wishes to emphasize.

Preview

1. Use a list within a paragraph whenever the list is short (fewer than six items) and you do not wish to emphasize the list.

2. Use numbers or letters to identify each item in a paragraph list. Enclose the number or letter within parentheses.

3. Capitalize the first word of each item in a paragraph list only if each item is a complete sentence or if an item begins with a proper noun.

4. In paragraph lists, do not precede the list with a colon if the list follows a preposition or a verb.

5. Use a displayed list for a long series of items and for any series you wish to emphasize.

6. Use numbers, letters, bullets, or dashes to identify each item in a displayed list.

7. Use bullets or dashes to identify each item in a displayed list when the list contains items of equal importance, the order of succession is not an issue, and those items will not have to be referred to by number or letter.

8. Capitalize the first word of each item in a displayed list.

9. Use a colon to introduce a list when the complete sentence preceding the list contains such anticipatory words or phrases as *the following, as follows, thus,* and *these.*

10. Do not end the introductory sentence with a colon if the sentence is lengthy and the anticipatory word or phrase occurs early in the sentence, or if another sentence comes between the introductory sentence and the list.

11. End items in a displayed list with periods if one or more of the items is a complete sentence.

12. Whenever one paragraph list occurs inside another list, use numbers for the outer list and letters for the inner list.

13. Ensure items in lists are parallel in structure. Begin each item with the same type of word (noun, verb, adjective, etc.).

Lists include a series of items embedded within a paragraph (called paragraph lists) or a series displayed vertically (called displayed lists). Occasionally it may be necessary to provide lists within lists. List items must be presented in parallel structure.

Lists

1. **Use a list within a paragraph whenever the list is short (fewer than six items) and you do not wish to emphasize the list.**

   For accounting purposes, you should be aware that the clothing store also offered donations to the shelter: (1) fifteen Healder long-sleeved shirts, (2) a dozen pairs of ski socks, and (3) eight pairs of Alderman fur-lined hiking boots.

2. **Use numbers or letters to identify each item in a paragraph list. Enclose the number or letter within parentheses.**

   The timesheet is in three color-coded sections: (1) blue—Date, (2) cream—Billable Project Title, and (3) yellow—Billable Hours.

   OR

   The timesheet is in three color-coded sections: (a) blue—Date, (b) cream—Billable Project Title, and (c) yellow—Billable Hours.

3. **Capitalize the first word of each item in a paragraph list only if each item is a complete sentence or if an item begins with a proper noun.**

   We suggest that the qualification program include (1) written results of testing on similar equipment, (2) videotape showing performance, and (3) Afton Laboratories' representative interview.

4. **In paragraph lists, do not precede the list with a colon if the list follows a preposition or a verb.**

   See COLONS.

Do This

The Atlantic accounting system is programmed **to** (a) cross-reference medical entries, (b) prevent duplication, (c) signal accounts needing collections, and (d) produce standard invoices.

The Atlantic accounting system is programmed to perform these tasks: (a) cross-reference medical entries, (b) prevent . . .

Not This

The Atlantic accounting system is programmed **to**: (a) cross-reference medical entries, (b) prevent . . .

The tasks the Atlantic accounting system performs **are**: (a) cross-referencing medical entries, (b) preventing . . .

NOTE: In the preceding two **Not This** examples, the two sentences are not complete before the colons. In the first, the preposition *to* requires one or more objects. Similarly, the verb *are* could not conclude a full sentence, so the colon is not correct. The test, then, is that a colon signals a paragraph list only when the lead-in words before the colon form a complete sentence.

5. **Use a displayed list for a long series of items and for any series you wish to emphasize.**

   The groundskeeper at the nursery explained the following plant structures and functions:

   1. Root
   2. Stem
   3. Leaf
   4. Flower
   5. Fruit
   6. Seed

Lists

6. Use numbers, letters, bullets, or dashes to identify each item in a displayed list.

Use numbers or letters whenever the list is lengthy, whenever the text must refer to items in the list, or whenever the items are listed in decreasing order of importance. The numbers or letters should not be enclosed by parentheses, but they should be followed by a period.

> The report defined our interests in the following options:
>
> a. Computer design
>
> b. Microelectronics
>
> c. Genetic engineering
>
> d. Laser optics

7. Use bullets or dashes to identify each item in a displayed list when the list contains items of equal importance, the order of succession is not an issue, and those items will not have to be referred to by number or letter.

> We selected the Reiner's software package for the following reasons:
>
> - It accepts our present files with no conversion loss.
> - It provides easy-to-follow, step-by-step on-line help.
> - It provides presentation guides our teachers can easily apply.

NOTE: On word processors and typewriters that do not have bullets, create bullets by typing a lowercase *o* and using a black ink pen to fill in the center.

8. Capitalize the first word of each item in a displayed list.

> Please address the following departmental issues:
>
> - Management of personnel files
> - Safety in the workplace
> - Effective proposal writing
> - Collection of data for updates

NOTE: The exception to this rule occurs whenever the listed items complete the thought begun in the introductory sentence (see NOTE 2 in Rule 11).

9. Use a colon to introduce a list when the complete sentence preceding the list contains such anticipatory words or phrases as *the following, as follows, thus,* and *these.*

> The manufacturers that develop the needed part are as follows:
>
> - Communications, Inc.
> - Connect Five
> - Electronics Unlimited
> - Glenn Fox Parts and Equipment

NOTE: In some writing, such as advertisements, the lead-in sentence for a displayed list will not contain anticipatory words (for example, *Our upgrade kit includes:* instead of *Our upgrade kit includes these features:* [followed by the displayed list]). As in this example, rewrite lead-in sentences to contain an anticipatory word or phrase.

Lists

10. Do not end the introductory sentence with a colon if the sentence is lengthy and the anticipatory word or phrase occurs early in the sentence, or if another sentence comes between the introductory sentence and the list.

The following steps are required to process the order received by the customer service department. Note that the order is important for the invoicing to occur properly.

1. Customer service representative enters and saves the order on the Xell computer system.
2. Customer service representative transfers a copy of the order to the order department.
3. Order clerk packs, labels, and ships the order.
4. Order clerk transfers a copy of the order to the billing department.
5. Billing clerk prepares and mails the invoice.

11. End items in a displayed list with periods if one or more of the items is a complete sentence.

Rolph's Bakery has a wide range of related experience:

- We developed five royal-tested lunch menus specifically for these occasions.
- We designed and constructed six multi-tiered cakes (on display in the Burdock Branch showroom).
- We produced the full range of after-dinner chocolate custards with layered designs.

NOTE 1: The above listed items are clearly sentences, so periods are necessary. Sometimes, however, items may not be clearly sentences.

    Convene.

    Caucus.

    Vote.

    Adjourn.

Strictly speaking, each of these words is an imperative sentence and should require a period, but their shortness has led some editors to prefer no periods. Items without periods also reflect a trend in advertising and in media documents to use lists without punctuation.

NOTE 2: Sometimes a displayed list completes the sentence begun with the introductory statement. In this instance, even though the listed items are not sentences, the final one will require a period. Also, note that such lists do not follow a colon and they use commas or semicolons after all but the last item.

The life of your automobile tires may be prolonged by

1. rotating front tires to the back (and the back to the front) every 5,000 miles,
2. performing a complete alignment every 10,000 miles,
3. balancing the tires every 5,000 miles, and
4. maintaining appropriate air pressure (checking the pressure each time you stop to get gas).

NOTE 3: Lists with continued punctuation (as in this example) are now rare, probably because writers, influenced by advertising, are using capitals and spacing to make lists more visually emphatic.

Lists

12. Whenever one paragraph list occurs inside another list, use numbers for the outer list and letters for the inner list.

1. The physical characteristics of the Butler cookware include (a) heavy-weight aluminum construction, (b) Mikelege nonstick interior surfaces, (c) all rustproof elements, and (d) easy-clean grease filter.

2. The performance data for aluminum heat conductivity and efficiency include (a) heat transfer levels, (b) energy efficiency ratings, and (c) timed tests.

NOTE: Whenever one displayed list occurs inside another list, use bullets for the outer list and check marks or dashes for the inner list.

To ensure quality billing, follow these requirements:

- Know your branch procedures.
- Assign proper account numbers.
- Watch for specials appearing on the Daily Special Sheet.
    - ✓ Specials shown on Service Orders document the date and monies charged.
    - ✓ Specials shown on the Vault Special Order form document the date and person giving approval.

Do This

Say good-bye to annoying or distracting noises by using this program in the following ways:

1. Connect a single 9-volt battery.
2. Plug into the headphone jack of your portable system at home.
3. Plug into your computer sound card.
4. Plug into the headphone jack on a plane.

NOTE: Each item begins not only with a verb, but also with the same kind of verb. The list would not be parallel if the verb or sentence forms were changed, as in the following bad example:

Not This

Say good-bye to annoying or distracting noises by using this program in the following ways:

1. Connection of a single 9-volt battery
2. Plug into the headphone jack of your portable system at home
3. Plugged into your computer sound card
4. Plugging into the headphone jack on a plane

13. Ensure items in lists are parallel in structure. Begin each item with the same type of word (noun, verb, adjective, etc.).

See PARALLELISM.

Memos are written communication to persons within the writer's organization and are often referred to as "interoffice correspondence."

M*emos* is a shortened version of *memoranda* or *memorandums*. The longer, formal versions are correct, but the more convenient *memos* is widely used and acceptable.

Memos are written communication to persons within the writer's organization. Hence, memos are often referred to as "interoffice correspondence."

Memo content and **memo format** vary, depending on the organization and the purpose of the memo. Some organizations insist memos be no longer than one page. They argue memos are for transmitting and storing day-to-day internal messages.

Other organizations allow memos to be as long as necessary. In longer memos, the writer must use summaries, headings, lists, and other emphatic devices to break up the content and make the memo readable. See EMPHASIS.

Memo content also varies considerably—from brief notices of meetings to full-fledged analyses of alternatives and recommendations for action. The fact is that memos are useful devices for transmitting any type of information to other persons within an organization.

The main difference between a memo and a letter is their heading or opening. A memo identifies the writer and the reader, but not the company or organization. A letter, in contrast, opens with the name, address, and phone number of the company or organization.

Preview

1. Begin with a subject line that clearly expresses the purpose of your memo.

2. Include your main point(s) in the first lines of your text.

3. Design and organize your memos so key points are immediately visible.

4. Make your memos personal and convincing.

5. Choose direct and simple memo closings.

Memo Model

Heading — Memorandum
To: _____ Date: _____
From: _____
Subject: _____

Body

Signature Line

Reference Initials

Attachment Notation

Courtesy Copy Notation

Memos

Memo

> **Memorandum**
>
> To: M. L. Abrams   Date: March 15, 1997
>
> From: Joan Abercrombie
>
> **Subject: Compliance with Accident Prevention Procedures in the Electronics Processing Laboratories**
>
> Please comply with the following accident prevention procedures in the Electronics Processing Laboratories. These procedures require careful attention . . .

Letter

> **Empire Electronics**
> 1234 South Main Street, Centertown, MD 21131
> 301-555-7771   Fax: 301-555-7779
>
> November 10, 1997
>
> Alex Lofgreen
> Anderson Laboratories
> 1834 Richmond Avenue
> Centertown, MD 21131
>
> Dear Alex Lofgreen:
>
> **Subject: Request to Resolve Unnecessary Shipping Delays**
>
> Please help us track down the cause or causes for the unnecessary shipping delays. Nearly 50 percent of the Anderson shipments . . .

Memo Content

Because memos are essentially letters that stay within an organization, the following principles of good letter writing apply equally to memos. See LETTERS.

1. Begin with a subject line that clearly expresses the purpose of your memo.

Test any memo by covering all but the subject line(s). Do the subject lines capture the major point(s)? Can you predict exactly what ideas will follow the subject lines? If readers can't make an accurate prediction, your memo invites misreading and misunderstanding.

Subject lines should be in boldface type, underlined, or emphasized with some other technique. An effective subject line gives both the purpose and the key facts related to that purpose, and often requires 6, 8, 10, or more words using 2 or more lines of type. See HEADINGS and EMPHASIS.

Do This

>Subject: Authorization to Advertise for an Additional Copy Editor for Our Marketing Team

>Subject: Request for Invoicing Turnaround Every 10 Working Days, Not Monthly

Not This

>Subject: Hiring a Copy Editor

>Subject: NEW INVOICING

NOTE: Sometimes the lead-in word *Subject* or the old-fashioned *Re* (*Regarding*) is omitted.

---

2. Include your main point(s) in the first lines of your text.

If you open your memo with your main points, readers will know the purpose of the memo immediately. If your opening lines are not informative, your readers are likely to skip and scan for a main point or supporting ideas. If they don't find anything of importance within 15 or 20 seconds, your memo will go on the bottom of their to-read stack.

The opening lines of text usually repeat words and phrases from the subject line. This repetition is desirable.

Do This

>**Subject: Authorization to Advertise for an Additional Copy Editor for the Marketing Team**
>
>Please **advertise** immediately **for an additional copy editor** for the Marketing team. As you noted, our current editor is unable to complete the work we need in a timely fashion. If possible, let's have the new person hired and trained by June 15.

Not This

>Subject: Copy Editor
>
>As you know, the marketing team has been asked to take on six new projects. These were not included when we set up our original staffing plan, and so we are having to absorb costly overtime payments. In addition, this situation is placing a tremendous burden on an already overworked staff. We are, therefore, asking you to **advertise** immediately **for an additional copy editor**.

---

3. Design and organize your memos so key points are immediately visible.

The design of your memo should naturally grow out of your strong opening (see Rules 1 and 2).

A solid, informative opening often outlines the supporting points to follow.

An effective visual design includes headings, lists, graphics, and other emphasis techniques. See EMPHASIS. A writer's goal is to design and organize a memo so every reader receives the writer's intended message.

Research has shown that the more visual the image, the more memorable the message.

Visually design your memos by answering these key questions:

- What are the key points you want your readers to remember?

- What subheadings and lists should you use?

Memos

- Which points come first? Which come next?
- How much repetition is useful?
- What tables and other graphics should you include?
- Does the page layout reinforce the message?

---

4. Make your memos personal and convincing.

Memos, like letters, rely on document design to reinforce the message conveyed by individual words and sentences. See LETTERS.

Still, your voice speaks through the words and phrases you choose, even if softly. You must, therefore, choose language that is personal and as convincing as possible.

Because memos are internal or interoffice letters, the message can be written in a less formal fashion than an external letter, making use of pronouns and contractions where appropriate. Assess your reader's interests and needs, and address these interests by speaking directly to the reader(s).

Do This

One of your priorities included an adjustment of the due date for contract renewal. Your estimate of dates also included associated cost savings. We agree with you.

Use contractions when they would normally occur in speech.

Do This

Once your program has been approved, we'll move ahead to hire the necessary professionals. We're doing this with existing funds because next year's budget has yet to be approved.

Avoid jargon and gobbledygook.

Not This

According to the aforementioned agreement, the elements of the items to be discussed are likely of some interest, yet they may well not be greatly and completely significant. These are of some concern because the agenda considered is primarily based on a priori assumptions generated and discussed by our committee of professionals.

As in this example of poor and insulting writing, writers of jargon and gobbledygook use language recklessly, without regard to the basic meanings beneath the language. The writer of this example takes 51 words to say nothing. Every phrase is weakened by an empty modifier. Every reader would take away a different, muddled message.

Prefer the common word or phrase—for example, *met* instead of *convened* and *plant* instead of *manufacturing facility*.

Do This

The committee **met** and made its recommendation Monday. The committee urged a new stock issue by January 1997. This issue would finance an expansion of the Hong Kong **plant**, which now runs three shifts a day.

As in this simple and direct example, average sentence length should be low—13 words in this instance.

Memos

If you make your writing personal, you will also be convincing. A convincing style arises as much from your tone or your implied credibility as it does from citing facts and figures. If you keep your language simple and direct, you will gain your readers' respect. See TONE.

5. Choose direct and simple memo closings.

Make your closing as simple and direct as you made your opening lines.

One option is to close your memo with a restatement of your main point.

> I hope you'll make room in your busy schedule for the coordination meeting on June 15 at 2:30 in the Human Resources conference room.

> All your tests, as outlined above, indicate we should identify a new vendor for our factory-installed CD player. We hope that you concur and that you'll authorize initial funding by September 22.

Another option is the standard reference to questions or problems. If you choose this option, keep it short and be sure to give your phone number.

> Please call or write Jack Owens (412-555-2245) if you have any questions about our proposed investment schedule. As our financial advisor, Jack can tell you how we generated the figures in our proposal.

Memo Format

Memo format varies from organization to organization. However, memos often have these standard components:

- Heading
- Body
- Signature line
- Reference initials
- Attachment notation
- Courtesy copy notation

HEADING

Use a heading with these elements:

TO:

FROM:

DATE:

SUBJECT:

REFERENCES:

The order of these elements, their spacing and punctuation, and their placement on the page vary considerably. In printed memo forms, the heading elements often do not have colons. Typed headings usually have colons.

Some memos open with *To* and then give the *Subject* line. Others place the *Date* after the *To* line. Still others arrange the items in two parallel lists such as the following:

TO	FROM
SUBJECT	DATE
REFERENCES	

Some memos omit the *From* line, opting instead for a typed name and signature at the end of the memo.

To/From   The names of both the sender and the receiver do not require courtesy titles (*Mr., Mrs., Ms.,* or *Miss*), but *Dr.* is sometimes used. Names should be as complete as possible and,

Memos

if appropriate, should include the person's title and department. Long after the memo has been filed, future readers will probably not know *Hank* or *Sue,* and their full names could be important.

Some memos are sent to so many people that it is impractical to list their names after *To.* When this occurs, the word *Distribution* is typed after *To,* and a list showing those who will receive copies is placed at the end. See the model memos at the back of this *Style Guide.*

Date The date is usually written with the month spelled out.

Do This
    March 15, 1997

Not This
    3/15/97

Subject The content of the subject line should be specific enough to tell readers exactly what the memo is about. The subject line may therefore include dates, invoice numbers, project information, loan agreement numbers, and other similar information.

NOTE: A specific enough subject line may make a reference line unnecessary.

> **Subject: Recommendation for Engine and Cylinder Overhaul, Management Summary Report 10/17/97**

References If a memo makes reference to other documents, the full title of these documents is usually provided on a reference line. If the date appears by itself just right of the center of the page, the reference line may be placed below it. Another option for multiple references is to place them on their own lines, usually before or after the subject line. See the model memos at the back of this *Style Guide.*

REFERENCES:

1. F. H. Howell, "Testing of the Wing Plate Assembly." 18 May 1990.
2. J. K. Jameson, "Design Options in the Wing Plate Assembly." 22 March 1990.

If several items appear in the reference list, number them for easy reference within the body of the memo.

> Reference 1 notes that all wing plate assemblies have passed inspection this year. However, reference 2 indicates that design modifications must be undertaken to improve reliability.

BODY
Paragraphs in the body of the memo are usually single-spaced with a double space between them. The first line of these paragraphs may or may not be indented (5 to 10 spaces). Both the indented and block forms are correct and usually acceptable; however, your company may have a preferred style.

Headings and lists are important devices, especially when a memo is more than a page or two long. See HEADINGS and LISTS.

The heading for continued pages should contain the recipient's name, the date, and the page number.

    M. J. Abrams   -2-   March 15, 1997

    OR

    M. J. Abrams
    March 15, 1997
    Page 2

Memos

SIGNATURE LINE

Traditional memos had no signature line. The author's name appeared after *From* in the heading.

Recently, however, because memos are photocopied for distribution or different versions may exist, many writers have begun signing their initials or their whole names two lines below the final line of the text, or next to the name on the From line. The name or initials may be typed, but they may also be handwritten.

Rarely do such signature lines contain titles, probably because the people within a company already know job titles or can easily look them up in a directory.

REFERENCE INITIALS

Reference initials in memos usually contain only the typist's initials. These initials appear flush with the left margin and either two lines below the signature line or two lines below the bottom line of text (if the memo has no signature line).

The initials are usually in lowercase letters:

   jtk

If the reference initials also contain the author's initials, the author's initials precede those of the typist and follow one of these forms:

   GLK/jtk   GLK:jtk   glk/jtk

When someone other than the sender writes the memo, the sender's initials come first, then the writer's initials, and then the typist's initials:

   GEL/TER/jtk   GLK:TER:jtk

NOTE: Individuals in organizations like to know who prepared the memo so they know who to contact if the sender is not available.

ATTACHMENT NOTATION

Attachment notations are not very common in memos. If used, they appear flush with and on the line immediately below the reference initials. The number of attachments appears within parentheses:

   GLK/jtk

   Attachments (3)

In some technical memos with a number of attachments (such as maps or charts), the attachments may be listed at the bottom of the memo following the attachment notation.

COURTESY COPY NOTATION

If used, *cc* (*courtesy copy* or *carbon copy*) notations appear two lines below the reference or attachment notations. The *cc* notation is placed at the bottom of the memo. It indicates who, in addition to the person listed in the heading, is receiving a copy of the memo. The form varies:

   cc

   cc:

   Copy to

   Copies to

Memos sent to a large number of readers often have a distribution list instead of a courtesy copy list. The word *Distribution* appears in the heading following *To*. *Distribution* also appears instead of *cc* in the courtesy copy notation, and following *Distribution* is a list of the names and (if appropriate) departments of those people who should receive copies of the memo.

103

Numbers

Numbers used in writing follow many rules for specific situations and provide added emphasis for facts, figures, and measurements.

Numbers can be written out as words (*nine*) or can appear as figures (*9*), depending on the size of the number, what it stands for, and how exact it is. The recommendations that follow are based on the current standard practice of business writing.

1. Use numerical figures for any number expressing time, measurement, or money.

3 A.M.

45 ft

1 in.

8 cm

34.17 m

$15

NOTE: A period following the unit of measurement (*cm* or *ft*) is generally not used today in business writing. However, if the abbreviated unit of measurement may be confused with an actual word (*in* or *am*) the period must be used (*in.* or *a.m.*).

Figures are easier to read and are remembered more accurately and longer than their spelled-out versions. Rules 2 through 12, which follow, show examples of when Rule 1 may not apply.

Preview

1. Use numerical figures for any number expressing time, measurement, or money.

2. Write out numbers if they are below 10. If they are 10 or above, use figures.

3. Write out numbers that begin a sentence.

4. Rewrite sentences beginning with a very large number.

5. Use figures to express estimates based on experience, evidence, or both.

6. Write out approximations that are obvious exaggerations for effect.

7. Use a combination of letters and figures for large round numbers (1 million or greater).

8. Be consistent.

9. Use figures for quantities containing both whole numbers and fractions.

10. Always use figures for percentages and decimal fractions.

11. Always use figures for dates.

12. Form the plural of a number expressed as a figure by adding a lowercase *s*.

13. Use a comma to separate groups of three digits when the group is over 4 digits.

104

Numbers

2. Write out numbers if they are below 10. If they are 10 or above, use figures.

five systems

15 systems

three job responsibilities

14 job responsibilities

two technicians

22 technicians

NOTE 1: Regardless of the number's size, use figures if they are followed by a unit of measurement (see Rule 1):

5 pounds

2 yards

1 kilometer

NOTE 2: In nontechnical writing, writers often write out numbers less than 100—for example, thirty-five, seventy-one, eighty-nine. Note the hyphens in these written-out forms. See HYPHENS. Writing out numbers less than 100 avoids overemphasizing double-digit numbers in nontechnical business documents, which typically contain few numbers.

3. Write out numbers that begin a sentence.

Twelve inches from the bottom are two slots for electrical connections.

Four years ago, we began a study of frozen foods.

These two examples do not use figures even though they are followed by units of measurement. Rule 3 overrules Rule 1.

4. Rewrite sentences beginning with a very large number.

Do This

Every second, the human brain receives 363 signals from the nerve endings.

Not This

363 times a second the human brain receives a signal from the nerve endings.

Three hundred sixty-three times a second the human brain receives a signal from the nerve endings.

5. Use figures to express estimates based on experience, evidence, or both.

about 3,000 samples

approximately 60 applicants

roughly 2 cubic feet per second

over 3 million orders this quarter

NOTE: Some editors would prefer the written-out forms in the example above. Others prefer numerals with such words as *nearly, about, around,* and *approximately.* Use your judgment. Figures convey a greater sense of precision than words, and you should be careful not to suggest what is untrue.

6. Write out approximations that are obvious exaggerations for effect.

That computer is not worth two cents.

The boss received a thousand telephone calls today.

His mother told him a million times to clean up that mess.

Numbers

7. Use a combination of letters and figures for large round numbers (1 million or greater).

We have invested over $45 million in laser research in the last 5 years.

Our annual marketing budget exceeds $16 million.

---

8. Be consistent.

Treat numbers of the same type equally within a sentence, paragraph, or section. However, **never** begin a sentence with a figure.

Do This

Model A will require 5 batteries; Model B, 17 batteries; Model C, 9 batteries; and Model D, 14 batteries.

Not This

Model A will require five batteries; Model B, 17 batteries; Model C, nine batteries; and Model D, 14 batteries.

Do This

Seven of the cable television companies carry 39 television channels. The other 14 cable companies carry only 8 channels.

Not This

7 of the cable television companies carry 39 television channels. The other 14 cable companies carry only eight channels.

Seven of the cable television companies carry thirty-nine television channels. The other fourteen cable companies carry only eight channels.

Seven of the cable television companies carry 39 television channels. The other fourteen cable companies carry only 8 channels.

---

9. Use figures for quantities containing both whole numbers and fractions.

The assignment calls for paper 8½ by 11 inches.

---

10. Always use figures for percentages and decimal fractions.

The rectangular frames are 7.25 in. high.

The maximum wheel diameter is 27.5 in.

The tests require an 8 percent participation rate.

NOTE: In the last example, *8%* would also be acceptable, although many style guides prefer that writers use the percent sign only in tables and graphics. In accounting and other financial documents, the percent sign is common in text.

---

11. Always use figures for dates.

June 14, 1989

14 June 1989

the 14th of June 1989

June 1989

NOTE: If you use the preferred style (month-day-year, as shown in the first example above), always separate the day and year with a comma. The second example shows the alternate style: day-month-year, with no punctuation.

Numbers

The third example is wordy but still acceptable in some contexts, such as in legal documents.

If you write only month and year (as in the last example above), use no punctuation. Separating the month and the year is unnecessary. See COMMAS.

---

12. Form the plural of a number expressed as a figure by adding a lowercase *s*.

>   before the 1970s
>
>   temperatures well into the 100s
>
>   the 5s represent actual strikes

NOTE: Do not include an apostrophe between the number and the letter *s*.

Plurals of numbers written out are formed like the plurals of other words:

>   in the twenties
>
>   groups of threes or fours

See PLURALS.

13. Use a comma to separate groups of three digits when over four digits.

>   55,344,500
>
>   10,001
>
>   9,999
>
>   678

NOTE 1: In some technical fields, the preferred style is to omit the comma separating digits in numbers only four digits long:

>   5600
>
>   9999

NOTE 2: A practice in a few countries outside the United States is to use a space instead of a comma to separate groups of three digits:

>   7 143
>
>   98 072.1
>
>   1 742 600 503

Organization

Structure the ideas in a document in a natural but emphatic order, providing the most important information first.

Organization is *the* key writing principle. If your documents are poorly organized, nothing can save them.

The principles of organization differ slightly from document to document, depending on the type of document, the readers, the content, and the writer's purpose. Letters, memos, and reports all differ somewhat in their organizational patterns, mostly because their readers differ.

- Readers of letters are typically outside the company or agency sending the letter. Their relationship to the writer is more distant, and consequently more formal, than the relationship between the writer and others within the writer's company. See LETTERS.

- Readers of memos, on the other hand, are typically within the writer's company or agency. They share the same assumptions, experiences, and knowledge—all of which tend to make memos less formal than letters. See MEMOS.

- Many companies have strict guidelines for organizing reports. Writers may have few options in varying that organization. Before writing a report, it is important to be familiar with your company's established procedures.

Carefully consider how to arrange your ideas and supporting details so the document serves its purpose and satisfies the readers' needs. You might organize the same information differently for different readers, depending on their needs and your purpose in writing to them.

For example, if you have been involved in a car accident, your report to the insurance company, a family member, or a friend will be different. If you were to write to the police requesting information, you would also have a different tone and style. Sample letter openings for each type of reader are provided on the following page.

The data and ideas you include in a document and the way you organize them depends on (1) to whom you are writing and (2) why you are writing to them.

Preview

1. Place your most important ideas at the top of the document and on the left side of the page.

2. In documents longer than a single page, preview your most important points to highlight the major ideas.

3. List items in descending order of importance.

4. Use informative headings that label the text under them and show logical divisions in the text.

5. Use emphasis techniques to provide cues to the document's organization.

6. Use graphics to emphasize important ideas.

7. Review (summarize) major points.

Organization

Reader	Document Opening
Insurance Company	Attached you will find two price quotes for repairs from Auto Body and from Watkins Brothers' Auto Repair as you requested. Please call me at 555-8886 with your decision so I can make the appointment for the repairs. The repairs are necessary because of the damage done to my car in an accident on Thursday, November 18, 1997, at the intersection of Brown and McKelleps. The driver of the other vehicle failed to stop at the stop sign . . .
Family Member	I was involved in a car accident on Thursday, November 18. I wasn't injured, but my car was heavily damaged. The driver of the other vehicle drove right past the stop sign—never even slowed down! It happened at the intersection of Brown and McKelleps . . .
Friend	I guess I can forget about the trip we planned next month. Some idiot plowed into my car last Thursday. I wasn't hurt but my car's a wreck . . .
Police Officer	Would you please send me a copy of the written report of the car accident I was involved in on Thursday, November 18, 1997, at the intersection of Brown and McKelleps. My insurance company is particularly interested in the section you wrote indicating the estimated speed of the other vehicle and showing . . .

Figure 1. Sample Letter Openings. *If you have been involved in a car accident, your report would be organized differently for different readers.*

1. Place your most important ideas at the top of the document and on the left side of the page.

In each section of text, begin with your most important ideas, then support those ideas by presenting your details afterwards—as shown in the 4-Box Organizer in Figure 2 and the memo in Figure 3.

Because readers read from left to right, and typically pay more attention at the beginning, place the most important ideas of the document at the top and on the left side of the page. The subject line, the opening paragraph, and headings are all important to readers.

A frequent problem with business and technical writing is the tendency to lead **to**, rather than **from**, major ideas. Many writers believe that skeptical readers will not agree with their conclusions unless they first explain how they arrived at those conclusions. This tendency results in documents that are non-emphatic, difficult to follow, and filled with unnecessary detail.

Most nonscientific readers are far more interested in the conclusions than they are in the steps leading to them. Placing the conclusions at the beginning of the document makes reading easier because the reader is given a viewpoint from which to understand the facts being presented.

Organization

4-Box Organizer for Effective Memos

Box 1
Purpose
To Know
To Do
Deadlines

- Write an informative subject line.
- Begin Paragraph 1 with your most important idea (**Know** and **Do** statements).

Box 2
Because
Why?

- Preview key content, listing points in order of importance. Use numbers or bullets.

Box 3
Proof
Who? What?
When? Where?
Why? How?

- Use informative headings that match the points listed in Box 2.
- Support each point (heading) by giving additional information.

Box 4
Summary
Summarize and Repeat.

- End by restating your most important ideas.

Figure 2. 4-Box Organizer for Effective Memos

Write a subject line informing readers of your message. This subject line is separate from the opening sentence of Paragraph 1 although they will contain some repeated points. See LETTERS and MEMOS.

Begin Paragraph 1 with your most important idea. Give your readers immediately the information they need. Write a **Know** statement presenting the most important reason for your request and a **Do** statement spelling out specifically what you would like done in response to your communication. If there is a deadline, include this in the first paragraph.

In rare instances you cannot begin by stating your most important idea because the reader either will not understand it or will not accept it.

Organization

```
                        Memorandum

          To:     Diana Marsh        Date:   July 17, 1997
          From:   Martin Andersen

          Subject:  Selecting New Software for Warner Preschool
          ─────────────────────────────────────────────────────

          The Delfa software supplied to Warner Preschool is currently not being used
          because it failed to meet the students' needs. We would like you to select and
          deliver new software to Warner by July 25.

          On July 15 the Delfa software was removed from the school's computers
          because students were becoming frustrated with its difficulty level. Teachers
          reported that their students were actually becoming aggressive and damaging
          the computers because the students could not respond rapidly enough to win
          any of the games. The software obviously requires motor skills and manual
          dexterity far beyond that of preschool children.

          We have contacted Delfa ourselves, but they do not have any other computer
          programs that would be more suitable. We need you to test other packages
          and select something appropriate for Warner.

          The computer program at Warner is one of the main reasons that parents
          select it as the preschool for their children. It is, therefore, very important that
          we have replacement software available as soon as possible. Please make a
          selection and personally deliver it to Warner no later than noon on Friday,
          July 25. Please also allow time at the school to demonstrate the software for
          the teachers and to check its effectiveness with their students. If you need
          assistance, call me at 555-6656.

                                                    Martin Andersen

          cc: Ralph Wills
```

Box 1 — To Know, to Do, and Deadlines.

Box 2 — Because—Why do it?

Box 3 — Prove the "Because" with who, what, when, where, how, and why.

Box 4 — Summarize and Repeat.

Figure 3. 4-Box Organizer Memorandum Example

In such a case, you will need to provide introductory information. Such introductory setups might mention previous meetings, a document, or other background details.

Keep your setups as short as possible. Do not unnecessarily delay presenting your major ideas. In the following letter the setup is unnecessary:

After we met in October, I spoke with several of our largest customers. They confirmed your view that our shipping procedures need updating. I am requesting, therefore, that you review and recommend changes.

Organization

A better version (without the opening setup):

> Please review and recommend changes to our shipping procedures. I have called several of our largest customers, who confirmed that our procedures need to be updated.

2. In documents longer than a single page, preview your most important points to highlight the major ideas.

In documents longer than a single page, use a bulleted or numbered list to establish the structure of the document. If you don't, readers may be overwhelmed by the document's size or complexity. Opening previews and concluding reviews are essential if you want readers to grasp your major points.

In short documents, you can preview content in the opening paragraphs.

3. List items in descending order of importance.

In the case of the long document, the bulleted or numbered preview list acts as a map giving your reader quick access to your entire message. This map lists the most important item first, least important last.

If numbering or lettering systems are used, they reinforce the order of importance. We all know that being *Number 1* is better than being *Number 6*. We know from school that an *A* is better than an *F*. Rightly or wrongly, we assume a natural ranking of items. Therefore, list items in descending order of importance, and group similar ideas where possible.

If you wish to create a list in which items are equally important, use bullets instead of numbers or letters, and state that the listed items are equal. See LISTS.

When you introduce items in a list, discuss them in the same order later. Saying that you are going to talk about *A*, *B*, and *C*, and then beginning with *B* violates the readers' sense of order. Follow these examples:

> The survey revealed three employee concerns: an increase in wages, shorter shifts, and more up-to-date equipment.
>
> Wages have consistently risen at an annual rate of . . .
>
> Shortening work shifts may be to our advantage . . .
>
> The packaging department received two major pieces of new equipment . . .

Do This

> The software cut costs while improving our accuracy and reducing the time needed for reports. Prior to using this software, we spent twice as much research money on fixing mistakes.

Not This

> The software cut costs while improving our accuracy and reducing the time needed for reports. Prior to using this software each report took six months to complete. . . .

This example demonstrates a subtle but important use of organization. The writer introduces three ideas: *cutting costs, improving accuracy,* and *reducing time*. To be consistent with the order in which these ideas were introduced, the writer must follow the introductory statement with *cutting costs*, not *improving accuracy* or *reducing time*, as occurs in the final version.

Organization

4. Use informative headings that label the text under them and show logical divisions in the text.

Headings break a document into pieces, revealing its organization. Readers can glance at the headings to determine where they need to read more closely and where they can skim. Also readers can gain an overall sense of the document even if they do not have the time, interest, or knowledge to read the entire text.

Headings are especially useful when you need to signal organizational shifts or abrupt changes in direction, such as the transition from one topic to another (unrelated) topic. If the shifts are too radical, you cannot easily indicate them in text.

In longer documents, turn the bulleted or numbered list into headings. Under each heading, provide detailed text discussing the *who, what, when, where, how,* and *why* of the key points. See HEADINGS.

5. Use emphasis techniques to provide cues to the document's organization.

Throughout documents, you should signal organization shifts or the placement of key ideas by the position and appearance of text.

Position refers to the placement of words within a sentence, paragraph, or section.

Appearance refers to how the words look on the page—for example, page layout, spacing, indentation, boldface type, underlining, type size, type style, color, etc. See EMPHASIS and PAGE LAYOUT.

6. Use graphics to emphasize important ideas.

Graphics help make information more understandable and more readable. Graphics can draw the reader's attention simply because they are different from text. One of the best ways to emphasize information is to make it visual. Create charts, graphs, drawings, diagrams, flow charts, or illustrations. See EMPHASIS and GRAPHICS.

7. Review (summarize) major points.

End by restating your most important ideas, including your **Do** statement.

The lengthier a document becomes, the more crucial this rule is. Readers of long documents need to be introduced to the subject, learn the most important points early, receive the supporting detail and explanation, and then have the important points all wrapped up in a tidy closing statement.

An old saying regarding oral presentations (but applicable to writing) is that you should tell the audience what you're going to tell them, tell them, and then tell them what you told them.

The following table reviews the seven quality standards of documents. Use these standards for any written document, especially longer documents. A maintenance manual or a procedure manual, which might contain over 100 pages, should follow these standards.

Organization

Standard	Action	Style Guide References
1. Up and Left	Put main points **at the top of the document and on the left side of the page.**	ORGANIZATION, Rule 1
2. Preview	Preview the content of long documents or sections.	ORGANIZATION, Rule 2
3. Lists	Use lists to promote easy access to information.	EMPHASIS LISTS ORGANIZATION, Rule 3
4. Headings	Use informative headings to clarify shifts in content.	HEADINGS ORGANIZATION, Rule 4
5. Emphasis	Use emphasis techniques to guide readers.	EMPHASIS PAGE LAYOUT ORGANIZATION, Rule 5
6. Visual Aids	Use tables, charts, or other visual aids to present complex or technical information.	GRAPHICS ORGANIZATION, Rule 6
7. Review	Review (repeat) your main points at the end of long documents or sections.	ORGANIZATION, Rule 7

Figure 4. The Seven Quality Standards for Documents. *Documents, particularly lengthy documents, should be organized following these standards.*

Page Layout

Page layout refers to the visual techniques (graphics, columns, etc.) used to enhance the effectiveness of a document.

Page layout is the design of the document—how the pages are laid out using visual or graphic design techniques to enhance and arrange the information on the page.

Page layout often includes choices that affect the entire document, such as margins, page size, and number of columns. Occasionally the layout may change for certain sections of a document to give special attention to important information, but a reader usually expects every page in a document to be similar in design.

NOTE: Rules 1 through 7 cover the basic tools to develop style sheets for documents. A style sheet is essentially a map of your intended page layout. Developing a style sheet (see Rule 8) is a good initial step when you are planning to write something. You can write your text to complement and to fit the style sheet. Figures 1a and 1b illustrate a style sheet for a large document. Simpler documents would need simpler, less-detailed style sheets.

Page layout choices depend on the purpose of the document and its intended audience. A good page layout ensures that language, graphics, and even color combine on the page to promote clear communication. Readers should find the document pleasing and easy to read even though they may not be conscious of all the page layout techniques. See EMPHASIS, GRAPHICS, and WRITING.

Preview

1. Select the page size, shape, and design features that will clearly and effectively communicate to your readers.

2. Set your margins and borders so you have enough white space to make the page attractive and readable.

3. Add headers and footers that help your readers know exactly where they are in the document as they are reading.

4. Use more than one column if you have the option available to you.

5. Choose a type size and style to complement your page layout decisions in the preceding rules.

6. Establish a consistent system of headings and lists and stick with it throughout your document.

7. Choose and place graphics and color for maximum impact and increased readability.

8. Develop a style sheet for any document you plan to write.

9. Avoid overloading pages with too much text and too many layout features.

10. Don't forget the basics just because you have a fancy design.

Page Layout

Headings allow you to divide text frequently and to highlight key ideas. Using uppercase and lowercase letters makes headings easier to read. The larger the point size, the higher the level of heading. See HEADINGS and ORGANIZATION.

A 0.5-point **divider line** separates the main text from the side questions or comments.

Boxes and **color** screens highlight and emphasize text and visuals. Well chosen use of color in the text can give maximum impact to main ideas. See EMPHASIS and GRAPHICS.

Many documents are enhanced by the use of more than one **column**.

Headers and footers help readers know exactly where they are in the document as they are reading.

Policies and Procedures Manual

First-Level Headings, Helvetica 18-Point Bold (centered)

Second-Level Headings, Helvetica 14-Point Bold (flush left)

Third-Level Headings, Helvetica 12-Point Bold (flush left)

Fourth-Level Headings. Fourth-level headings lead into paragraphs. Times 12-point bold, period, and one space to the paragraph first word.

Double-space after the first-, second-, and third-level headings and to begin a new paragraph.

The text is formatted on pages with a 1/3- to 2/3-column layout. The 1/3 column is 2 in. wide. Space between columns is 0.167 in. A 0.5-point divider line separates the two columns.

Text is Times 12-point for all normal text. Use **boldface** for emphasis. Text is unjustified.

The header of each page contains the manual title 0.5 in. down from the top of the page with a 1-point line directly below extending to the left and right margins.

The footer of each page contains the company logo at the left margin with a 1-point line extending to the right margin. The 1-point footer line is placed 0.875 in. up from the bottom of the page.

Inside margin is set at 1.0 in., top margin at 0.75 in., outside margin at 0.5 in., and the bottom margin at 0.75 in.

Point size refers to the size of the type. The higher the number, the bigger the type.

Safety cautions are placed in 10-percent screened 0.5-point line boxes in the left 1/3 column. Boxed text is Times 10-point bold italic.

Powder Peaks
Ski Manufacturers

Figure 1a. A Typical Style Sheet. *A good style sheet provides clear and specific instruction to contributors so all contributors' material is consistent.*

Page Layout

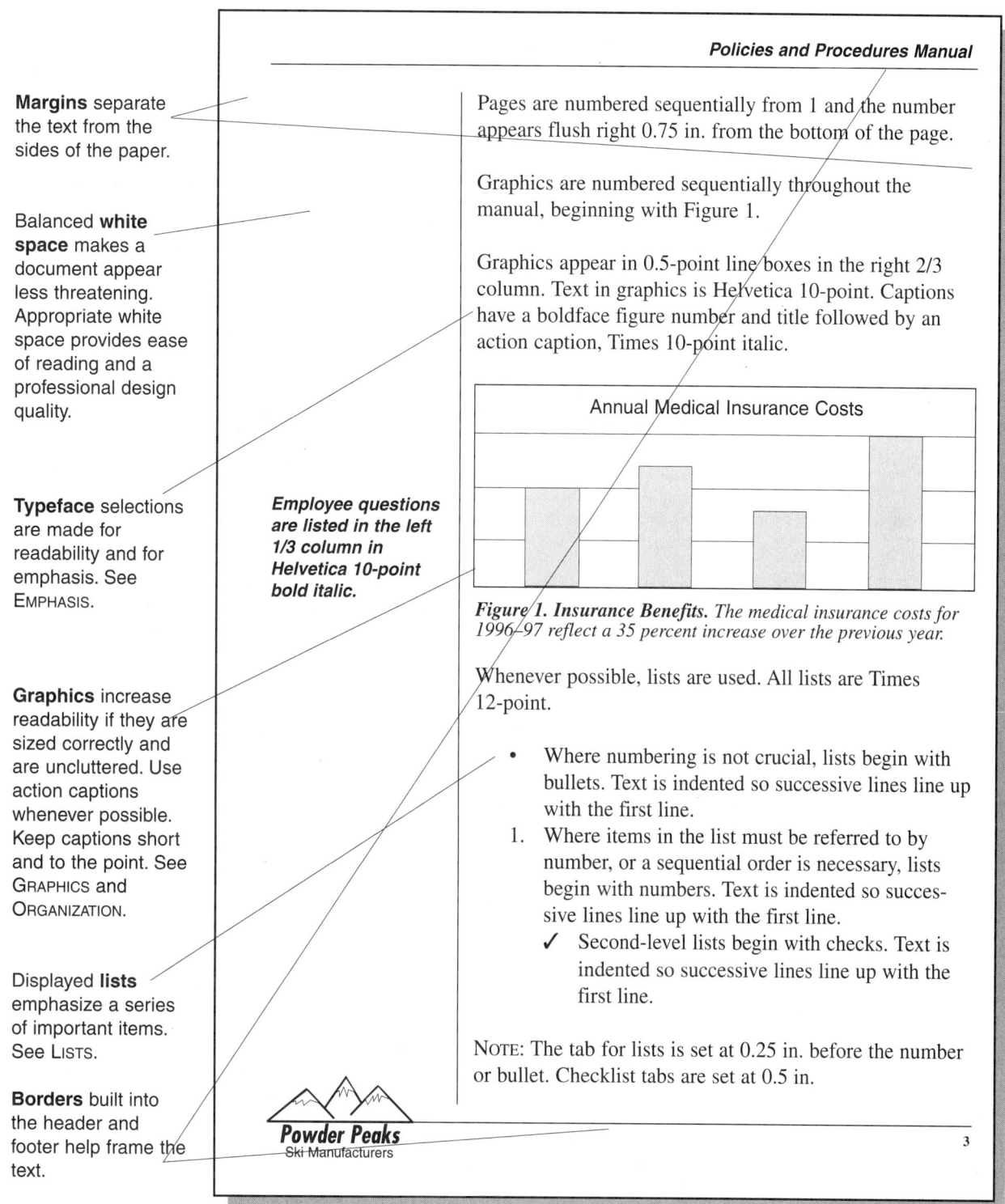

Figure 1b. A Typical Style Sheet (continued).

Page Layout

Although computers make it possible for everyone to design and produce documents, not all do-it-yourself page layouts are successful. The production of a high-quality, professional document takes many hours and a lot of money. Recognizing these difficulties, some companies and agencies choose to use contract professionals (graphics specialists and writers from outside the company) to do the work when a document is significant or urgent.

1. Select the page size, shape, and design features that will clearly and effectively communicate to your readers.

Normal business letter or memo pages (and most book and magazine pages) are longer than they are wide. This shape is called a vertical or **portrait** format. This *Style Guide* uses a portrait format for its pages. However, if you use many charts and graphs, or if you expect to use the material on a video screen, you may want to choose a horizontal or **landscape** format. In a horizontal format, pages are wider than they are long.

After you choose a page size and shape, you need to choose the design features to use on that page. Design features for a page include the following options:

- Margins
- Borders or divider lines
- White space
- Headers and footers
- Columns
- Typefaces
- Headings and lists
- Graphics and color

See Figures 1a and 1b for illustrations of these design options in a portrait format. Each of these options is addressed in separate rules.

2. Set your margins and borders so you have enough white space to make the page attractive and readable.

Each page and each section of a page has margins—the white space separating pieces of text from each other or from the sides of the paper. Your computer may have default (standard) margins, but these are often too narrow or too wide. Try different margins to see the difference in the look of the page.

Setting margins for letters can be a problem, especially if the text is brief. The overall rule is to center a letter on the page so the page looks balanced. Make the left and right margins equal, and if the letter is very short, the text should be dropped down so the white space at the top roughly equals the white space at the bottom. See LETTERS.

Borders or divider lines can help frame your text. They can be as simple as a line around the entire text on a page. They can also be a part of the header or footer.

Divider lines are lines used to divide or set off a column or a section of text. Printers call these lines *rules*. Rules can be very fine (called hairlines, ¼ point) to extremely heavy (72 points). See Figure 2 for a sample of divider lines, with their point sizes indicated.

Remember that you want your page to look simple. Plenty of white space can contribute to the simplicity of your page. Remember, also, that too many borders and divider lines can make the page cluttered and ineffective.

Page Layout

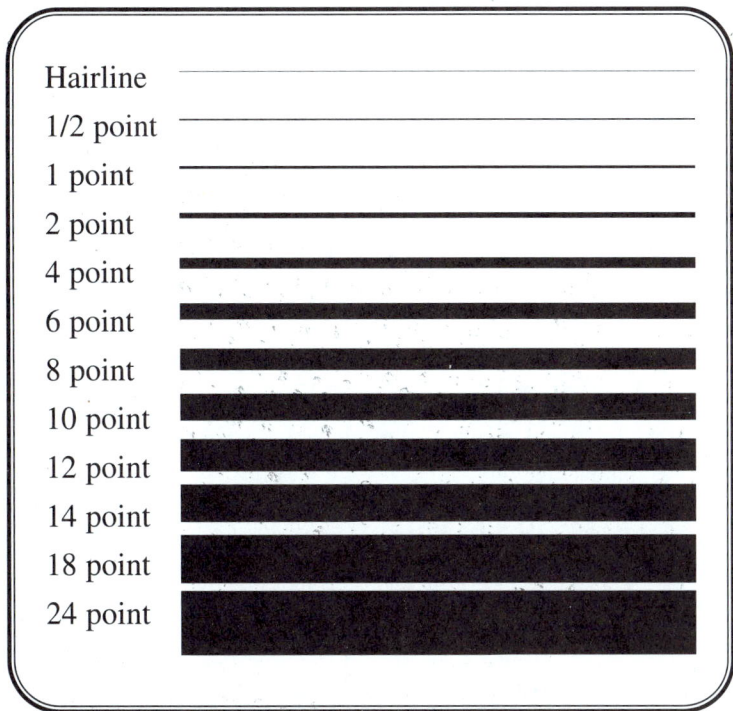

Figure 2. Several Divider Lines or Rules, of Differing Widths, Labeled with Their Point Sizes. *Rules can be set in a wide range of widths, either horizontally or vertically.*

but the following elements can be helpful to the reader:

- Page number
- Name of the manual or report
- Number and title of a chapter or of a subsection in a lengthy chapter
- Name of the company or organization publishing the document
- Organizational logo or symbol, such as a trademark
- Issue date
- Revision date

See INTELLECTUAL PROPERTY.

See Figure 3 on the following page for an illustration of header/footer elements.

3. Add headers and footers that help your readers know exactly where they are in the document as they are reading.

Headers and footers are like road signs. They tell readers which section, subsection, and page they are reading. Most published books have headers and footers. Notice the header and footer on this page.

Most documents in the past did not use headers and footers, except for a page number. But computers and word processing software have made headers and footers a common feature on brief reports, informal memos, and other common business documents.

There is no rule stating specifically what should be included in a header and a footer,

4. Use more than one column if you have the option available to you.

Using two (and in some instances, three) columns on a normal page gives your text a more professional and attractive appearance than a single column. Multiple columns have shorter lines of text, which make them more readable than text that moves all the way across a page. The eye can read a narrow column about 50 characters wide (six or seven words) faster than lines as wide as a full page (about 75 characters).

Two or three columns are basic to most desktop publishing situations, but the columns do not have to be equal. Notice in Figure 1a that one column is about two thirds of the page.

119

Page Layout

Labels (pointing to elements of the sample page):
- Name of Manual
- Number and Title of a Chapter
- Page Number
- Organizational Logo
- Issue Date
- Revision Date

Sample Page:

McKinley Sales Training Workbook   5.0 Sales Process Overview

5.0 Sales Process Overview

McKinley sales and process overview information is presented in the following order:

5.1   Responsibilities of the Sales Representative

5.2   Responsibilities of Billing Personnel

5.3   Sales Process Flow Chart

5.1 Responsibilities of the Sales Representative

A quality sale begins with an effective, well-communicated sales proposal. The sales representative performs the following steps to develop the sales proposal, write the contract, and intitate the service:

1. Gather as much information as possible about a potential customer (as it applies to McKinley services), i.e., customer locations, type of service provided at each location, and frequency of service at each location.

2. Contact the operations supervisor and ask if the service can be provided.

3. Develop a service profile, translating customer service requirements into quality McKinley deliverables. The deliverables are standard McKinley services fulfilling the customer's service needs.

The written sales proposal contains all necessary information to capture a customer's business and complete a contract.

4. Write and present to the customer the sales proposal (including pricing and terms). At this meeting, the sales representative is prepared to complete a contract with the customer to ensure timely service and billing.

5. Familiarize the customer's billing contact with McKinley invoice formats and billing processes (when the contract and terms are agreed).

6. Write and present to the McKinley operations supervisor a complete service order.

Issue 1: August 1997
Revision: September 9, 1997

McKinley Sales

5-1

Figure 3. A Typical Page Illustrating Header/Footer Elements. *Page numbers are best set on the outside (either in the header or the footer) for easy reader reference.*

Page Layout

5. Choose a type size and style to complement your page layout decisions in the preceding rules.

A typeface includes letters, numbers, and symbols of the same design. A font is a complete set of type of one size and one typeface.

Use a plain typeface when quick comprehension is needed. A fancy or display typeface should only be used when fast grasp is not important or to make a point—for example, **STOP**. The examples in the following discussion suggest some of the options you have for either plain or fancy typefaces.

Choose a type size and typeface and then stick to your choices. Too many options or choices on the same page become busy-looking or cluttered.

Desktop publishing, word processing, and computer authoring programs provide a wide selection of typefaces and styles. See Figure 4 for a list of typical proportional typefaces. Usually, these typefaces also allow a wide selection of sizes.

Proportional typefaces are available on many computer programs. In proportional typefaces, the space used by a letter is variable depending on the appearance of the letter. The *i* is narrower than the *n* while the *m* is wider still. Capital letters also have different widths—for example, a *W* is wider than an *I*.

To make the letters of different widths flow together in a pleasing manner, programs use proportional spacing to make the letters seem to be equally spaced even though the actual spacing is variable depending on which letters are next to each other.

Proportional typefaces are called laser fonts, postscript fonts, truetype fonts, or other similar names. Several of the currently popular proportional fonts are Bookman, Century, Times, and Helvetica. These names come from old printing fonts, which had to be set up character by character in the days before typesetting machines and computers. See Figure 4 for examples of these and other common proportional typefaces.

Proportional Typefaces	Letterforms
Avant Garde	Sans serif
Bookman	Serif
Century Gothic	Sans serif
Futura	Sans serif
Garamond	Serif
Helvetica	Sans serif
Helvetica Condensed	Sans serif
Korinna	Serif
Minion	Serif
Optima	Serif
Palatino	Serif
Sabon	Serif
Times	Serif

Figure 4. Typical Proportional Typefaces. *Many popular proportional typeface fonts are based on old printing font families. Although these faces are all shown in 12-point size, some look smaller because the descenders (the parts of letters that hang below the baseline) on p and y are part of the typeface height.*

Page Layout

Sometimes two typefaces look almost alike but have different names. There are, however, differences in some characters. Look particularly at *a, e, f, g,* and *q*. These differences are important because artists designed the typefaces, and these designs are often copyrighted. See INTELLECTUAL PROPERTY.

Mono-spaced typefaces are nonproportional type. The letters are all the same width.

Mono-Spaced Typefaces	Letterforms
Courier	Serif
Letter Gothic	San Serif
Prestige Elite	Serif

Figure 5. Typical Mono-Spaced Typefaces. *Nonproportional typefaces are mono-spaced, meaning all letters are the same width.*

Typewriters, with the exception of some special machines, have mono-spaced type. Courier typeface is a reproduction of a traditional typewriter font. See Figure 5 showing Courier and other mono-spaced typefaces.

We recommend that you avoid using mono-spaced fonts if you have proportional fonts available on your computer or word processor. Today mono-spaced typefaces look old fashioned and less professional.

The development of the shape of an alphabet letter is a letterform. **Serif** and **sans-serif** letterforms differ in their shape or design.

A **serif** letterform has extra finishing lines (feet or hooks) on letters which make them more stylistic and make them lead or run into each other. For example, in Figure 4, the Bookman typeface is a serif font, as illustrated in the lines at the base of the *m* or the *n* and the feet or hooks on the *B* or the *k*. Serif letterforms make the eye move smoothly from one letter to the next. Because serif type can ease the reading and eyestrain associated with studying lengthy papers, it is the preferred letterform for long documents.

A **sans-serif** letterform does not have the finishing lines of the serif typeface. For example, in Figure 4, the Avant Garde typeface is a sans-serif typeface. Note that both the *A* and *d* are plain in appearance and have no finishing feet or hooks. *Sans* means "without" in the French language—the typeface is without the feet or hooks.

Different **styles** of letters exist for both serif and sans-serif typefaces. The common optional styles include bold, italic, condensed or narrow, and outline. See Figure 6 showing various styles available in the Times New Roman typeface.

Times New Roman

Times New Roman Bold

Times New Roman Italic

Times New Roman Condensed

Times New Roman Outline

TIMES NEW ROMAN SMALL CAPS

Times New Roman Shadow

Figure 6. Times New Roman Typeface Shown in Several Different Styles (16-point).

Page Layout

Type size is also an option on most computers. The size is measured in points—from the tallest ascender (parts of lowercase letters above the mean line, such as on *d, l,* or *h*) to the deepest descender (parts of letters below the baseline, such as on *g, p,* or *y*). There are 72 points in one inch. See Figure 7 showing the measurement of type.

A common mistake is to assume that bigger typefaces are always easier to read. Most business documents should not have running text larger than 12 points.

6. Establish a consistent system of headings and lists and stick with it throughout your document.

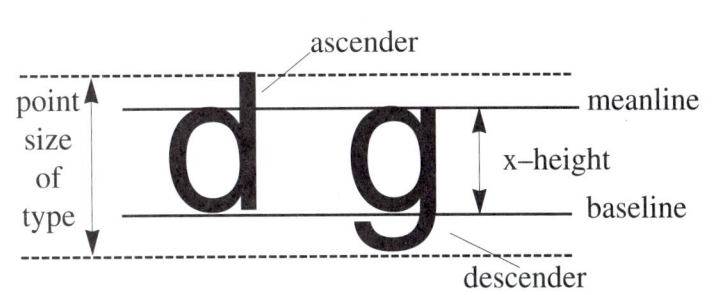

Figure 7. Measurement of Type. *Times typeface is shown in 36-point size to 8-point size. Most computer programs permit type size changes in 1-point increments.*

Design a system of headings and lists that allows you to divide the text frequently to signal the different sections of your text and to highlight key ideas. A consistent, well-designed set of headlines is helpful to readers. Headings are also valuable in business letters and memos, especially if a letter or memo is longer than a single page.

Deciding on a system of headings includes selecting the typeface to use, the size, and other distinguishing features, such as bold, capital letters, numbering, or placement. See Figure 8 on the next page for a simple list of possible headings. See HEADINGS and LISTS.

A common pattern is to use sans-serif typefaces for headings and a serif typeface for text (see Rule 5 for a definition of *serif* and *sans serif*). This is the practice followed in the *Style Guide*.

Lists also allow for a number of options. At the simplest, decide whether you will number lists, use bullets, or use checks. Also, you need to decide how you intend to indent or frame lists using white space. See Figure 1b and LISTS.

7. Choose and place graphics and color for maximum impact and increased readability.

A well-chosen, high-quality graphic is worth a thousand words. Graphics are 10 times more

Page Layout

> # FIRST-LEVEL HEADINGS
>
> ## Second-Level Headings
>
> **Third-Level Headings**
> Text begins below the heading.
>
> **Fourth-Level Headings.**   Text begins on the same line.

Figure 8. Possible Headings Using Various Typeface Options. *Typeface options might include all capitals, different sizes, boldface, and even sometimes italics. An optional feature is to number headings—for example, 2.0, 2.1, 2.1.1, etc. See Figure 3.*

memorable than mere text. So plan for and prepare high-quality graphics.

Your style sheet (see Figures 1a and 1b and Rule 8) should plan for graphics and the placement of captions as a part of graphics. See GRAPHICS.

Decide what your main point is before you decide what graphics you want to include. If your goal is to present a trend or a contrast between two different methods, you might want to use a bar graph or a graph with a plot of two trends.

In other cases—for example, if you want to describe a piece of unfamiliar equipment—consider either a photograph or an illustration (perhaps a schematic of the equipment).

Finally, you might want to use a flowchart or other tree diagram to illustrate the steps in a process or to show who is serving on different committees.

Make your graphics fit your main point or document purpose.

Placing graphics is often a subjective skill, but the following suggestions are generally true:

- Mention a graphic in the text before it appears.
- Make a graphic and its caption largely independent from the text.
- Make a graphic large enough to be readable, and don't expect readers to turn the page to read the caption or notes.
- If a graphic is too complex or cluttered, break it into two graphics or consider making it an attachment to your document.

---

8. Develop a style sheet for any document you plan to write.

Style sheets are essential whether one writer or many will be working on the document. If several writers are contributing to a single document, they should all receive a style sheet **before** they begin writing the text.

Page Layout

Even a writer working alone will profit from working up a style sheet before beginning to write the text.

A good style sheet shows and tells writers exactly what the page layout or page format is, how to break up the text using headings, how long (roughly) the paragraphs should be, and what sorts and sizes of graphics work best. In short, a good style sheet helps ensure that what the writer produces will fit the chosen style and format.

As Figures 1a and 1b show, a style sheet is a road map to the document you intend to write. Remember to include typefaces, type sizes, and any other information you or someone else would need to use to prepare a computer version of your text.

NOTE 1: Style sheets are helpful even if you are not directly writing on a computer. If a computer version is likely, work out a style sheet for this version and then write your text to fit in with this style sheet.

NOTE 2: On most computers the best way to develop a style sheet is to prepare an electronic template for yourself and all writers to use. The template will contain all the format options you want in your style sheet. This template or file is the starting point whenever you start a new document. You will access or call up the template, write some text, and then save the file using another file name.

9. Avoid overloading pages with too much text and too many layout features.

Writers often cram too much writing onto a page, trying to stay within a certain page limit. Writers may even ignore the appearance of the document because they believe that page layout is someone else's concern. They may think an editor or publisher should take care of the layout.

Later they (or many weeks later an editor) will have to go through the text shortening a discussion, changing an introduction, and adjusting all the graphics. Time and money are wasted because much of the text must be rewritten to match the page layout (or style sheet).

10. Don't forget the basics just because you have a fancy design.

Final proofreading and checking are essential.

Errors creep into the best of documents. For instance, changing the subheading text in the middle of a chapter may also require changes in many other places: the introduction to the chapter, the table of contents for the document, the index, the summary of key points in the chapter, etc.

Most computer word processing programs permit tagging of text (attaching invisible programming characters). A special subprogram copies tagged text, later incorporating it into indexes or tables of contents. However, some other changes may not occur automatically. With word processing, the ease of changing something can cause some problems. Moving text often results in leftover letters, punctuation, or spaces. There is no substitute for a final, complete proofreading before publication. This step will save you embarrassment—and possibly your job.

Parallelism

Ideas and items in lists should be written with parallel construction to increase readers' understanding of a document.

Parallelism ensures that ideas are expressed in a similar fashion. This way of presenting ideas emphasizes their similarity and makes reading easier.

Do This

The study will include **organizing**, **dividing**, and **assessing** the workflow.

Not This

The study will include **organizing**, **dividing**, and **assessment** of the workflow.

The sentence verb *include* is followed by three key words: *organizING, dividING,* and *assessMENT*. These three words appear in a series. They are equal in purpose and use in the sentence. Therefore, they should have the same grammatical form.

> **Preview**
>
> 1. Ensure that two or more words or phrases that behave similarly in a sentence or are coordinated (connected) in some way are parallel in construction.
>
> 2. Make items in lists parallel.

---

1. Ensure that two or more words or phrases that behave similarly in a sentence or are coordinated (connected) in some way are parallel in construction.

Parallelism applies not only to verbs, but also to nouns, adjectives, phrases, and every other part of a sentence.

> The Human Resource Representative will be responsible for **distributing** the survey developed by the Marketing Team and for **gathering** and **recording** complete survey results.

> The moving company applied great **preparation**, good **organization**, and proper item **identification** on each load they delivered to the office.

Figure 2.2-1 shows the relationships: **where things happen, why things happen,** and **how things happen**.

Training was necessary to meet the needs of **managers, designers,** and **programmers**.

A final report **describing** the process and **referencing** the documents was mailed on Friday.

---

2. Make items in lists parallel.

Parallelism is especially important in lists. A list, whether displayed vertically on the page or embedded within a paragraph, is a series. To make it parallel, each item should be constructed similarly and should begin with the same kind of word (noun, verb, etc.).

This file will include the following items:

1. Company letters
2. Company memos
3. Mailing address lists
4. Department reports
5. Employee evaluations
6. Sales representatives' assignments

Parallelism

The following list is also parallel. Note that each item begins with the same kind of verb. See COLONS, CONJUNCTIONS, and LISTS.

A study concluded that for our purposes the keyboard must have the raised dots built into the following keys:

1. Escape (**Esc**)
2. Shift (**Shift**)
3. F key (**F**)
4. J key (**J**)
5. Delete (**Delete**)

NOTE: Although now rare, some individuals would not capitalize the first word of each item in a displayed list. But in the business world today, the preferred convention is to capitalize the first letter of the first word or phrase displayed in a list. See LISTS and CAPITALS.

Parentheses and Brackets

Parentheses insert comments or explanatory material into a sentence.

Parentheses ( ) are used to insert (in a strong way) comments, explanatory material, or less important information into a sentence. Brackets [ ], like parentheses, also set off comments, corrections, or explanatory material, but they are used inside of parentheses or inside quoted material. Dashes—which are stronger than parentheses—are also used to insert material. Commas, which are also used to insert material, are weaker than either dashes or parentheses.

Note how the strength of the explanation increases in the following examples:

> Stadium owners using both TV and vending fees helped fund a study reviewing the impact of different sports on their facilities.

> Stadium owners, using both TV and vending fees, helped fund a study reviewing the impact of different sports on their facilities.

> Stadium owners (using both TV and vending fees) helped fund a study reviewing the impact of different sports on their facilities.

> Stadium owners—using both TV and vending fees—helped fund a study reviewing the impact of different sports on their facilities.

See COMMAS and DASHES.

Preview

1. Use parentheses to include explanatory sentences in a paragraph.

2. Use parentheses to enclose references, examples, ideas, and citations that are not part of the main thought of a sentence.

3. Use parentheses to enclose numbers in a paragraph list.

4. Use parentheses to enclose acronyms, abbreviations, definitions, and figures that have been written out.

5. Use proper punctuation when your parenthetical information includes commas, dashes, periods, and question marks.

6. Use brackets to insert comments or corrections in quoted material.

7. Use brackets to enclose parenthetical or explanatory material occurring within material already enclosed within parentheses.

8. For mathematical expressions, place parentheses ( ) inside brackets [ ] inside braces { } inside parentheses ( ).

9. No other marks of punctuation need to come before or after brackets unless the bracketed material has its own mark of punctuation or the overall sentence needs punctuation.

Parentheses and Brackets

1. Use parentheses to include explanatory sentences in a paragraph.

Current company policies do not allow sales associates to bargain with or make exchanges for a new line of clothes without consent from the manager. If you are approached by a salesperson for a new line of clothing, contact the store manager or clothing buyer immediately. (The procedures for buying a new line of clothes are found on p. 89 of the *Policies and Procedures* manual.)

2. Use parentheses to enclose references, examples, ideas, and citations that are not part of the main thought of a sentence.

Our analysis (see Figure 9.4) illustrates how your car has performed over the past 2 years.

Our insurance offers you complete coverage from natural and other disasters (fires, earthquakes, floods, and damage from faulty home appliances).

Our previous survey (conducted over a 3-month period in 1996) suggested that your current marketing program is losing money.

The most recent research (Bridge 1994) revealed pollution problems from nearby gasoline storage tanks.

NOTE: Do not use commas to offset the parenthetical statements. See CITATIONS.

3. Use parentheses to enclose numbers in a paragraph list.

During training, you will learn company policy about (1) customer service, (2) new job training, and (3) promotions.

See LISTS.

4. Use parentheses to enclose acronyms, abbreviations, definitions, and figures that have been written out.

The CARP (Capital Area Renovation Project) will have enough money as long as the contractor trims costs.

The South Fork plant uses over 20,000 kwh (kilowatt hours) of electricity every month.

Artesian water (water naturally confined in the ground under pressure) is used for the city's drinking water.

By the project deadline date, Narwood will deliver fifty (50) pumps to the San Diego facility.

See ABBREVIATIONS.

NOTE: Whenever you write a legal document—a contract, a requisition order, or any other legal material—you should write out the numbers and enclose the figures in parentheses. This protects your document from unauthorized changes. See NUMBERS.

5. Use proper punctuation when your parenthetical information includes commas, dashes, periods, and question marks.

If the information in the parentheses ends with a comma or a dash, do not place the comma or dash inside the parentheses.

Parentheses and Brackets

Do This

She entered the room (by the side door) and ignored us completely.

Not This

She entered the room (by the side door,) and ignored us completely.

If the entire sentence is enclosed by parentheses, place the period inside the closing parentheses.

(See Appendix 2 for the complete test results.)

If only part of a sentence is enclosed by parentheses and the closing parenthesis occurs at the end of the sentence, place the period outside the closing parenthesis.

Electronic cameras help us ensure customer and store safety (see Figure 5-15 for camera locations).

If the information in the parentheses ends in a question mark, place the question mark inside the parentheses.

Do This

The project deadline (April 1?) is never stated in the contract.

Not This

The project deadline (April 1)? is never stated in the contract.

If the parenthetical statement does not include a question mark, but the idea you are expressing is a question, place the question mark at the end of the sentence.

Do This

Is the project deadline (supposedly April 1) stated in the contract?

Not This

Is the project deadline (supposedly April 1?) stated in the contract.

---

6. Use brackets to insert comments or corrections in quoted material.

"Your quoted price [$3,750] is far more than our budget allows."

"Our engineers surveyed the cite [site] for its suitability as a new building cite [site]."

See QUOTATION MARKS.

NOTE 1: In these examples, the brackets indicate that the quoted material did not directly mention the information included within the brackets.

NOTE 2: A common use of brackets, especially in published articles, is to insert *sic* in brackets following an error:

"We studied the affect [sic] of the new design on production outputs."

Sic, borrowed from Latin, means "thus" or "so." It tells readers that the text quoted appears exactly as it did in the original, including the error. In the example above, the word preceding *[sic]* should have been *effect*.

Parentheses and Brackets

7. Use brackets to enclose parenthetical or explanatory material occurring within material already enclosed within parentheses.

We decided to reject the bid from Gull Industries. (Actually the bid [$58,000] was tempting because it was far below our estimate and because Gull Industries usually does good work.)

NOTE: You can sometimes use dashes instead of the outer parentheses and then replace the brackets with parentheses:

Do This

The Board of Directors—or more accurately, a committee of the actual owners (Hyatt, Burke, and Drake)—answer to no one but themselves.

Not This

The Board of Directors (or more accurately, a committee of the actual owners [Hyatt, Burke, and Drake]) answer to no one but themselves.

NOTE: Most writers and editors prefer the version without brackets because it is easier to understand. See DASHES.

8. For mathematical expressions, place parentheses ( ) inside brackets [ ] inside braces { } inside parentheses ( ).

$(2 + 2y\{2 + 4x[2(x + y)]\}) = 16xy^2 + 16x^2y + 4y + 2.$

9. No other marks of punctuation need to come before or after brackets unless the bracketed material has its own mark of punctuation or the overall sentence needs punctuation.

Do This

The carpet was probably costly. (Actually, the cost [$38 per yard] included the padding and a warranty for 5 years.)

Not This

The carpet was probably costly. (Actually, the cost, [$38 per yard], included the padding and a warranty for 5 years.)

Persuasion

Persuasion is the technique of using logical, factual, and emotional appeals to win agreement with or support for an idea.

Persuasion is any technique used by a writer or speaker to gain agreement or to win support for an idea. The most obvious persuasive technique is an appeal based on solid, logical reasons. But most effective persuasive writing also enlists the reader's or listener's emotional support.

Some documents are all persuasion—for example, a sales letter or a proposed plan to hire more employees. Other documents may not be as obviously persuasive, yet they usually have a persuasive intent. A scientific study or a financial report may be primarily factual, but the writers still want to convince readers that the information being presented is reliable. In this sense, most business writing includes persuasive elements.

Preview

1. Determine your readers' needs and objectives.

2. Define your role and objectives in relation to those of your readers.

3. Work with readers to generate persuasive solutions and benefits.

4. Design a message that speaks clearly, effectively, and persuasively to your readers.

5. Maintain a credible position so readers have reasons to agree with you and your ideas.

1. Determine your readers' needs and objectives.

The readers' needs and objectives are important starting points because persuasion must be a two-way process. The old model of the salesperson with a pitch is gone. Today's persuasive writing is based on problem solving and consultation, not pitching a canned presentation to skeptical customers.

Initially, list your readers, both internal ones (within the company) and external ones (customers). Next, profile each of them by asking yourself the following questions to determine what your readers' needs are.

- What are their jobs and professional responsibilities?
- What level and type of decisions can they make?
- Whom do they work for and whom do they supervise?
- What problems or questions are they working on now?
- What do they already know about your services or your ideas?
- How likely are they to use the information you can provide?

Example

Recommendation Document Suppose you are trying to get a contract with a sporting goods company to supply ice skates. After investigating, you discover that three people will make the decision: the president, who cares most about the company's name and reputation; the chief financial officer, who cares most about the

Persuasion

company's profits; and the head buyer, who cares most about the performance of the skates. Your proposal must include persuasive arguments designed to appeal to each of the three and to capture their votes.

As in the example above, you must identify your readers' needs before you can begin to design persuasive documents.

2. Define your role and objectives in relation to those of your readers.

Effective persuasive writing is a two-way communication. It requires you to know your role and objectives as well as the readers'.

NOTE: The following example expands on the example introduced under Rule 1.

Example

Recommendation Document (continued)
To be effective, your proposal to sell ice skates must identify your company as sharing the goals of each of the three people who will vote on the proposal. For the president, who is image conscious, you might want to stress the long history of your company and its investment in sponsoring activities such as the Olympics. For the chief financial officer, you might want to emphasize the price/value relationship of your product. You will want to present the argument that the prestige of your product line will justify a higher price and that your national advertising campaign will save them the cost of local advertising. For the head buyer, you will want to point out that the last three national champions all wore skates made by your company. You will want to mention the features of the skates that have made them the choice of champions.

The role you want to select for yourself in this situation is that of a partner. You must get each of the three people who will vote on your proposal to see you as more than a salesperson. Each person must believe you are offering a partnership in which you will help them achieve their goals.

At times, your role in relation to your readers may lead you to question your honesty. For instance, do you need to admit to the reader that you made a mistake or that your equipment won't meet the written specifications? Such questions and problems are essentially ethical issues and it is important to remember that lasting business relationships are based on honesty and trust. See Rule 5.

3. Work with readers to generate persuasive solutions and benefits.

This step means you continue to work with your readers, confirming your original observations and checking your progress. You never want your customer to feel neglected.

NOTE: The following example builds on details already introduced in Rules 1 and 2.

Example

Recommendation Document (continued)
As you build the case for selling your product, you will want to maintain contact with your potential customers. A part of this maintenance is deciding if one person will have more influence on the vote than another. In the example of the sporting goods store, a quick analysis will show that the head buyer is probably going to be the most influential member of the committee. Unless he or she is convinced your skates are a quality product, the president proba-

133

Persuasion

bly won't believe they will help build the company's image. If the skates aren't a quality product, the financial officer probably will believe that the company may have trouble selling them or may even face lawsuits for injuries.

You should contact the buyer in order to get as much information as possible. It is a good idea to discuss issues thoroughly with people such as the head buyer before submitting any written document.

See the discussion on reviewing in WRITING.

---

4. Design a message that speaks clearly, effectively, and persuasively to your readers.

Make your message reader-centered. An effective and persuasive message has the reader in the foreground. You and your interests remain in the background. Test yourself by looking at a recent persuasive letter or sales document: The *you*'s in a message should outnumber 2 to 1 the *I*'s and *we*'s.

The following three writing principles illustrate what is meant by *reader-centered writing*.

- Be as clear as possible.
- Organize your information with your readers' needs in mind.
- Choose effective and forceful examples.

Be as clear as possible. An undefined term or an unclear explanation allows readers to dismiss your ideas for the simple reason they do not understand you. Do everything you can (or need to) to communicate your intent clearly. Carefully define all technical terms and assumptions. Use page layout, boldface, headings, lists, and other format options to make your message as obvious and as effective as possible. See EMPHASIS and PAGE LAYOUT.

Organize your information with your readers' needs in mind. Organization means you consider both the logic of your points and the arrangement of these points for the maximum effectiveness on your readers. See ORGANIZATION.

Example

Recommendation Document (continued)
If you have decided the head buyer is the most influential voter on the committee, you will want to organize your letter so the major emphasis is on the quality of your product. Concentrate on the issues important to the customer, not to you.

Choose effective and forceful examples. Persuasive writing requires an interaction between general principles and good examples. Choose examples that match the backgrounds of your readers. If your readers have a limited technical background, choose nontechnical examples.

Example

Recommendation Document (continued)
The head buyer is probably not concerned with very technical information about how the skates are made, but she almost certainly is interested in how well the skates perform in competition. In your letter, you must provide evidence that your skates hold up to the demands of competitive skating.

NOTE: No rules exist about which examples or details are the most effective and most desirable. You should choose appropriate ones based on the profile of your readers. For example, try to select samples that will be interesting and meaningful for the age group of your readers.

Persuasion

5. Maintain a credible position so readers have reasons to agree with you and your ideas.

Establish and maintain your credentials from your first discussion with your customer to the writing of your final document. Your persuasive case stands or falls depending upon your readers' perception of your credibility.

Will the readers see you as honest? Knowledgeable? Professional? A good listener? Sympathetic? In other words, should the readers trust what you have to say or to recommend? Honesty and trust are the basis of any persuasive relationship. Without these virtues, you will have little success developing a logical case.

Don't rely on purely personal facts about yourself or your organization to establish your credibility. You can occasionally refer to your background or your prior business experiences. But these references will not buy you any credibility if you can't, for instance, produce a document that appears professional and presents sound arguments in favor of your position.

You establish your persuasive credibility by providing the following features or information in your documents:

- Careful, well-designed format—one that is professional in appearance
- Clear, persuasive, organization and examples (see Rule 4)
- Technically sound, accurate study of data and examples
- Correct spelling and punctuation

135

Plurals

The plural forms of most nouns and pronouns follow simple rules, but many irregular words and coined phrases require special treatment.

Plurals of most nouns and pronouns are signaled by their spelling. Such changes are no problem if they follow the regular pattern: an *–s* or an *–es* added to the singular form makes the plural form:

book	+	s	=	books
church	+	es	=	churches
report	+	s	=	reports
tax	+	es	=	taxes

Problems arise when the plural does not follow the regular pattern:

Singular	Plural
chassis	chassis
fungus	fungi
he, she, it	they
I	we
matrix	matrices
mouse	mice

The following discussion covers these and other irregular plurals. The best guide, however, is a good recent dictionary, such as the *Merriam-Webster Concise School and Office Dictionary*. See SPELLING.

> ### Preview
>
> 1. Use a dictionary to determine the plurals of many irregular forms, especially those technical terms borrowed from Latin or other languages.
>
> 2. In compound terms add the plural ending (usually *–s* or *–es*) to the most significant word.
>
> 3. Nouns ending in *–o* preceded by a consonant usually add *–es* for the plural.
>
> 4. The coined plurals of abbreviations, titles, figures, letters, and symbols require an *–s* and sometimes an apostrophe plus an *–s*.
>
> 5. Plurals of pronouns, when they exist, are likely to be very irregular.

---

1. Use a dictionary to determine the plurals of many irregular forms, especially those technical terms borrowed from Latin or other languages.

addendum, addenda

agendum, agenda

alga, algae

alumna, alumnae (*fem.*)

alumnus, alumni (*masc.*)

antenna, antennas (antennae, *zoology*)

appendix, appendixes (*or* appendices)

axis, axes

basis, bases

Co., Cos.

crisis, crises

criterion, criteria

datum, data

ellipsis, ellipses

Plurals

focus, focuses (*or* foci)

formula, formulas

fungus, fungi

gladiolus (*singular and plural*)

hypothesis, hypotheses

index, indexes (indices, *scientific*)

larva, larvae

larynx, larynxes

lens, lenses

matrix, matrices

medium, mediums (*or* media)

memorandum, memorandums (*or* memoranda)

minutia, minutiae

nucleus, nuclei

oasis, oases

parenthesis, parentheses

plateau, plateaus

radius, radii

referendum, referendums

stimulus, stimuli

stratum, strata

synopsis, synopses

terminus, termini

thesaurus, thesauri

thesis, theses

thorax, thoraxes

vertebra, vertebras (vertebrae, *zoology*)

virtuoso, virtuosos

vortex, vortexes (*or* vortices)

NOTE 1: Many of the above forms now have regular plurals (*appendix, appendixes* or *memorandum, memorandums*). However, some editors still prefer the irregular forms (usually based on the word's origin in Latin or another language: *appendices, memoranda*). The longer a word is in English, the stronger the tendency is to make the plural conform to the regular English pattern (adding an –*s* or –*es* to the singular form).

NOTE 2: Though many of these words come from other languages, they are now sufficiently English and do not need underlining or italics.

2. In compound terms add the plural ending (usually –*s* or –*es*) to the most significant word.

assistant attorneys

assistant chiefs of staff

attorneys at law

bills of fare

brothers-in-law

comptrollers general

daughters-in-law

deputy judges

goings-on

grants in aid

lieutenant colonels

lookers-on

trade unions

Plurals

3. Nouns ending in *–o* preceded by a consonant usually add *–es* for the plural.

   echo, echoes

   potato, potatoes

   veto, vetoes

NOTE: This rule has many exceptions, so if in doubt, check a good dictionary, such as the *Merriam-Webster Concise School and Office Dictionary*. Here are some of the common exceptions:

   dynamo, dynamos

   Eskimo, Eskimos

   ghetto, ghettos

   halo, halos

   indigo, indigos

   magneto, magnetos

   piano, pianos

   two, twos

   zero, zeros

4. The coined plurals of abbreviations, titles, figures, letters, and symbols require an *–s* and sometimes an apostrophe plus an *–s*.

   OKs

   ABCs

   CODs

   the three Rs

   SOSs

   g's

   1's and 2's

NOTE: Use the apostrophe only if necessary to avoid confusion, as in lowercase letters and some number combinations (without an apostrophe, the plural of *g* would look awkward, and the plural of *1* could be confused with *Is*). Save the apostrophe to show possession, as in *John's hat*. The trend is for the apostrophe to vanish, leaving the simple *–s* to signal that the item is a plural. See APOSTROPHES.

5. Plurals of pronouns, when they exist, are likely to be very irregular.

<u>Singular</u>	<u>Plural</u>
I	we
you	you
he, she, it	they

Possessives are forms of nouns and pronouns that follow specific rules to show ownership or other relationships.

Possessives are forms of nouns and pronouns that show ownership or other relationships. The following are examples of ownership:

> **WWW's** building
>
> **Mr. Wilson's** store
>
> **his** store
>
> **Susan's** desk
>
> **her** desk
>
> **Lewis'** report
>
> the **Lewises'** house

The following are examples of relationship:

> the **book's** cover
>
> **its** cover
>
> the **company's** support
>
> the **captain's** story
>
> a **summer's** day
>
> a **doctor's** degree

NOTE: Noun possessive forms usually need an apostrophe or an apostrophe plus an *–s*. See APOSTROPHES.

Preview

1. Add an apostrophe and an *–s* to form the possessive for both singular and plural nouns that do not end in *–s*.

2. Add an apostrophe to form the possessive for singular nouns ending in *–s* or an *–s* sound (although some writers still add an *–s* after the apostrophe).

3. Add only an apostrophe to form the possessive for plural nouns ending in *–s*.

4. Add an apostrophe plus an *–s* to the last word in personal and organizational names showing possession, a group showing joint possession, and hyphenated words.

5. Do not use an apostrophe with possessive personal pronouns or with the relative pronoun *whose*.

6. Add an apostrophe and an *–s* to make the possessive forms of indefinite pronouns.

7. You can sometimes use possessives without a following noun.

8. You can use a possessive to modify an *–ing* form of a verb used as a noun.

---

1. Add an apostrophe and an *–s* to form the possessive for both singular and plural nouns that do not end in *–s*.

The following are examples of singular noun possessives:

> the **cat's** paw
>
> **Anne's** statement
>
> a **man's** coat
>
> an **accountant's** books

139

Possessives

The following are examples of plural noun possessives:

>**men's** coats
>
>the **children's** toys

NOTE: The names of countries, government units, and organized groups ending in –s do not need apostrophes:

>**United States** plan
>
>**Massachusetts** statutes
>
>**Mineworkers** court case
>
>**United Nations** publication

---

2. Add an apostrophe to form the possessive for singular nouns ending in –s or an –s sound (although some writers still add an –s after the apostrophe).

>the **actress'** (*or* actress's) script
>
>the **boss'** (*or* boss's) idea
>
>**James'** (*or* James's) speech

NOTE: Add only an apostrophe if the new word has more than two syllables and if the addition of the –s would make the word hard to pronounce.

>**Baby Cosmetics'** (not Cosmetics's) proposal
>
>**W.R. Reynolds'** (not Reynolds's) reaction

---

3. Add only an apostrophe to form the possessive for plural nouns ending in –s.

>the **actresses'** dressing room
>
>the **bosses'** meeting
>
>the **cars'** owners

NOTE: Do not use an apostrophe to make the plural of a noun.

Do This

>All of the **Smiths** were home to greet us.

Not This

>All of the **Smith's** were home to greet us.

---

4. Add an apostrophe plus an –s to the last word in personal and organizational names showing possession, a group showing joint possession, and hyphenated words.

>**Charles F. Shook's** decision
>
>**Nip & Tuck's** policy
>
>**Dewey, Cheatum, and Howe's** corporate policy
>
>my **sister-in-law's** shoes

NOTE: Corporate and organizational practices vary, so check the letterhead or other letters for exceptions:

>Plastic **Welders** Club
>
>**Rolliers** Profit Sharing

Possessives

5. Do not use an apostrophe with possessive personal pronouns or with the relative pronoun *whose*.

The company lost **its** lawsuit.

We refused to pay for **ours**.

They lost **theirs** when the tornado came.

He mentioned **his**.

Whose report is this?

NOTE 1: The possessive forms of personal pronouns are *my/mine, your/yours, his, her/hers, its, our/ours, their/theirs*. Except for *his* and *its*, which have a single spelling, the two forms have different uses. The first forms (*my, your, her, our,* and *their*) come before nouns. The second forms (*mine, yours, hers, ours,* and *theirs*) come after a verb, but the noun does not follow the pronoun.

They were **her** ideas. (The noun ideas follows her.)

The ideas were **hers**. (No noun follows hers.)

NOTE 2: Distinguish between possessives without apostrophes and contractions with apostrophes. See APOSTROPHES.

The pump had lost **its** cover.

We decided that **it's** (it is) time to start over.

He changed **his** job recently.

He's (he is) changing his job.

Whose idea was this?

Who's (who is) going to the meeting?

6. Add an apostrophe and an –s to make the possessive forms of indefinite pronouns.

anyone else's task

one's ideas

the **other's** notion

the **others'** schedules

anybody's recommendation

someone else's job

7. You can sometimes use possessives without a following noun.

My ideas are like **Sue's**. (Ideas is not repeated, but you understand that it follows Sue's.)

His nose is like a **bloodhound's**. (Nose is not repeated.)

I'll be at **Jim's**. (A location is not shown.)

She was at the **doctor's**. (Office is understood.)

WW's is good, but **YY's** is better. (Both nouns are understood.)

8. You can use a possessive to modify an –ing form of a verb used as a noun.

Bill's speaking to my boss helped.

I objected to **his** working on the rig overnight.

I admired **Sue's** planning.

Quotation Marks

Quotation marks enclose direct quotations, indicate the title of a reference, or highlight special words.

Quotation marks have multiple uses. The most common use (enclosing direct quotations) gives them their name. In earlier centuries, quotation marks did not exist, and the reader could not tell easily the writer's words from the quoted words. Today, the conventions for using quotation marks are well established.

1. Use quotation marks to enclose direct quotations.

Direct quotations include the actual words and phrases from a document or from a person speaking:

> The Policy Manual says, "Refer all customers with credit or return problems to the manager."

Indirect quotations do **not** take quotation marks:

> The Policy Manual says that we should refer all customers that have credit or return problems to the manager.

Indirect quotations do not give every word and phrase in the direct quotation. Often an indirect quotation is only a paraphrase:

> The Policy Manual says that we should send customers with any problems to the manager.

NOTE: Single quotation marks are used to indicate a quotation within a quotation:

Preview

1. Use quotation marks to enclose direct quotations.

2. If you use quotation marks for a long quotation that extends for more than one paragraph, place quotation marks at the beginning and ending of the entire quotation and at the beginning of each new paragraph within the quotation.

3. Use quotation marks to indicate the title of an article, section, volume, or other part of a longer document.

4. Use quotation marks to indicate that a word is used in a special or unusual sense.

5. Always place periods and commas inside closing quotation marks.

6. Always place semicolons and colons outside closing quotation marks.

7. Place dashes, exclamation marks, and question marks inside quotation marks if they are part of the quotation; otherwise, place them outside quotation marks.

> According to the Policy Manual, "Nichelle Carowan, the Fashion Farm's owner, wants all employees to 'enjoy the Fashion Farm experience.'"

Quotation Marks

2. If you use quotation marks for a long quotation that extends for more than one paragraph, place quotation marks at the beginning and ending of the entire quotation and at the beginning of each new paragraph within the quotation.

> "As we put out the fire that evening, we all snuggled into our down sleeping bags and prepared for a good night's rest.
>
> "About 20 minutes later, I was almost asleep when I heard a twig snap outside my tent.
>
> "I lay very still, trying to listen for any sound. Almost immediately, I tensed from the pungent smell of smoldering, rotted leaves."

NOTE: You can use long quotations in two formats: (1) Enclose them with quotation marks, or (2) indent them from both the left and right margins (in which case they do **not** require quotation marks).

3. Use quotation marks to indicate the title of an article, section, volume, or other part of a longer document.

> The accountant must approve all expenses specified under "Special Expenses" in the Policy Manual.
>
> This purchase order must include a completed and signed Standard Form 212, "Service Requisition Order."

See TITLES.

4. Use quotation marks to indicate that a word is used in a special or unusual sense.

> The 1993 audit showed that the company's definition of "wholesale" meant tripling the prices before selling anything.
>
> Only in English do "slim chance" and "fat chance" mean the same.

NOTE: Italics (or underlining) can replace quotation marks when you want to refer to a word as a word:

> In the contract, *employee* refers only to those people officially hired by the company.

OR

> In the contract, employee refers only to those people officially hired by the company.

5. Always place periods and commas inside closing quotation marks.

> We have completed the section entitled "Hooks, Lines, and Sinkers."
>
> Chris read John's short story, "Fechner's Night Out."
>
> "Employees only," read the sign on the door.

NOTE: This convention is standard in the United States. The convention developed because printers wanted to make their pages look nicer, so they put the periods and commas inside of the closing quotation marks.

143

Quotation Marks

British usage places commas and periods inside or outside the quotation marks, depending on whether they are or are not part of the quotation.

6. Always place semicolons and colons outside closing quotation marks.

The company's experience belongs under "Related Experience"; the store manager's experience belongs under "Résumés of Key Personnel."

Include the following under "Materials":

a. Purchase orders

b. Employee work schedules

c. Materials/equipment required

7. Place dashes, exclamation marks, and question marks inside quotation marks if they are part of the quotation; otherwise, place them outside quotation marks.

The section entitled "Work Experience"—the part of the resume where you detail how your past work experience applies to the job you want—should be no longer than two pages.

He said, "Can we improve the kind of service we give our customers without losing our profit margin?"

Is it possible to get a copy of her article, "The End of the Cold War"?

A résumé is a summary of a person's job experience and skills given to a potential employer when a person applies for a job.

Résumés

Résumés are summaries of job experience and skills. When given to a potential employer, the résumé provides a way for the employer to get a first impression of a job candidate. Based on the résumé, employers may decide they want to interview the candidate. Usually people looking to hire a new employee are very busy. Thus, résumés must convey a lot of information quickly.

The formal spelling for *résumé* includes accents over both *e*'s in the word. These accents, which are carried over from the French spelling, are becoming optional in English. Often, for example, they are omitted when the word is in all capitals: *RESUME*. We retain the accents so you can see how they would appear in more formal business contexts.

There are two types of résumés: the **chronological résumé** and the **functional résumé**. A chronological résumé lists experience by job title and employment. A functional résumé is organized by job skills or personal abilities. Both types contain much of the same information, but they are organized differently to highlight specific qualifications.

Chronological Résumé

The chronological résumé is also known as a traditional résumé. It lists experience in chronological order by job title and dates of employment, with the most recent experience listed first. See the model of a chronological résumé among the model documents at the back of the *Style Guide*.

Preview

1. Design and organize your résumé (and cover letter) so readers can easily identify and remember your experience and skills.

2. Write your résumé to target the specific job you seek.

3. Use action verbs and descriptive phrases to describe your experience and skills.

4. Describe with specifics the successes you have had in jobs or activities.

5. Keep your résumé concise; if possible, limit your résumé to one page.

6. Use proper grammar, mechanics, and spelling.

7. Prepare (publish) your résumé so it has a clean, professional look.

Use a chronological résumé if your job history fits these criteria:

- You have had a series of jobs, with dates that show an employment history.

- The jobs you have had directly support your job objective and related skills.

- Even if you have had jobs unrelated to your job objective, you decide to list these jobs because you want to show your employment history.

The chronological résumé is good for demonstrating a progression of jobs with dates and a

Résumés

variety of skills. A chronological résumé is **not** effective for someone still in school, for someone just out of school and without a job history, or for someone changing careers.

Functional Résumé

The functional résumé organizes experience according to function, skill, or abilities. See the model of a functional résumé among the model documents at the back of the *Style Guide*.

Use a functional résumé if your job history and skills fit these criteria:

- You are an entry-level job seeker who has no job history (or a limited history).
- Many of the skills that qualify you for a particular job come from school activities or hobbies, not from actual jobs.
- You want to link your skills and abilities with the requirements for a specific job.

The functional résumé highlights qualifications for a job based on the skills and successes you have, whether these occurred in jobs or in school. The functional résumé allows you to emphasize your skills and abilities because these become the major headings in your résumé.

1. Design and organize your résumé (and cover letter) so readers can easily identify and remember your experience and skills.

This rule applies equally to both the chronological résumé and the functional résumé. Both should be well-designed documents. The cover letter to your résumé should also be well designed. See PAGE LAYOUT, LETTERS, and the model résumés and cover letters among the model documents at the back of the *Style Guide*.

If the layout or design is ineffective, your résumé may not survive an employer's initial screening. Most employers spend less than 60 seconds looking at a résumé before they decide whether to discard the résumé or to read it more carefully.

Layout or design features include the following:

- An attractive and open page design. See PAGE LAYOUT.
- Clear and informative headings and subheadings. See HEADINGS.
- Displayed lists and paragraph lists. See LISTS.
- Specific content that emphasizes your skills and abilities. See Rules 2, 3, and 4 in the following discussion.

An effective layout helps you sell yourself as a skilled and desirable potential employee.

Your résumé and attached cover letter allow you to present yourself in a well-thought-out manner. In your job application, however, you often have to respond in writing without a great deal of time to plan what you need to say and how to say it.

2. Write your résumé to target the specific job you seek.

Your résumé should use design, wording, and facts that focus on the specific job you seek. The content of your résumé should include the work experience, activities, skills, and education related to the targeted job.

Many people have, for example, two or even three different versions of their résumés—each version tailored to the specific requirements of different jobs. For example, you might have one résumé that highlights your skills as a clerk or general office worker. A second résumé might highlight your skills as a retail sales person. Both résumés would have the same facts and dates, but their headings and their supporting text would be quite different.

Choose a short, effective job objective that describes the job you want. Be as detailed as possible. Your job objective is the first opportunity for employers to see if you fit the job opening.

NOTE: You may want to mention in your job objective the company or firm to which you are applying. This level of detail is now possible because, if your résumé is written on a computer, such specific references take no more than a minute or two to insert or change.

Do This

Objective: To bring my skills working with the sick and the elderly to a position as a nurse's aide at the Cumberland Care Center.

Objective: To be an apprentice electrician for Greenbriar Electrical Contractors.

OR

Objective: To bring my skills working with the sick and the elderly to a position as a nurses's aide.

Objective: To serve as an apprentice to a licensed master electrician.

Not This

To work in nursing.

To help people.

To work in sales.

To be an electrician.

Summarize your experience in a way that supports your job objective. If one of your previous jobs does not directly relate to your job objective, identify any elements of that job that do relate to the job you want.

Then, include in your résumé only those elements that contribute to proving that you are qualified for the job. Either omit irrelevant job information or limit it to minor items in your résumé.

On the following pages you will find two sample résumés, one that effectively communicates all relevant information, and a second that is an example of what not to do in a résumé.

The résumé in Figure 1 highlights customer service skills throughout. Every fact and line supports the specific job objective.

The résumé in Figure 2 lacks any such highlighting, and fails to sell its writer's skills because it presents only bare facts and dates.

Résumés

Do This   **Chronological Résumé**

Angela R. Stevenson
1572 Big Piney Road, #283
Indianapolis, IN 46290
317–555–1234

Objective

Make objective statements specific to the company and the job desired.

A position as a customer service representative for Media Marketing, Inc.

Work Experience

Write explanations of responsibilities in a bulleted list using action verbs to invite the reader to continue reading. See LISTS, EMPHASIS, and ACTIVE/PASSIVE VOICE.

Customer Service Representative   1996–1997
Abbott Labels, Milwaukee, WI
- Responded to customer inquiries and complaints
- Entered or corrected client information in TASK database
- Provided complete customer satisfaction
- Received two unsolicited letters of commendation from satisfied customers

List responsibilities to include only those that relate specifically to the desired job.

Receptionist   1994–1996
Office Supply Mart, Framingham, MA
- Answered all client calls
- Ensured clients received prompt and courteous response
- Performed light typing and filing duties

Activities

Include activities that support and extend work experience listed above and demonstrate further qualification for the job.

Help-Line Volunteer   1993–1994
Beckins Junior College, Beckins, MA
- Answered activities line and referred students to appropriate resources
- Trained other volunteers

Business Manager   1991–1992
Beckinspeak Newspaper, Beckins, MA
- Managed financials, equipment ordering, and invoicing for 15-person staff
- Assisted with interviews and staffing of the volunteers

Highlight skills from abilities that apply directly to the requirements of the desired job.

Skills
- Type 45 wpm
- Use TASK database and WordWhiz software

Figure 1. A Résumé Example Showing How to Slant Your Content Toward a Specific Job.
Notice that all the listed responsibilities and activities support the job objective listed in the opening lines—Objective: A position as a customer service representative for Media Marketing, Inc. Because this résumé is prepared on a computer word processor, the Objective statement is easily customized to include the name of the company receiving the résumé. This résumé may be only one of several versions prepared by the same person to target specific job openings directly.

Résumés

Not This **Chronological Résumé**

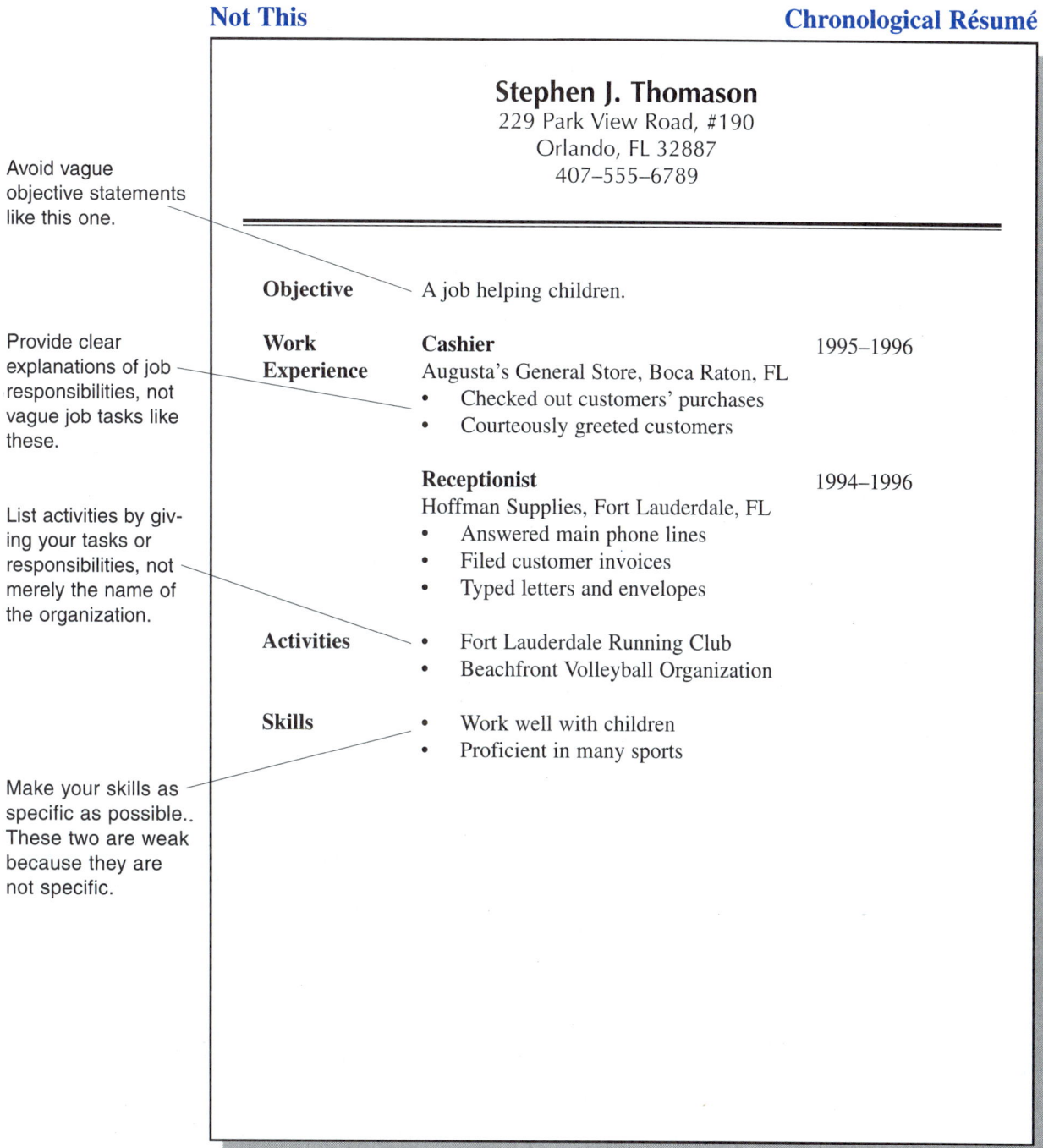

Avoid vague objective statements like this one.

Provide clear explanations of job responsibilities, not vague job tasks like these.

List activities by giving your tasks or responsibilities, not merely the name of the organization.

Make your skills as specific as possible. These two are weak because they are not specific.

Stephen J. Thomason
229 Park View Road, #190
Orlando, FL 32887
407–555–6789

Objective — A job helping children.

Work Experience

Cashier 1995–1996
Augusta's General Store, Boca Raton, FL
- Checked out customers' purchases
- Courteously greeted customers

Receptionist 1994–1996
Hoffman Supplies, Fort Lauderdale, FL
- Answered main phone lines
- Filed customer invoices
- Typed letters and envelopes

Activities
- Fort Lauderdale Running Club
- Beachfront Volleyball Organization

Skills
- Work well with children
- Proficient in many sports

Figure 2. An Example of What Not to Do in a Résumé. *Job experiences and activities are presented as mere facts. They do not support the objective, which itself is weak and vague— Objective: A job helping children. Not only is this résumé weak in terms of targeting, but it is seriously lacking in content development. The key to a successful résumé is to provide valuable information in an attractive manner to support a well-developed job objective. The person who prepared this résumé may have experiences identical to those of the applicant in the previous example, but an employer would not see that fact.*

149

Resumés

3. Use action verbs and descriptive phrases to describe your experience and skills.

Action verbs and other descriptive phrases help your readers visualize you and your job activities.

Do not assume readers know what skills or tasks are included in a job. For instance, saying you were a "sales clerk" doesn't specify the job skills. Did you order new stock and then restock the shelves? Did you answer customers' phone questions? Did you close out your computer register each day and turn in all signed credit card receipts? Did you help train new clerks? Specify these and any other special duties or responsibilities.

Action verbs are verbs that convey action. For example, *survey, manage, organize,* and *close out* are action verbs. The common helping verbs convey little or no action. For example, *do, does, have, has, is, are, was,* and *were* are nonaction verbs. Use action verbs to lead off your list of job skills or tasks.

Do This

Wrote and **coordinated** the sending of collection letters

Surveyed the site for hazards

Managed six employees

Not This

Was involved in preparing and coordinating collection letters

Was a surveyor of the site for hazards

Had a position as night shift manager of six employees

State your experience in past-tense action verbs. If you currently are performing a task, use the present tense, for example, *supervise three workers on the loading dock* or *open the front office and sort the incoming mail.*

Do This

Resolved customers' problems

Designed landscaping plans based on customers' needs (past tense version)

OR

Resolve customers' problems

Design landscaping plans based on customers' needs (present tense version)

Not This

Customers' complaints were sent to me

Landscaping plans

Use verb phrases, beginning with a past-tense action verb, rather than narrative passages.

Action Verbs for a Resumé	
Managed	Implemented
Oversaw	Developed
Led	Recommended
Supervised	Used (machine or software)
Performed	Assisted
Completed	Helped
Acted	Supported
Negotiated	Filed
Communicated	Typed
Wrote	Proofread
Answered	Collaborated
Resolved	Edited

Résumés

Do This

Determined source of computer problems; **solved** all simple problems

Not This

As a computer technician, I **worked** with people's computers that had problems. I **tried** to tell what was wrong with them. If I could, I **fixed** the problems.

---

4. Describe with specifics the successes you have had in jobs or activities.

Wherever possible, include information about how you have been successful. Include all successes that directly relate to your desired job. Try to give your reader a sense of your major accomplishments; if possible, use numerical quantities.

Do This

Trained new retail associates, usually three a month

Led all telemarketers in sales; sold $93,873 in last fiscal year

Met fast-paced distribution system requirements; filled an average of 50 orders each day

Maintained 1996–1997 financial accounts for a Junior Achievement company ($12,500 annual budget)

Not This

Worked with other retail associates

Sold floral equipment on the telephone

Filled orders by pulling packages off the shelf and putting them in boxes

Kept Junior Achievement accounts

5. Keep your résumé concise; if possible, limit your résumé to one page.

Unless you have extensive job experience, limit your résumé to one page. State your qualifications in action verb phrases. Where appropriate, use bulleted lists (beginning with action verbs) to describe your experience. (See Figure 3 on the following page.) See LISTS.

---

6. Use proper grammar, mechanics, and spelling.

Your résumé must present the best possible picture of you. Never include grammatical mistakes or spelling errors. Proofread your document, and then proofread it again.

Whenever possible, ask a friend or a relative to proofread your résumé. Their eyes will be fresh, so they will see things you may have overlooked.

Résumés include many titles and proper nouns. A proper noun is the actual name of a company or place, for example, *Acme Shoe Manufacturing Company* in *Albany, Georgia*. Proper nouns are always capitalized. See CAPITALS and TITLES. In a résumé, treat a job title as a proper noun.

Do This

Technical Writer, Vidcom Graphics, San Jose, CA

Office Manager, Computeria, Cupertino, CA

Not This

technical writer, Vidom graphics, San Jose, Ca

office manager, Computeria, Cupertino, CA

Résumés

Do This

Objective	To obtain a position as Office Manager of TicketSource's New Jersey office.
Work Experience	**Shift Supervisor** TicketBooth Ticket Service, Newark, NJ 1992–1997 • Sold theater and concert tickets; exceeded goal every year • Helped callers choose seats and dates • Accurately processed ticket requests within 2-minute time limit **Office Assistant**

Not This

Objective	To obtain a position as Office Manager of TicketSource's New Jersey office.
Work Experience	**Shift Supervisor** TicketBooth Ticket Service 1238 Cargo Street Newark, NJ 1992–1997 • I worked for TicketBooth for three years, 1992–1997. • I exceeded my goal every year I worked for TicketBooth. I exceeded my 700/month goal in 1992 by 75 tickets a month. In 1993, I passed my dollar goal of $21,000 by $900. In 1994, they raised my goal to $23,000, and I beat that by $675. • I talked to callers on the phone and found out what tickets they wanted. Then, I asked them what seats they wanted. Once I got them seats, I would process the ticket order. We had to do this in 2 minutes, which I was normally able to do. Then, we would send the order to Processing, and answer a new call. **Office Assistant**

Figure 3. Use Action Verbs in Bulleted Lists to Energize a Résumé. *The top example in this figure shows how to effectively use action verbs and bulleted lists to highlight specific job responsibilities and skills. The second example illustrates the problems with using narrative.*

Résumés

When using verb phrases, lists, and headings, choose one form and use it throughout your résumé. Be consistent. Follow the rules of parallelism to ensure your résumé maintains consistency. See PARALLELISM.

Do This

Dependable

Managed food bank hotline over 12-month period

Delivered food to 20 recipients

Team Player

Participated on varsity basketball team

Worked successfully with six other food bank volunteers

NOTE: *Dependable* and *Team Player* might be required job applicant characteristics listed in a work-for-hire newspaper ad. See the résumé model in the back of the *Style Guide* which emphasizes the applicant's qualifications in those required areas. Note that the verb phrases below the headings are parallel—*Managed, Delivered, Participated, Worked.*

Not This

Hard Worker

Worked 12-hour shifts for summer job

Lifting heavy objects was part of my job

Worked in hot manufacturing environment

Flexible

Can do many office tasks efficiently

New tasks and skills **are welcomed**

NOTE: *Worked, Lifting, Can do*, and *are welcomed* are not parallel verb phrases.

7. Prepare (publish) your résumé so it has a clean, professional look.

Choose a format and appearance that is appropriate and professional. Choose high-quality white or cream paper (at least 20-pound paper). Avoid unusually colored papers.

Use a variety of fonts to help emphasize the important points, but avoid unusual fonts. Also, do not use too many fonts (i.e., not more than three fonts). See PAGE LAYOUT.

Proofread your résumé to ensure there are **absolutely no grammatical or typographical errors.** Grammatical and typographical errors give the impression you are sloppy or careless.

We recommend you take your completed résumé to a résumé service shop or photocopying shop where they can publish your résumé using the latest desktop publishing and high-quality photocopying machines. This step, while optional, will cost you little and will help set your résumé apart from the majority of résumés a company will receive.

Résumé Format

Whichever type of résumé you decide to prepare, you will have to decide how to record your information.

The following subsections suggest ways for you to gather information for your résumé, and they illustrate how to write different sections of a résumé. Remember, however, that the seven rules in the preceding discussion of résumés apply to any résumé you write, regardless of the sections you choose to include or the format you use.

Résumés

A good résumé will contain most of the following sections. The first four sections are usually required, while the last three are optional. Also, note that the order of the sections can vary after the first two, which always lead off a résumé.

- Personal Information (required)
- Job Objective (required)
- Work Experience (required)
- Education (required)
- Activities (optional)
- Skills (optional)
- References (optional)

Cover letters for résumés are also optional, but we recommend you prepare a cover letter even if the job ad does not request one. The cover letter allows an employer to see how you would handle routine business correspondence. See LETTERS and see the model cover letters for résumés among the model documents at the back of the *Style Guide*.

PERSONAL INFORMATION (REQUIRED)

Start your résumé by listing your personal information, much as a letter starts with the sender's name and address.

- Name
- Address
- Telephone Number
- Other Personal Information

Make this information accurate and up-to-date. An employer needs this information to contact you if you are selected to come in for an interview. Incomplete or inaccurate information implies you are careless and perhaps irresponsible.

Name Include your full legal name.

Do This

Susan Roberta Arnold

Not This

Suzy Arnold

If you prefer a nickname, include it in parentheses:

Susan (**Suzy**) Roberta Arnold

Address Include your complete mailing address. Be sure to provide your apartment number (if applicable) and ZIP code (preferably the ZIP code plus 4).

2897 Oakland Lane, Apartment 305
Silver Lake, Kansas 36051-2988

A common practice is to use the U.S. Post Office abbreviations for the state. See LETTERS for a list of these capitalized, two-letter abbreviations.

2897 Oakland Lane, Apartment 305
Silver Lake, KS 36051-2988

NOTE: Do not use a business address unless you want or expect letters to come to that address.

Telephone Number If you have more than one telephone number at which you can be reached, include both and label them. However, if you cannot receive calls or do not want potential employers to contact you at a daytime number, do not include that number. Include the area code when you give your phone number(s).

203–555–2001 (Home)

203–555–1100 (Work)

Resumés

NOTE: If you do not want to be called at work, say so on your resumé. Otherwise, an employer might look at your job history and try to reach you at your current job.

Other Personal Information Do not include personal information about your gender, race, age, religion, physical handicaps, sexual orientation, height, or weight. Unless these directly affect your ability to perform a job, equal employment opportunity laws (both federal and state) prohibit an employer from considering these factors when hiring an employee.

Questions to Develop Your Personal Information
What is your full name?
What is your personal mailing address?
At which telephone numbers can you be reached?

JOB OBJECTIVE (REQUIRED)

A job objective is similar to a subject line in a letter or memo. It tells the reader why you have assembled and sent this information. A job objective should be as specific as possible—tailored to the job for which you are applying. In addition, it should keep the reader's (the potential employer's) needs in mind.

Do This

> Objective: To use my advanced clerical skills in a position as an office assistant or an administrative assistant.

Not This

> Objective: To obtain a job that will challenge me and let me learn a lot about the legal world.

The more focused the job objective, the more focused the applicant appears to potential employers.

> Objective: To contribute my experience as a medical technician to Diagnostic Services Company's new testing laboratory.

Questions to Develop Your Job Objective
What type of job do you want?
In what industry do you want to work?
What level of responsibility do you want in a job?
What contributions can you bring to this job?
For what kind of company (large/small/growing/international/private/public) do you want to work?

WORK EXPERIENCE (REQUIRED)

Include a description of your work experience, starting with the most recent. Include the job title, company name and location, and the dates you worked there. See Figure 4 on the following page. You need not include your supervisor's name here; you might want to include the name, however, in your list of references (see the discussion of references at the end of this section).

Questions to Develop Your Work Experience
For what company did you work?
What was the address of the company (city and state)?
What was your title?
When did you work there?
What were your responsibilities?
What were your accomplishments?

155

Résumés

Do This

- Recreation Assistant, Merryvale Hospital, Craig, CO — 1996–1997
- Assistant, Mother Hubbard Nursery School, Seattle, WA — 1994–1995

Not This

- Recreation Assistant — 1996–1997
- Assistant — 1994–1995

Figure 4. **Provide Complete Listings for All Work Experience.** *While the job title in a person's work experience is an important indication of responsibilities, the name of the company and its location are equally important to establishing credibility and must be included.*

If you are using a chronological format, follow each job title with a description of your job duties and successes. See Figure 5 for an example of how to correctly list job duties in a bulleted list.

If you are using a functional format, include most of the same job information, listing the duties or skills in major headings, with the names of the companies as supporting information.

Work Experience

Office Manager — 1996–Present
Smithson Accounting, Bridgeport, PA
- Manage administrative staff of six people
- Order supplies; reduced office supply budget by $3,500 annually
- Oversee all office logistics
- Write letters and proposals for senior partner

Secretary — 1994–1996
Joe Brown Accounting, Norristown, PA
- Managed all customer invoices; implemented new billing system
- Provided comprehensive administrative support for two accountants
- Answered main phone line; interacted daily with customers and vendors

Figure 5. **Job Duties and Successes Written in a Bulleted List.** *This concise format for listing responsibilities and accomplishments allows readers to understand immediately the most important facts about your work experience and how they relate to the desired job.*

Résumés

EDUCATION (REQUIRED)
List all education relevant to the job you want. Start with your most recent education.

> Lubbock Technical College, Lubbock, TX, Landscape Design Certification Program, 1996–Present
>
> Lubbock Junior College, Lubbock, TX, AA Degree, 1996
>
> Lubbock High School, Lubbock, TX, 1994

Include majors or class titles if they relate to your job objective.

> Frankfurt Nurses College, Frankfurt, KY, LPN Degree, 1995–1997
>
> San Marcos College, San Marcos, CA, Paralegal Program, 1994–1996

If you have taken a course that contributes to your qualifications for a particular job, include it under EDUCATION.

> Emergency Medical Technician Training, 1994–Present
> Projected completion: 1997
>
> Basic Hotel Administration Course
> Cleveland High School, Cleveland, OH
> Continuing Education Program, 1993

Include grade point averages or class rank only if they are higher than average:

> Springfield High School, Springfield, MA
> 1994–1998
> Graduated in top third of class
>
> Spokane Technical College, Spokane, WA
> 1996–present
> Cumulative GPA: 3.23 (out of 4.0)

Include awards and honors received:

> Coolidge High, Alexandria, VA
> Graduated 1994
> Awarded "Business Challenge Award"

Questions to Develop Your Education
Which schools have you attended?
Where are these schools located?
What were the dates when you attended these schools?
What degree or certificate did you receive?
What was your grade point average?
What awards or recognitions did you receive?
Have you received any training outside of these schools?
Was a certificate involved in this outside training?
What course work did you do in this training?

ACTIVITIES (OPTIONAL)
List any activities relevant to your job objective. These activities can include professional organizations, civic organizations, or activities where you performed tasks similar to those required by the job you want. Do not include information that does not relate to your desired job.

For an example of how related activities can be woven into a résumé to reinforce a writer's work experience and qualifications, see Figure 6 on the following page.

Résumés

Activities	**Newspaper Writer** Stetson High School Deerfield, IL	1995–1997
	President **Member** Junior Achievement Buffalo Grove, IL	1996 1993–1995
	Volunteer Office Manager Deerfield Arts Center Deerfield, IL	1994–Present

Figure 6. Activities Included as Additional Experience on a Résumé. *While including activities on a résumé is optional, activities that are related to the résumé objective can enhance the image of the writer's qualifications. But only include activities if they support the objective.*

Questions to Develop Your Activities
To what professional associations do you belong?
To what social associations do you belong?
How do these professional or social associations relate to your job objective?
In what sports or hobbies do you participate?
How do these sports or hobbies relate to your job objective?
What offices did you hold in these clubs or associations?
What were your accomplishments in these activities?
What business skills did you practice?
What recognition did you receive?

NOTE: Only include social associations, sports, and hobbies if they relate to your job objective.

SKILLS (OPTIONAL)

Include any skills pertinent to your job objective. These can include language skills, office skills, software proficiency, or other aptitudes.

> Proficient in the use of MicroDot Write, AniWord, and NumberWiz Spreadsheet
>
> Fluent in Spanish
>
> Typing speed of 65 wpm
>
> Able to meet apprentice-level electrician needs

If you are using the functional résumé format, you will include the most important information organized by subject under SKILLS. See Figure 7 on the following page for an example of how to effectively present job-related skills.

Résumés

Skills	**Advanced Clerical Skills** • Typed letters, memos, reports, and invoices for lawyers • Accurately filed case information and employee records • Used MicroDot Write software to create newspaper layouts, basketball rosters, and school papers **Customer Service Skills** • Answered Daddy's Daycare main line; enrolled callers in daycare services • Volunteered at Community Service holiday gift wrap service; wrapped gifts according to customers' wishes • Answered law office main telephone line; correctly forwarded callers to appropriate person

Figure 7. Job-Related Skills Listed in a Functional Résumé. *A functional résumé is most effective for job applicants who do not have an extensive work history but have gained important skills through jobs, activities, school, etc. In this type of résumé, list skills as headings.*

Questions to Develop Your Skills
Do you read, write, or speak any languages other than English?
At what office skills are you proficient?
What business machines do you know how to use?
Do you type? If so, how fast?
Do you know any computer programming languages?
What computer software do you know how to use?
What computer platforms do you know how to use?
At what trade skills are you proficient?

REFERENCES (OPTIONAL)

References are almost never included in résumés. At most, the writer of a résumé may add a note that a list of references is available if the potential employer wishes to request it. This note itself is now optional.

We recommend you prepare a separate list of references for use if an employer requests it. **Be sure to list only people who have given you permission to use their names.** Asking people for permission is a courtesy. Also, sometimes you may ask someone who prefers not to give you a reference, perhaps because they feel they don't know enough about your abilities.

When you list references, include the person's full name, title, address, and phone number. If appropriate, add a note about the person's relationship to you or your job history.

Résumés

Mrs. Berta R. Smith, Assistant Manager
The Fashion Farm
Framingham, MA 98502
831-555-4403
(Immediate supervisor from 1995–1996)

Type your list of references on a single page, being sure to proofread the list for accuracy. The appearance of this list is just as important as the appearance of your résumé.

Usually, you should list at least three people as references. The most important one is the name of a recent job supervisor. If you have no job history or a limited history, consider asking three of the following people for references:

- Teacher
- Coach
- Family friend who is in business and can speak about your personal qualities
- Clergyman
- Physician or dentist, if they can speak about your personal qualities
- Advisor for a club or other after-school group

COVER LETTER (OPTIONAL)

Although not actually part of a résumé, the cover letter is an important (though optional) feature to go along with your résumé. See LETTERS and see the model cover letters among the model documents at the back of the *Style Guide*.

The cover letter allows you to speak directly to a specific job, even if your résumé is more general. For instance, you may have prepared a résumé targeted for a job in retail sales. If you are involved in a lengthy job search, you might submit this same résumé to several dozen companies. For each, however, you should prepare a specific cover letter mentioning a specific want ad and any features in the want ad your qualifications match.

Semicolons can be used to link closely related thoughts or to separate independent but coordinated thoughts.

Semicolons have two primary functions—linking thoughts and separating thoughts.

> **Preview**
>
> 1. Use semicolons to link complete thoughts that are closely related but are not joined by a conjunction (*and, but, for, nor, or, so, yet*).
>
> 2. Use semicolons to separate independent clauses joined by a conjunctive adverb or transitional expression.
>
> 3. Use semicolons to link complete thoughts that are closely related and joined by a coordinating conjunction if the complete thoughts are lengthy and already contain commas.
>
> 4. Use semicolons to separate items in a series when one or more of the items has a comma.

1. Use semicolons to link complete thoughts that are closely related but are not joined by a conjunction (*and, but, for, nor, or, so, yet*).

Color Graphics Co. has completed more than 20 projects this week; in all 20 projects they used a quality control inspector.

Typically, the complete thoughts linked by a semicolon are equal in structure and importance. Writers could separate the complete thoughts with a period and create two sentences.

Color Graphics Co. has completed more than 20 projects this week. In all 20 projects they used a quality control inspector.

As you can see from these two examples, the semicolon shows a closer relationship between the thoughts than a period does. The semicolon says, "These thoughts are closely related."

2. Use semicolons to separate independent clauses joined by a conjunctive adverb or transitional expression.

A transitional word or phrase indicates or clarifies the relationship between the thoughts before and after the semicolon.

Some commonly used conjunctive adverbs and transitional phrases include the following:

accordingly	consequently
for example	for instance
further	furthermore
however	in addition
indeed	moreover
nevertheless	nonetheless
on the contrary	on the other hand
therefore	thus

Heavy rainfall flooded highways near the river; **consequently,** Mark could not drive the shortest route to the business college.

Julio thought accounting was a difficult subject; **however,** he completed his homework.

161

Semicolons

NOTE: When a conjunctive adverb or transitional expression is used to join two complete sentences, it is preceded by a semicolon and followed by a comma.

---

3. Use semicolons to link complete thoughts that are closely related and joined by a coordinating conjunction if the complete thoughts are lengthy and already contain commas.

See COMMAS, CONJUNCTIONS, and TRANSITIONS.

> The committee began a careful inspection of the preliminary design study, which General Landscaping submitted upon just two weeks' notice; and they found that the sprinkling system analysis, although obviously hurried, was still superior to those of other designers who had had much more time.

---

4. Use semicolons to separate items in a series when one or more of the items has a comma.

> Runners in the relay are Jody Hansen, first leg; Alicia Williams, second leg; Sondra Thompson, third leg; and Vonnie Walker, fourth leg.

> The store sells ice; food such as carrots, tomatoes, and corn; and all types of soft drinks.

Every word in a document must be spelled correctly to ensure clarity for readers and to develop credibility for the writer.

Spelling every word correctly is important in any professional document—from formal report to everyday letter or memo.

Spelling is important for the sake of both clarity and credibility. Most misspellings do not cause readers to misinterpret the sentence in which the misspelling occurs, but the misspelled word draws attention to itself. This slows down readers and diverts their attention away from the ideas being expressed.

Language is a medium. When the medium draws attention to itself, it detracts from the message.

Misspelling words may also cause readers to question the writer's competence, intelligence, and credibility.

How much confidence would you have in this writer's engineering abilities?

> Raw seawater has been consider as a possible alternate source for the principal water supply. However, bench scale tests indicate that the high consentration of dissolved salts in seawater interfeer in the efficient recovery of mineral from the ore.

Misspellings in a document make the writer and the writer's organization look incompetent, sloppy, careless, and potentially untrustworthy.

However, spelling in English is far from simple. Roughly 90 percent of the words in English are regular, but the other 10 percent are demons.

Preview

1. Challenge the spelling of every word in your document, especially those words with which you have difficulty.

2. Use the spelling rules you find helpful.

3. Form plurals carefully. Many irregular forms exist.

4. Keep a list of the words you have trouble spelling.

5. Use word-processing software that checks spelling.

Which words in the following pairs are correct?

accomodate/accommodate

committment/commitment

concientious/conscientious

changable/changeable

indispensible/indispensable

inevitible/inevitable

irresistable/irresistible

occurence/occurrence

preceed/precede

prefered/preferred

privlege/privilege

seperate/separate

transfered/transferred

truely/truly

163

Spelling

If you are like most people, you had to pause on at least two or three of the pairs. Perhaps you still aren't sure. Did you look up any of them in a dictionary?

English evolved over centuries of influence from the languages of all the ethnic groups in the world. Because English is derived from the borrowed, rich resources of international languages, it has an inconsistent base system of words. That's why English pronunciation and spelling are inconsistent.

1. Challenge the spelling of every word in your document, especially those words with which you have difficulty.

The best proofreaders and editors challenge every word, especially those known to be difficult (such as those listed previously).

If the word is common enough, you can trust yourself to recognize correct spelling. If you are unsure, however, check a dictionary.

2. Use the spelling rules you find helpful.

The spelling rules are difficult to remember, and most have many exceptions. If you take the time to memorize the rules, you should probably also memorize the exceptions. At some point, the exercise becomes tiresome, and the rewards are questionable.

However, you should use the rules you have found helpful and can remember well enough to apply. Probably the most well known and most useful rule is "–i before –e except after –c." Here are some of the exceptions:

counterfeit

foreign

freight

height

neighbor

sleigh

weight

Some of the other common rules are briefly summarized below:

- Change a final –y to –i before adding a suffix to a word, but keep the –y before –ing.

activity	activities
deny	denies, denying
happy	happily, happier, happiest, happiness
likely	likelihood, likeliest
study	studies, studied, studying

- Drop a silent final –e before a suffix beginning with a vowel but not before a suffix beginning with a consonant.

age	aging
desire	desirable
mobile	mobility
notice	noticing
scarce	scarcity
care	careful
manage	management
safe	safety

Spelling

Some exceptions to this rule are as follows:

acreage

argument

changeable

courageous

judgment

mileage

ninth

truly

- Double a final consonant before a suffix beginning with a vowel (1) if the consonant ends a stressed syllable (or a single-syllable word) and (2) if the consonant is preceded by a single vowel.

bag	bagged
brag	bragged
shop	shopped, shopper
stop	stopped
begin	beginning
occur	occurred
prefer	preferred
regret	regretting, regretted

3. Form plurals carefully. Many irregular forms exist.

man	men
analysis	analyses
matrix	matrices
potato	potatoes
mouse	mice

See PLURALS for a discussion of these irregular forms as well as a list of the most common irregular plurals.

4. Keep a list of the words you have trouble spelling.

Remembering spelling rules and their exceptions is difficult. A simpler and nearly foolproof method for improving your spelling is to keep a list of the words you commonly misspell. Look up the correct spellings and list the words alphabetically.

When you see that you have misspelled a word, add it to your list. Then refer to the list when you need to use one of those words. Over time, your mind will come to recognize the look of the word with its correct spelling, and you will no longer need the list.

Until you no longer need it, keep the list in a convenient place where you can see it easily as you write. Tuck the list inside your dictionary, or tape it inside your notebook or on the wall in front of your desk or writing area.

5. Use word-processing software that checks spelling.

Whenever possible use word-processing software to check your spelling. Spell-checking software is a valuable tool for improving and proofreading your writing. See WRITING.

Remember that a computer spell checker may not discover all your errors. For example, a spell checker will not identify *their* as the wrong spelling when the writer meant to write *there*.

Titles

Titles of people, organizations, governments, and publications often require special treatment for capitalization.

Titles of people, organizations, governments, and publications often require special capitalization, punctuation, and other format conventions. See CAPITALS.

Preview

1. Capitalize the first letter of titles when they **immediately** precede personal names. Do not capitalize the first letter of a title when it follows a personal name.

2. Capitalize the first letter of names of companies, schools, organizations, and religious bodies.

3. Capitalize the first letter of names of government bodies.

4. Capitalize and italicize (or underline) the titles of books, magazines, newspapers, plays, movies, television series, and other separately published works.

5. Capitalize and use quotation marks for chapters of books, articles in magazines, news stories or editorials, acts within a play, episodes of a television series, or other sections of something separately produced or published.

---

1. Capitalize the first letter of titles when they *immediately* precede personal names. Do not capitalize the first letter of a title when it follows a personal name.

Mrs. Robert T. Evans

Mr. Edward Johnson

Ms. Josephine Kukor

President Amy Kaufmann

Assistant Professor Ned Davies

Lieutenant Cynthia Wagner

the **Reverend** John Tyler

Rabbi Tochterman

Amy Kaufmann, the **president** of Union College, spoke to the press.

Ned Davies is an **assistant professor** at Columbia University.

Our **lieutenant** was Cynthia Wagner. (Here was separates the title from the name.)

NOTE 1: The titles of high-ranking international, national, and state officials often retain their capitalization, even when the name of the individual is either absent or does not follow the title.

> The **President** spoke before the Congress.
>
> We wrote to the **Vice President**.
>
> The **Pope** toured South America.

NOTE 2: Titles of company or corporation executives as well as titles of lesser federal and state officials are sometimes capitalized. Such capitalization is unnecessary, but you should follow company or agency practice.

> The **Mayor** announced an end to the New York transit strike. (*or* The mayor)
>
> The **Vice President of Finance** is resigning Monday, September 18. (*or* The vice president of finance)

Titles

NOTE 3: Titles used in a general sense are not capitalized.

> a U.S. **representative**
>
> a **king**
>
> a **prime minister**

2. Capitalize the first letter of names of companies, schools, organizations, and religious bodies.

> the **Wilson Restaurant Supply Company**
>
> the **University of Oregon**
>
> the **Young Men's Christian Association**
>
> the **Republican Party**
>
> **St. John's Lutheran Church**

NOTE: The words capitalized are those normally capitalized in any title. See CAPITALS. *The* in most titles is not capitalized unless the company, school, organization, or religious body has established *the* as part of its legal name: *The Johns Hopkins University, The Travelers Insurance Company.*

3. Capitalize the first letter of names of government bodies.

> the **United Nations**
>
> the **Cabinet**
>
> the **California Legislature**
>
> the **Ohio Board of Education**
>
> the **Davis County Commission**
>
> the **House** (for House of Representatives)
>
> the **Department** (for Department of Agriculture)

NOTE: Except for international and national bodies, shortened forms of these government bodies or common terms are not capitalized:

> the **police department**
>
> the **county council**
>
> the **board of education**

4. Capitalize and italicize (or underline) the titles of books, magazines, newspapers, plays, movies, television series, and other separately published works.

> *Oliver Twist* (book or movie)
>
> *Newsweek*
>
> *The New York Times*
>
> *West Side Story*
>
> *Superman*
>
> *NOVA*

5. Capitalize and use quotation marks for chapters of books, articles in magazines, news stories or editorials, acts within a play, episodes of a television series, or other sections of something separately produced or published.

> The last chapter was called "The Final Irony."
>
> "The Colombian Connection" was the lead article in last week's *Time*.
>
> We supported his editorial, "A Streamlined Election System."
>
> We watched "The Fatal Circle" last night on *Gunsmoke*.

 **Tone** — *Tone reflects a writer's attitude toward the subject or audience, and can have an important effect on how well a message is understood.*

Tone reflects your attitude toward your subject and your readers. Your writing may strike your readers as personal or impersonal, friendly or distant. You may sound warm and engaging or cold and abrupt.

Your style reflects your mood as a writer and the choices you make while writing. The words you choose, the length and structure of your sentences, and the use of personal pronouns or contractions are all a part of your style.

Style and *tone* are often confused. Some people use the terms interchangeably, but one is the cause and the other the effect:

> ### Preview
> 1. Use pronouns to establish a personal, human tone in letters and memos.
> 2. Use the language you would choose if you were actually talking with your readers.
> 3. Choose sentence structures that reflect a friendly, conversational tone.
> 4. Include personal information and personal references.
> 5. Choose your paper, typeface, and format to reflect a personal, friendly tone.

- **Style** refers to those choices that create the tone readers perceive. Style is your "manner of speaking," the way you use language to express ideas.
- **Tone** refers to the feeling or impression a document conveys to its readers. It is one of the products of your style.

We usually describe the tone of a piece of writing with words such as these:

abrasive	formal
assertive	friendly
authoritative	impersonal
blunt	informal
bureaucratic	informative
casual	objective
cold	officious

condescending	personal
courteous	polite
demanding	sincere
discourteous	stiff
distant	subjective
earnest	threatening
engaging	warm

Most of the time, your business letters and memos should be

courteous	informative
forthright	personal
friendly	polite
helpful	sincere
informal	warm

168

Tone

The extent to which your documents are personal will depend on your relationship with the reader. But never fail to be courteous, polite, informative, sincere, and helpful—especially when you don't know the reader. Good business writing—no matter how tough the subject is—should **never** be discourteous.

Below are the style choices that will help you write business letters and memos with an effective tone. These are the same rules that make writing clear, concise, and easy to read.

1. Use pronouns to establish a personal, human tone in letters and memos.

Probably no single writing choice is as effective in making business documents sound personal as well-chosen pronouns. Of the pronouns possible, *you* is the most important. Always be aware of your readers and address them directly:

Do This

> During our discussion of **your** April bill, **you** mentioned **you** had called **your** local service person at least three times during the month. Do **you** remember the service person's name and the dates when **you** called?

Not This

> Concerning the April bill, the local service representative may have been called, but these calls cannot be verified unless the representative's name and the dates when the representative was called are provided to this office.

The ineffective version has no personal pronouns; thus, the reader is ignored. Not using personal pronouns makes the letter cold and informal. Passive verbs contribute to the impersonal tone and make the letter sound unfriendly at best. See ACTIVE/PASSIVE.

The pronouns *I* and *we* are essential for effective letters and memos. Some people argue the writer should not be mentioned in business letters and memos. They argue that letters and memos should not reflect personal opinions or the personality of the author. This argument fails to distinguish between personal opinions and personal responsibility for one's actions. Compare these two examples:

Do This

> Based on the survey, **I** (*or* **we**) suggest that Martin Fitness Equipment should offer a wider range of colors in its 1997 product catalog.

Not This

> Based on the data, it is concluded that Martin Fitness Equipment should offer a wider range of colors in its 1997 product catalog.

The second version is mechanical, almost robotic. No person seems to have acted. The conclusion simply occurred. The result is a faceless, anonymous tone. This tone makes it seem as if the writer is deliberately avoiding responsibility.

2. Use the language you would choose if you were actually talking with your readers.

Read your document out loud. Would you be comfortable saying those words to someone in person? If you talked to your readers, would you talk this way?

Tone

The tone of a good business letter or memo is a natural one. It isn't full of slang or conversational expressions *(Well shucks, I reckon, ain't),* but it should sound natural, not forced or fake. If the document does not sound natural, if it is stiff and complex, if it is formal and faceless, rethink your tone.

The words, phrases, and sentences you use should be simple and direct, even though you have edited and revised them.

Do This

I recommend that we immediately replace the roof on the Bradley building.

Not This

It is recommended that the roof on the Bradley building be replaced forthwith.

Do This

Before leaving the room, turn out the lights.

Not This

Prior to evacuating the premises, ensure the illumination has been terminated.

The simplest remedy for overly stiff writing is to write like a human being. Don't write like an official, faceless machine. Just be yourself. Imagine you're talking to people in person. Try to sound human, not mechanical.

Using personal pronouns helps considerably. Here are some other suggestions:

- **Keep your sentences short and direct.** Rewrite any sentence that is longer than 30 words, and try to limit average sentence length to about 20 words. You can often break a long sentence into two shorter sentences. Make sure each sentence, whatever its length, is as clear and direct as possible.

- **Avoid long, complex words and unnecessary technical terms.** Never use words because you think they are impressive. The writer who tries to sound intelligent and educated (often by using a thesaurus) often winds up sounding silly.

Do This

We think your water pipes have corroded so much that only a trickle of water can flow through them.

Not This

Our hypothesis is that your water supply system has undergone severe corrosion and reached the debilitating point where water normally available is unavailable in the quantity and at the pressure provided for in the original specifications for your domicile.

Leaving aside the laughable words (*debilitating* and *domicile*), the second version still suffers from wordiness. Isn't *pipes* better than *water supply system*? And isn't *corroded* so much better than *undergone severe corrosion*? What do the inexact references to *quantity* and *pressure* accomplish that the word *trickle* doesn't do more vividly? The idea being expressed does not require technical terms, especially if the reader is a homeowner, not an engineer.

Legal documents often suffer from the same kind of wordiness and unnecessary complexity.

Tone

Do This

According to the directions outlined above, please sign all three copies of the contract and have your signature notarized. Then return the completed forms to this office by Friday, May 23.

Not This

In accordance with the provisions of the aforementioned procedure, the attached conveyance should be executed by you in triplicate, with the signature duly witnessed and attested to by a Notary Public, and the executed set of conveyance forms should then be returned to this office on or before, and no later than, Friday, May 23.

---

3. Choose sentence structures that reflect a friendly, conversational tone.

Avoid passive sentences. See ACTIVE/PASSIVE.

Do This

Our review of your account indicates you should receive a refund of $72. This refund would apply to 1997 charges.

Not This

Your claim has been reviewed, and it has been determined that $72 should be refunded to you for the period January to December 1997.

Do This

We reviewed the spending reports to find the problem. Over 90 percent of the mistakes turned out to be simple errors in daily recording.

Not This

The departmental accounting reports have been analyzed to determine the source of the discrepancies. It is concluded that over 90 percent of the discrepancies were caused by simple errors in daily recording.

---

4. Include personal information and personal references.

Readers like to know you have addressed their needs. So, if appropriate, include information from previous letters, memos, or discussions in your document. Or include information your reader has either requested or will need:

> I suggest you file a complaint with the County Commission. Your outline of previous conversations with the company convinced me you have a case.

A mechanical, yet easy, way to make a letter or memo personal is to include the reader's name in the body of the letter:

> So, Beth, if you have any more suggestions, please call me at my office.

> If we go forward, Cal, you should ask Marketing for a copy of their assessment form. I think you'd find it helpful.

NOTE: An occasional contraction (*you'd*) makes the tone conversational and informal. If you know your reader well, this may be acceptable; however, you should avoid contractions in more formal correspondence.

Tone

5. Choose your paper, typeface, and format to reflect a personal, friendly tone.

Even decisions about physical options can affect the tone of your letter or memo.

Choose quality paper (usually 20-pound paper) and a pleasing typeface. With word processors and computers, typeface options are growing. Know your options. Your goal is to capture the personal, friendly quality of the content of your letter (consider Times Roman or Palatino typefaces). Some typefaces are too rigid and stark (for example, American Typewriter). Others are too informal (for example, Script, which mimics cursive writing).

Next, design your document so it has a clean and open look, one conveying a personal, friendly tone. This means using generous margins, short paragraphs (on the average), headings, lists, and lots of white space. See EMPHASIS and PAGE LAYOUT.

Transitions connect ideas and show how they are related. Transitions make writing more logical and easier to follow.

Transitions are words or phrases that connect ideas and show how they are related. Used between two sentences or paragraphs, a transition shows how the sentences or paragraphs are connected. This makes the writing smoother and more logical. A transition creates a point of reference for readers, allowing them to see how your thoughts are organized.

Following is a list of functions and commonly used transitions. See CONJUNCTIONS and ORGANIZATION.

Preview

1. Use a comma to separate a transitional expression from the main body of a sentence.

2. If the transition interrupts the flow of a sentence, place commas on both sides of the transitional word or phrase.

3. When a transitional word or phrase comes between two complete sentences, place a semicolon before it and a comma after.

- **Addition**

additionally	again
also	besides
further	furthermore
in addition	likewise
moreover	next
too	what is more

- **Comparison or Contrast**

by contrast	by the same token
conversely	however
in contrast	in spite of
instead	in such a manner
likewise	nevertheless
otherwise	on the contrary
on the one hand	on the other hand
rather	similarly
still	yet

- **Concession**

anyway	at any rate
even so	however
in any case	in any event
of course	still

- **Consequence**

accordingly	as a result
consequently	hence
otherwise	so, then
therefore	thus

- **Diversion**

by the way	incidentally

- **Generalization**

as a rule	as usual
for the most part	generally
in general	ordinarily

Transitions

- **Illustration**

for example	for instance

- **Place**

close	here
near	nearby
there	

- **Restatement**

in essence	in other words
namely	that is

- **Summary**

after all	all in all
briefly	by and large
finally	in any case
in any event	in brief
in conclusion	in short
in summary	on balance
on the whole	ultimately

- **Time and Sequence**

after a while	afterward
at first, at last	at the same time
currently, finally	first (second, third, etc.)
first of all	for now
for the time being	immediately
instantly	in conclusion
in the first place	in the meantime
in time	in turn
later	meanwhile
next	presently
soon	subsequently
then	to begin with

---

1. Use a comma to separate a transitional expression from the main body of a sentence.

See COMMAS.

On the other hand, inexpensive skating equipment that does not provide quality performance may be of little value.

As a result, the equipment costs more and cannot be delivered overnight.

---

2. If the transition interrupts the flow of a sentence, place commas on both sides of the transitional word or phrase.

See COMMAS.

A lightweight plastic, **for instance**, will be the best choice.

The team equipment is, **however**, normally shipped overnight to arrive at the next tournament location.

---

3. When a transitional word or phrase comes between two complete sentences, place a semicolon before it and a comma after.

We wanted to accept their offer; **however**, our budget was not adequate.

The president was supposed to arrive Tuesday; **instead**, he won't be here until Wednesday.

Writing is a process of discovery that requires creativity, planning, organization, teamwork, and revision to produce the best results.

Writing is a process of discovery, creation, and surprise. As such, its steps overlap and repeat themselves, but most writers would recognize the following steps or stages in the writing of a document:

- Prewriting
- Writing a First Draft
- Evaluating and Revising
- Proofreading and Publishing

Collaboration is essential throughout the writing process. More and more writing tasks in the world of business require a team of writers. Teams plan documents and brainstorm ideas (prewriting). Team members write sections of draft documents. Teams then evaluate, review, and proofread each draft or version until the document is finally published.

Brainstorming is a valuable technique for you and members of your team of writers to use as you collaborate. One benefit of brainstorming is that you get a richer set of ideas and options—often ideas you alone might not have discovered. Another benefit is that the ideas are recorded early and then evaluated so you don't waste time on dead ends.

Brainstorming is a team activity, and the first step is to include people with different responsibilities and ideas. In the world of business, this step would mean inviting engineers, scientists, managers, legal staff, manufacturing specialists, sales personnel, government regulators, and customers to participate.

Preview

1. Determine all requirements for a document as early as possible.

2. Develop a prototype of your document and use this prototype to monitor your changes and progress.

3. Develop your own personal strategies for making the writing of a draft a comfortable, repeatable task.

4. Provide for early and frequent evaluations of your writing.

5. Set evaluation priorities and strategies. Tell reviewers what to look for and how to record their suggestions.

6. Writers and reviewers should meet face-to-face for most evaluation sessions, but record the results of such a meeting in writing.

7. Set revision priorities for yourself and for others who will help you revise and edit.

8. Use up-to-date references to guide your proofreading decisions.

In a school class, ask several students to be on your writing team. One student might be more interested in drawing graphics. Another student might know how to work on a computer. A third might be especially good as a proofreader. Include them all because you want a rich source of both ideas and skills.

Figure 1 summarizes brainstorming techniques that a team could use to plan a document.

Writing

Brainstorming Techniques

Use the following checklist to guide you during brainstorming sessions. Change or adjust these techniques as you and your brainstorming team members learn to work together.

- ❏ Work together so that everyone has a chance to speak and to contribute ideas.
- ❏ Appoint someone to record all ideas on a chalkboard, whiteboard, or pad of paper. (See Figures 2 and 3 for examples of how to record ideas.)
- ❏ Accept every idea without judging it or criticizing the person suggesting it.
- ❏ Don't worry about correct phrasing or proper spelling. The team goal is to get as many ideas as possible recorded. Editing can come later.
- ❏ Avoid discussions (or arguments) between individuals unless the whole team wants to clarify something.
- ❏ Make brainstorming sessions fast and productive, often no more than 10 or 15 minutes at one time.
- ❏ Most of all, have fun and make the process a success for everyone who participates.

Figure 1. Brainstorming Techniques. *The key to successful brainstorming is the free exchange of ideas about a specific topic. Do not worry how good the ideas are or in what order they are suggested. Follow these few simple steps to ensure your brainstorming sessions are successful and enjoyable.*

Figures 2 and 3 illustrate two ways for you to record your team notes during early brainstorming sessions.

Prewriting

Prewriting is an essential step in the writing process. Prewriting means more than merely discovering possible content. It means that as early as possible you state (and then write) your purpose for writing. You also begin to visualize the final document—its content, its length, and even the appearance of each page.

1. Determine all requirements for a document as early as possible.

In the business world, most documents fit some general pattern: a newsletter, a memo, a report, a letter, etc. Before you begin to write, you should have an idea of what the final document type will be. Try to visualize the finished product. Doing this will help you decide such things as the length and overall format. It will also help you make sensible decisions and avoid wasted time.

You will also need to know how the document will be produced. Will there be one copy or 10,000? Will the document be produced in black and white, two colors, or four colors? Will you be using photographs or other graphics? Is there a budget for how much money can be spent to create and print your document? See PAGE LAYOUT.

Be sure everyone who will be involved is notified and included in the planning process. Are there tests that must be run before the memo can be completed? Is someone supposed to conduct a survey that will be included in the report? Is your newsletter going to contain letters from satisfied customers?

It is unlikely that a single department is doing engineering studies, conducting research, and collecting marketing information. If you want cooperation from other departments to complete your assignment, you must give them plenty of time to do the work. Remember that each department has its own workload and its own deadlines—don't count on people being immediately available.

Writing

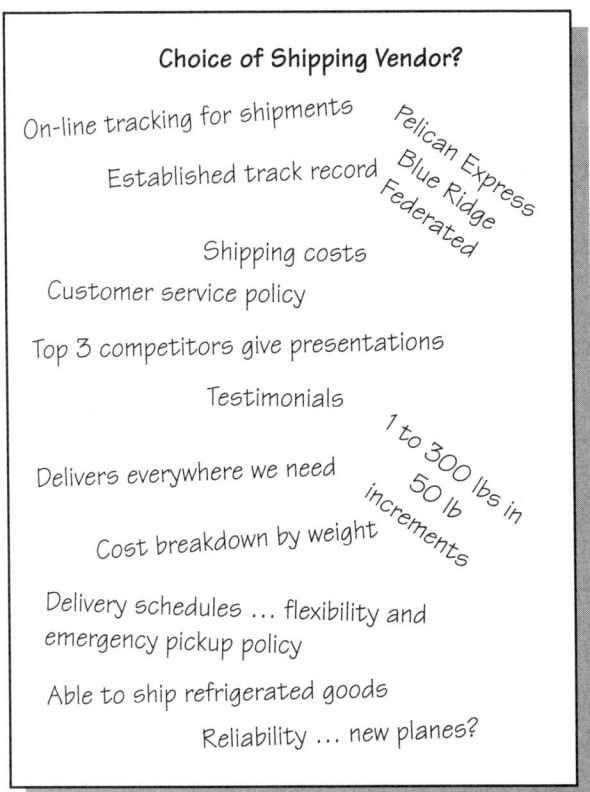

Figure 2. Brainstorming Notes. *The simplest way to record ideas is to list them in no particular order or sequence. Be sure to record everything said, or at least the key words or concepts. Don't cross out or erase. Don't worry if your list isn't neat.*

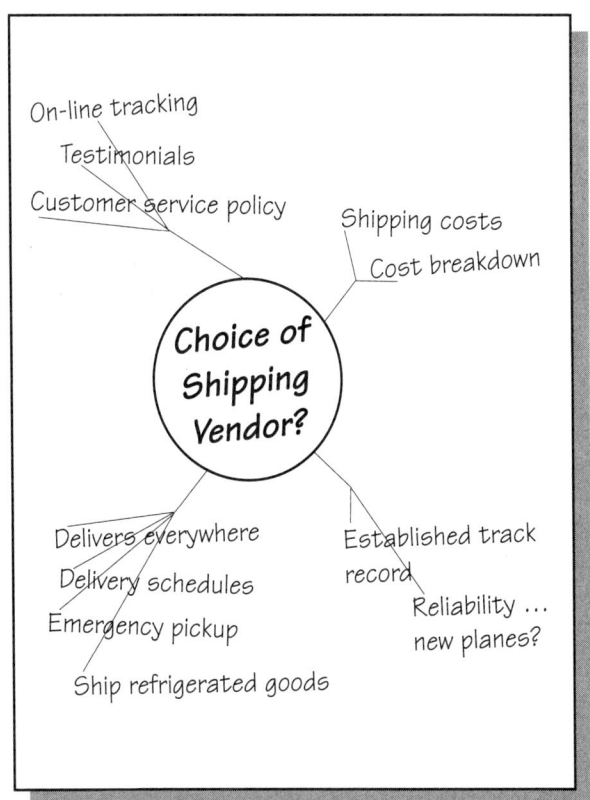

Figure 3. Clustering Notes. *This variation of brainstorming notes uses clustering to arrange ideas and show how they link to each other. The idea in the center (i.e., choice of shipping vendor) would be the main idea of the brainstorming. As ideas occur to participants, they are added to the figure, with lines drawn to connect—or cluster— related ideas.*

To begin the prewriting phase of writing, ask your team to brainstorm answers to the following questions. Use the techniques presented in Figure 1 to help make your brainstorming sessions productive.

- What is our main purpose?
- Who will read the document and what are their priorities?
- What sort of document (length, format, graphics, and content) do we intend to write?
- Who else can help gather and interpret information?
- Who can help with each later step in the writing process?

Don't ignore the preceding questions even if you are working alone. Too often writers begin to draft a document before they have decided what the document should accomplish and how it should look. Take time to answer in writing the preceding questions. The answers should help keep you (and other team members) on track.

177

Writing

2. Develop a prototype of your document and use this prototype to monitor your changes and progress.

A prototype is a full-scale model of a document. Often document prototypes are called mockups or storyboards. Regardless of the terminology used, a document prototype has these features:

- A full page-by-page model of the final document. For example, a prototype for a four-page memo report would begin with four blank pages.
- A page layout (or style sheet) to guide how text is written and how it appears on the page. Do you intend to use two columns on a page? A single column? See PAGE LAYOUT.
- Headings and subheadings that show the organization and scope of the text to be written. See HEADINGS.
- Sketches of graphics that will highlight key points. See GRAPHICS.

A brainstorming session is often a good way to begin to design a prototype. Remind yourself and your collaborators not to be judgmental or negative and to maintain a productive brainstorming mentality.

Avoid thinking of the prototype as your first draft. It is a model that exists to be challenged and tested. Everyone participating is free (without criticism) to play the "game." There are no fixed assumptions. This session is an idea-generating activity, and you may want to look at several options before deciding on your prototype design.

A document prototype saves time and money if it guides all later stages of document preparation, including the writing of text. A document prototype evolves as a team's vision of the final document matures.

Use your preliminary brainstorming notes to guide you as you prepare an **initial prototype** (a visualization of the page layout)—perhaps little more than blank pages with the header and footer sketched in and a few key headings and illustration blocks. (See Figure 4.)

As your prototyping activities continue, you will prepare an **interim prototype**, which will contain most headings and several subheadings, as well as more complete sketches of key graphics. This prototype still has little text. See Figure 5 for an example of an interim prototype.

A **mature prototype**—which may be the product of days of teamwork—begins to look like a rough draft. A mature prototype has full headings and subheadings, final versions of all graphics, and even much of the possible text. See Figure 6 for an example of a mature prototype.

The mature prototype becomes a rough draft when the text is complete. The design and scope of the document should be final by the time the rough draft is ready for review.

NOTE: An example of a final memo report developed from the preceding three prototypes appears among the model documents at the back of the *Style Guide*. See MEMO REPORT, pp. 214–217.

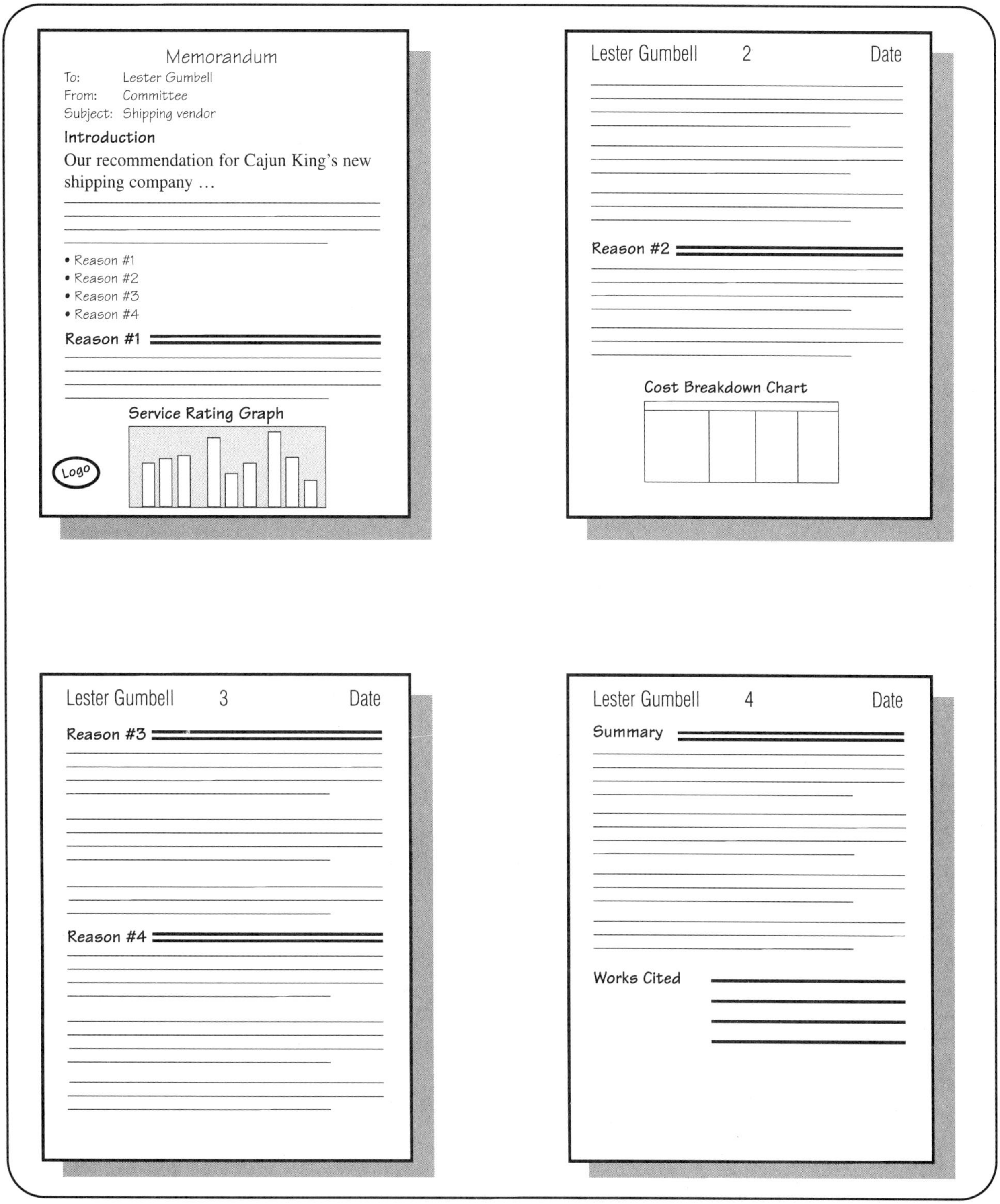

Figure 4. The Initial Prototype. *An initial prototype shows what content will be included in a document and how it will appear on the page. At this stage, the prototype may include little more than page headers and footers, rough sketches of graphics, and indications of where major headings and subheadings will appear. Do not try to write the document now; simply indicate where text will flow by drawing lines or shaded areas.*

Writing

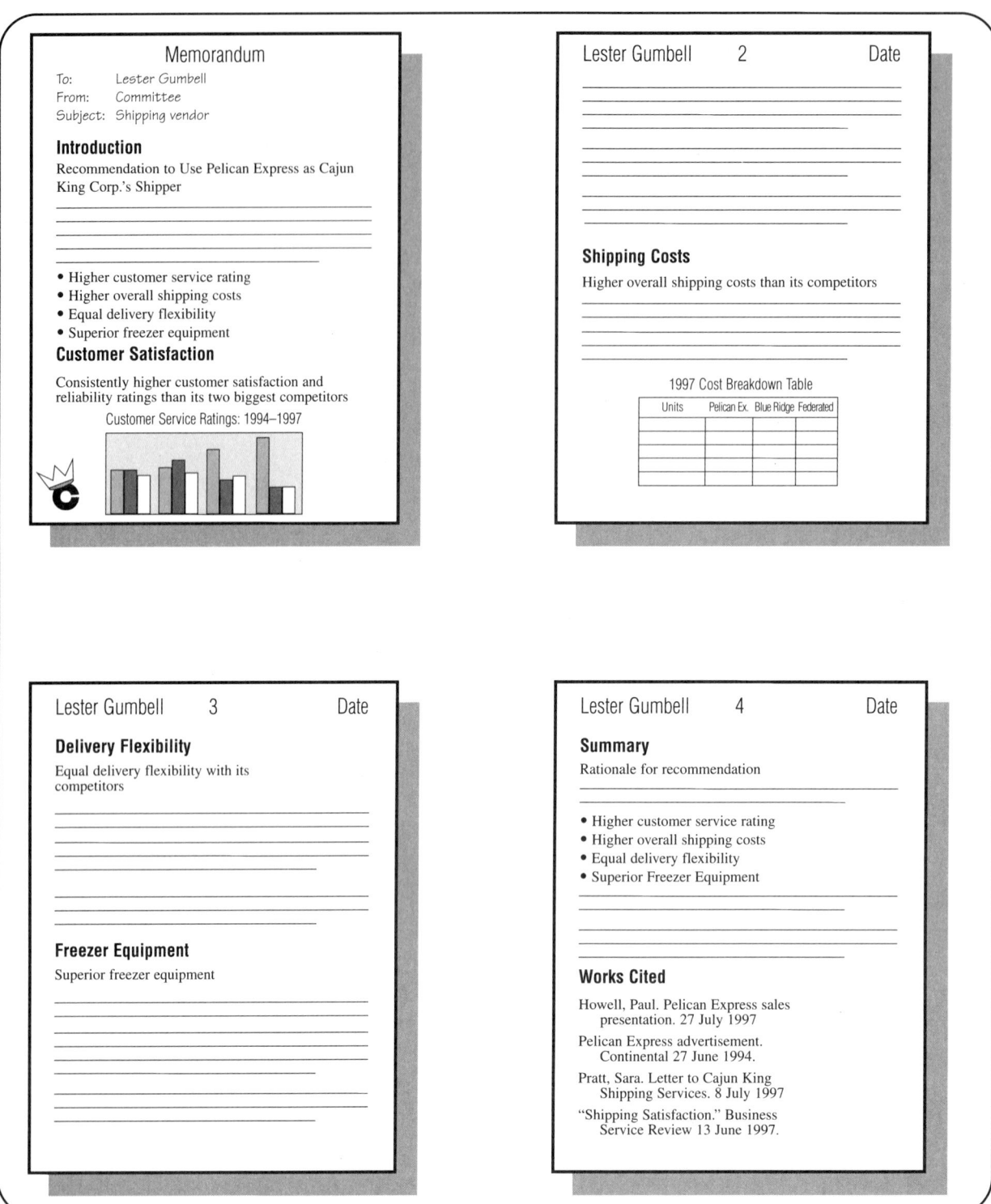

Figure 5. The Interim Prototype. *At this stage little text has been written. Instead, attention is paid to developing all major headings and subheadings, as well as creating more detailed sketches of key graphics. Content will be written later to fill in the gaps between section headings and to explain the graphics. The purpose for an interim prototype is to gain a clearer understanding of how much information a document will contain and in what order it will appear.*

Writing

Figure 6. The Mature Prototype. *At this stage a document begins to look like a rough draft. In addition to the final versions of all headings, subheadings, and key graphics, the document contains some text in all sections. A mature prototype is not a final document; rather, the text is written in rough form to put the ideas on the page. Later revisions will edit the text into a final version. Once the format is final, the content can receive the writer's undivided attention.*

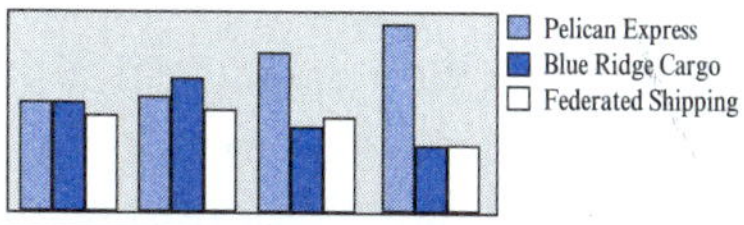

181

Writing

Writing a First Draft

Writing a draft begins when you make your initial planning notes (Rule 1). It continues as you work to flesh out your prototype (Rule 2). It does not end until you are ready to have reviewers read the document and suggest final revisions.

A key principle of time management is that you manage a complex task by breaking it into shorter tasks. Use the same approach in your writing.

3. Develop your own personal strategies for making the writing of a draft a comfortable, repeatable task.

Successful writing is 50 percent psychology and 50 percent skill with words. Ask yourself what frustrates you most about writing. Consider ways to lessen your frustrations and to make writing a pleasant task.

Your strategies may be unique, but some possible ones to consider are the following:

- Write the easy sections first. This gets your creative thoughts flowing.

- Don't worry about writing the draft in one sitting. Instead, work on your draft section by section, sentence by sentence. If you have a prototype in front of you, you can choose a section or paragraph on which to work.

- Turn off the internal voice that judges each word you write. Instead, view each word as an accomplishment and try to write at least a paragraph before pausing to read what you have written.

- Visualize yourself talking to your readers. Your thoughts and language should be just as natural and as free-flowing as your talk would be. There will be time to edit later.

- When you complete a section, take time to compliment yourself.

Evaluating and Revising

Evaluating means that, in addition to the writer, other people should review a draft. Collaboration is essential if you want your document to be as rich and as effective as possible. If you wait too long to ask for someone to evaluate a document, any major changes will cost you time (and money, in the business world).

4. Provide for early and frequent evaluations of your writing.

Schedule evaluation or review sessions during the earliest sessions working on the prototype. Continue to schedule sessions until the final draft is ready to be published.

Late reviews are wasteful and costly. If you wait until you have polished your draft to have someone other than yourself review the material, you run the risk of having reviewers tell you that all or part of your draft needs major work. The sections you have polished may need to be changed or even cut out entirely. These major changes will affect both your schedule and your budget.

Writing

5. Set evaluation priorities and strategies. Tell reviewers what to look for and how to record their suggestions.

Give reviewers specific written directions. Tell them what to look for during their review and how they should record their observations. If the review is an oral one (the preferred format), they may not need to record much on the prototype or draft. If you want annotated copies back, however, tell them.

As part of your directions, tell reviewers whether you want comments about the content and approach or whether you want them to check spelling and punctuation.

Notice that comments about content and approach are more important early in the writing process. Later, spelling and punctuation become more important.

6. Writers and reviewers should meet face-to-face for most evaluation sessions, but record the results of such a meeting in writing.

A face-to-face meeting between evaluators and the writer(s) is efficient and productive, if properly conducted. Such a meeting works well, whether the review is between peers or with a manager.

Written comments on draft materials are time consuming to write, not to mention being difficult to read. Reviewers may disagree and it is helpful to discuss organizational issues with everyone at the same time.

See Figure 7 for a checklist of procedures for conducting an efficient oral review session.

Review Procedures for Documents

- Reviewers must have time to review a copy of the prototype or draft before discussion. This copy is stamped *PROTOTYPE* or *DRAFT*.
- The writer(s) conducts the review session, setting ground rules and monitoring time.
- Review time is limited by agreement with the participants. A 1- or 2-page document should take no more than 6 or 7 minutes to review.
- Reviewers give their comments and observations briefly, with no explanations of details or their rationale, unless the writer asks for clarification.
- Comments are as constructive and as positive as possible.
- Comments need not be repeated unless reviewers disagree about a point. Discussions of the disagreement are not allowed unless the writer asks for clarification.
- A single person records comments. If appropriate, this person records and circulates a summary of comments or items to be researched.

Figure 7. Document Review Procedures. *Every major document needs to be reviewed, preferably by several people other than the writer. These meetings should not become critical complaint sessions where comments are directed at the writer instead of the document. Keep your comments positive and constructive, and help each other write better documents.*

---

7. Set revision priorities for yourself and for others who will help you revise and edit.

Most people cannot read and revise everything in a single reading. Instead, plan to use multiple readings, each reading directed toward a different reviewing/revision priority.

Writing

First, consider the overall content, design, and organization of your document. Next, focus on revising or expanding the most significant document sections, such as the conclusions or recommendations. As you work through the document, you may play with the headings and subheadings to make them more informative. Throughout the process of revision, you may also rework or add graphics.

Proofreading and Publishing

Proofreading and publishing are the final steps in creating an effective document. Without attention to these details, the best-planned document will fail.

As in early steps in the writing process, get assistance proofreading your document. It is always to your advantage to have a different set of eyes review the material because someone else will read and edit the document more objectively.

8. Use up-to-date references to guide your proofreading decisions.

No one can remember all the rules and guidelines of document preparation and language correctness.

Keep a set of basic and up-to-date reference books next to your computer or on a nearby bookshelf. At the least, obtain and use the following:

- A recent dictionary, such as the *Merriam-Webster Student's Dictionary*.
- One or more general style guides. (This *Style Guide* is an illustration of the sort of guide to acquire.)
- Specialized professional guides or glossaries.

Model Documents

Table of Contents

Job Applications/Résumés

Job Applications, Completed	187–189
Job Application, Blank Form	190–192
Job Description	193–194
Résumé, Experienced Functional	195
Résumé, Experienced Chronological	196
Cover Letter, Experienced Applicant	197
Résumé, Inexperienced Functional	198
Cover Letter, Inexperienced Applicant	199
Thank You Letter	200

Letters

Commendation	201
Complaint	202
Persuasive Sales	203–204
Proposal	205
Proposal Acceptance	206
Proposal Rejection	207
Sales	208
Survey Data	209

Memos

Personnel Notice	210
Procedure	211–212
Recommendation	213
Report	214–217
Request	218
Request for Clarification	219

Others

Abstract, Descriptive	220
Abstract, Informative	221
Minutes, Action	222–223
Minutes, Traditional	224–225
Newsletter Item	226
Policy, Customer Service	227
Procedure, Incomplete Order	228
Shift Report, Computer Company	229

Job Application, Completed

▶ See RÉSUMÉS, pp. 145–160

Read all directions carefully. Take an extra minute to survey the entire form for any special sections.

Print carefully and, if necessary, go back to connect a loop or clarify a letter.

Use your job objective to help you provide these reasons. See RÉSUMÉS.

Citizenship information and the minimum age requirement are federal employment requirements. Fill this section in completely, if applicable.

Use a dash (—) or *NA* for *"not applicable"* when a question does not apply. Either one signals you have looked at that question or item and not simply skipped answering it.

Confidential Application for Employment

Applicant: Thank you for your interest in Razor's Edge Fitness. Your application will be considered regardless of race, color, religion, sex, national origin, age, marital or veteran status, medical condition or disability, or any other legally protected status. To enable us to evaluate this application, please answer all questions carefully and as completely as possible. **Please print.** Before submitting this application, read and sign the acknowledgement at the end of the application.

Application for: ☑ Full-time ☐ Part-time ☐ On-call ☐ Temporary

Hours available to work:

PERSONAL INFORMATION

Date: 05-15-97   Soc. Sec. No.: 955-21-0000

Name (Last, First, Middle): Bennett, Mary

Present Address (Street, City, State, ZIP): 102 West Central Park, New York, NY 01009

Mailing Address (Street, City, State, ZIP): Same as above

Telephone: A.M. (212) 555-6578   P.M. (212) 555-0908

Referred by: Mrs. Julie Evans, guidance counselor

Position(s) applying for: 1. receptionist   2.

Date you can start: immediately   Salary desired: negotiable

Are you currently employed? ☑ Yes ☐ No   If yes, may we contact your present employer? ☑ Yes ☐ No

Have you applied previously for employment at Razor's Edge? ☐ Yes ☑ No   If yes, when?

Have you been previously employed by Razor's Edge or its affiliates? ☐ Yes ☑ No   If yes, when?

Do any of your relatives work at Razor's Edge? ☑ Yes ☐ No   If yes, list name, relationship, and department:

Rosemary Giles, aunt, Accounting Department

Please list your reasons for wanting a position with this company:

I would like to use my communication and teaming skills in a receptionist position that offers challenging opportunities and that demands work versatility, dependability, and ingenuity.

CITIZENSHIP

Are you prevented lawfully from becoming employed in the United States because of Visa or immigration status?

☐ Yes ☑ No   (Proof of citizenship or immigration status will be required upon employment.)

If you are a resident alien, please give your alien number found on your resident alien card (Form I-551):

N/A

Are you at least 18 years of age? ☑ Yes ☐ No

If you have ever been convicted of an offense (excluding minor traffic violations), please complete the following:

Charge: N/A   Place of Arrest: Date:

Result or outcome:

EDUCATION

	Name of Institution	City/State	Years Completed	Degree	G.P.A.
High School	West Central	New York, NY	1990-1994	Diploma	3.58
College					
Graduate					
Trade					

An attractive and completely filled-in job application is essential in any successful job search. Not all job applications are as long as the one above, but be prepared for detailed questions by taking along a filled-in sample form with all the names, dates, and other facts you might need. See pp. 190-192 for a blank job application form; practice filling it in, and take it with you when you apply for a job. See RÉSUMÉS.

Job Application, Completed

Explain your physical abilities only if this information would affect your ability to do a specific job. Otherwise, an employer cannot ask about your physical abilities.

Only list references who have given you permission to use their names. Always identify their occupations and provide their phone numbers.

Do not mention the name of a club or a church that would signal you belong to a specific religion or have a specific national origin. You can still mention, for example, that you were the treasurer of your church youth group, but the name of the church need not be specified.

Be sure to list any and all skills that would aid you in getting a job. See RÉSUMÉS for suggestions about how to identify skills.

Are you under the care of a physician or currently receiving medical treatment for any injury, physical defect, chronic ailment, or any other condition which could affect your ability to perform the essential functions of the job for which you are applying?
☐ Yes ☑ No   If yes, please explain fully:

REFERENCES
(List at least three—do not include employers or relatives)

Name and address	Occupation	Telephone No.
1. Mrs. Julie Evans, 1800 Eagle's Landing, New York, NY	Guidance Counselor	(212) 555-5410
2. Mr. Bob Hernandez, 121 E 6509, New York, NY	Clergy	(212) 555-0809
3. Mrs. Rose Morris, 105 Continental Lane, New York, NY	FBLA Advisor	(212) 555-0347

Name of person to be notified in case of emergency: Robert Bennett
Relationship: Father   Telephone: (212) 555-0908
Address (Street, City, State, ZIP): 102 West Central Park, New York, NY 01009

Please include any other information you think would be helpful to us in considering you for employment, such as additional experience, articles/books published, activities, accomplishments, etc. (You may exclude all information indicative of age, sex, race, religion, color, national origin, or disability.) Distributed meals to poor families in the West Central Park area of Manhattan, participated regularly on the varsity basketball team, created a basketball program on the computer and distributed it to the Physical Education department on a monthly basis.

SKILLS
Typing speed (words per minute): 60 wpm   Steno speed (words per minute): 90 wpm
Ten-key speed: 100 pm   By touch? ☑ Yes ☐ No   Are you familiar with word processing? ☑ Yes ☐ No
Business machines you can operate: Adding machine, fax machine
Check computer operating systems in which you are literate:
☑ Macintosh   ☐ Mainframe   ☑ IBM or compatible   ☐ Unix   ☐ OS2

Please explain any additional skills you feel are important to your consideration for employment with Razor's Edge. Use this space to list special abilities, hobbies, talents, interests, professional training, and other items regarding your job skills.

I answered up to 10 phone lines at one time for Parcels Plus. I attended business workshops during my membership in Future Business Leaders of America (FBLA). I processed invoices on the computer and filed invoices correctly.

Filling in a job application form is tricky because you often will mistakenly write information in a line above or below the line where it should go. If this happens, you have two choices. You can ask for a clean form and begin again. Or, if you can do so neatly, draw an arrow to show where the information goes. Do not cross out or blacken a line; such marks will make your application appear messy.

Job Application, Completed

Notice that your employment history should have no gaps. So be sure to note time spent, for example, looking for a job or attending school when these cause a gap in your employment.

List your immediate supervisor's name unless you want to list someone else in the company. For instance, you might list the owner instead of your immediate supervisor. If so, provide the person's title or position.

Notice that you are responsible for the accuracy and completeness of all information in the application. You could lose your job if you have not been honest.

EXPERIENCE

Please provide information covering your complete employment experience (with the most recent job or occupation listed first). Include time spent in military service, if any. If necessary, please attach an additional sheet to account for any gaps in your employment history or to explain any special awards, accomplishments, or job-related achievements. Please fill in this section as completely as possible, including mailing addresses, telephone numbers, and appropriate names. By listing supervisors' names, you are granting Razor's Edge permission to contact them regarding your employment history.

Please complete this section even if you are submitting a résumé.

Name of Company	From	To	Starting Salary	Last Salary	Reason for Leaving
West Central Food Bank	1996	1997	Volunteer	Volunteer	The program ended
Address	**Job Responsibilities** Distributed meals to poor families in the West				
894 Harrison, New York, NY	Central Park area of Manhattan, ensured each meal got to the				
Supervisor's Name	right family by a pre-determined time, and worked well with				
Tonya Cuado	Telephone (212) 555-4882				other volunteers.
Name of Company	From	To	Starting Salary	Last Salary	Reason for Leaving
Parcels Plus	1995	1997	$4.25/hour	$4.85/hour	To pursue receptionist jobs
Address	**Job Responsibilities** Processed invoices on the computer, took customer				
714 Albany Dr, New York, NY	orders via phone, helped bookkeeper with account receivable				
Supervisor's Name	administration and answered 10 phone lines.				
June Smith	Telephone (212) 555-1015				
Name of Company	From	To	Starting Salary	Last Salary	Reason for Leaving
Address	Job Responsibilities				
Supervisor's Name					
	Telephone ( )				

May Razor's Edge contact each of these companies? ☒ Yes ☐ No

Exceptions and reasons:

Have you ever gone by another name? ☐ Yes ☒ No

If yes, give the name(s):

ACKNOWLEDGMENT

I acknowledge that as an applicant for employment with Razor's Edge (1) no offer of employment is being made to me at this time; and (2) any material misrepresentation, falsification or deliberate omission of a fact in my application may be justification for refusal or, if employed, termination of employment. If an offer of employment is extended and I accept this offer, I acknowledge that (1) I will abide by the policies and procedures set forth in the Razor's Edge Employee Handbook; and (2) my employment will be "at will," which means it may be terminated at any time by me or Razor's Edge without any liability except to pay salary and benefits accrued up to the time of my departure.

Signature: *Mary Bennett*   Date: *May 15, 1997*

RAZOR'S EDGE FITNESS IS AN EQUAL OPPORTUNITY EMPLOYER.

Before turning in your job application, reread your answers carefully one final time. Be sure you have filled everything out as completely as possible. If appropriate, insert a clarifying note or comment. Even take time to tidy up any of your printing that does not look clear.

Job Application, Blank Form

Confidential Application for Employment

Applicant: Thank you for your interest in Razor's Edge Fitness. Your application will be considered regardless of race, color, religion, sex, national origin, age, marital or veteran status, medical condition or disability, or any other legally protected status. To enable us to evaluate this application, please answer all questions carefully and as completely as possible. **Please print.** Before submitting this application, read and sign the acknowledgement at the end of the application.

Application for:	❏ Full-time	❏ Part-time	❏ On-call	❏ Temporary

Hours available to work:

PERSONAL INFORMATION

Date: Soc. Sec. No.:

Name (Last, First, Middle):

Present Address (Street, City, State, ZIP):

Mailing Address (Street, City, State, ZIP):

Telephone: A.M. (   )   P.M. (   )

Referred by:

Position(s) applying for: 1.   2.

Date you can start: Salary desired:

Are you currently employed? ❏ Yes ❏ No   If yes, may we contact your present employer? ❏ Yes ❏ No

Have you applied previously for employment at Razor's Edge? ❏ Yes ❏ No   If yes, when?

Have you been previously employed by Razor's Edge or its affiliates? ❏ Yes ❏ No   If yes, when?

Do any of your relatives work at Razor's Edge? ❏ Yes ❏ No   If yes, list name, relationship, and department:

Please list your reasons for wanting a position with this company:

CITIZENSHIP

Are you prevented lawfully from becoming employed in the United States because of Visa or immigration status?

❏ Yes ❏ No   (Proof of citizenship or immigration status will be required upon employment.)

If you are a resident alien, please give your alien number found on your resident alien card (Form I-551):

Are you at least 18 years of age? ❏ Yes ❏ No

If you have ever been convicted of an offense (excluding minor traffic violations), please complete the following:

Charge: Place of Arrest: Date:

Result or outcome:

EDUCATION

	Name of Institution	City/State	Years Completed	Degree	G.P.A.
High School					
College					
Graduate					
Trade					

Job Application, Blank Form

Are you under the care of a physician or currently receiving medical treatment for any injury, physical defect, chronic ailment, or any other condition which could affect your ability to perform the essential functions of the job for which you are applying?
❏ Yes ❏ No If yes, please explain fully:

REFERENCES

(List at least three—do not include employers or relatives)

Name and address	Occupation	Telephone No.
1.		( )
2.		( )
3.		( )

Name of person to be notified in case of emergency:

Relationship: Telephone: ( )

Address (Street, City, State, ZIP):

Please include any other information you think would be helpful to us in considering you for employment, such as additional experience, articles/books published, activities, accomplishments, etc. (You may exclude all information indicative of age, sex, race, religion, color, national origin, or disability.)

SKILLS

Typing speed (words per minute):   Steno speed (words per minute):

Ten-key speed: By touch? ❏ Yes ❏ No Are you familiar with word processing? ❏ Yes ❏ No

Business machines you can operate:

Check computer operating systems in which you are literate:

❏ Macintosh   ❏ Mainframe   ❏ IBM or compatible   ❏ Unix   ❏ OS2

Please explain any additional skills you feel are important to your consideration for employment with Razor's Edge. Use this space to list special abilities, hobbies, talents, interests, professional training, and other items regarding your job skills.

Job Application, Blank Form

EXPERIENCE

Please provide information covering your complete employment experience (with the most recent job or occupation listed first). Include time spent in military service, if any. If necessary, please attach an additional sheet to account for any gaps in your employment history or to explain any special awards, accomplishments, or job-related achievements. Please fill in this section as completely as possible, including mailing addresses, telephone numbers, and appropriate names. By listing supervisors' names, you are granting Razor's Edge permission to contact them regarding your employment history.

Please complete this section even if you are submitting a résumé.

Name of Company	From	To	Starting Salary	Last Salary	Reason for Leaving
Address	Job Responsibilities				
Supervisor's Name					
	Telephone ( )				
Name of Company	From	To	Starting Salary	Last Salary	Reason for Leaving
Address	Job Responsibilities				
Supervisor's Name					
	Telephone ( )				
Name of Company	From	To	Starting Salary	Last Salary	Reason for Leaving
Address	Job Responsibilities				
Supervisor's Name					
	Telephone ( )				

May Razor's Edge contact each of these companies? ❑ Yes ❑ No

Exceptions and reasons:

Have you ever gone by another name? ❑ Yes ❑ No

If yes, give the name(s):

ACKNOWLEDGMENT

I acknowledge that as an applicant for employment with Razor's Edge (1) no offer of employment is being made to me at this time; and (2) any material misrepresentation, falsification or deliberate omission of a fact in my application may be justification for refusal or, if employed, termination of employment. If an offer of employment is extended and I accept this offer, I acknowledge that (1) I will abide by the policies and procedures set forth in the Razor's Edge Employee Handbook; and (2) my employment will be "at will," which means it may be terminated at any time by me or Razor's Edge without any liability except to pay salary and benefits accrued up to the time of my departure.

Signature: Date:

RAZOR'S EDGE FITNESS IS AN EQUAL OPPORTUNITY EMPLOYER.

Job Description

> These initial facts will vary from company to company, but job-level codes and the pay range are usually desirable pieces of information.

> The opening section (and its heading) highlights those personnel traits usually valued in any employee.

> The traits are listed beginning with a verb. This eliminates much needed repetition— for instance, "The employee will . . ." See PARALLELISM.

> The numbering system (and the lists) allows for easy reference to a particular duty or responsibility. See LISTS.

> The revision date allows users to keep track of updates.

Job Description

Job Title	
Hospitality Sales Assistant	
Job Level	Pay Range
15B	10
Department	Group or Area
Sales	Ithaca Hotel

GENERAL REQUIREMENTS

A. Contributes to client sales and service

1. Communicates courteously with customers at all times
2. Attends all customer events and contributes to enjoyable atmosphere
3. Reads all general sales inquiries; writes appropriate letters in response
4. Listens to any customer questions received via the main sales line; responds accurately
5. Selects and delivers welcome gifts to all star customers' rooms
6. Completes special sales projects as necessary
7. Provides any additional services required by Ithaca Hotel's sales staff

B. Provides general support to Account Managers as necessary

1. Uses DataMaster database to update and maintain Account Managers' records
2. Helps Account Managers write sales letters
3. Answers Account Managers' phones when they are unavailable; accurately records any messages from customers

Last Revised _September 3, 1995_   Page __1__ of __2__

Job descriptions are difficult to write because they should be as specific as possible, and writers (often the employees themselves) don't want to be too specific about the duties. Many companies, however, require a written job description be on file for every position in the company. This helps to ensure fairness and equity.

Job Description

Annotation	Form Content
The specific duties and responsibilities are organized almost chronologically—from the beginning of client contact to payment after service. Other organizations would be possible. See ORGANIZATION.	**Job Title:** Hospitality Sales Assistant

Job Title
Hospitality Sales Assistant

SPECIFIC DUTIES AND RESPONSIBILITIES

C. Enters and updates customer reservations

1. Gathers client information via phone conversations or letters
2. Accurately enters client data into Rhombus Computer Reservation system
3. Uses computer system to update customer profiles and billing information once a day
4. Prints billing information before customer check-out
5. Maintains customer reservation system; trouble-shoots any reservation system problems

D. Works at front desk when necessary

1. Uses Rhombus Computer Reservation system to check in clients
2. Asks clients if their reservations are correct; corrects any problems
3. Provides keys and hotel introductory materials; shows client on map the location of hotel room
4. Courteously answers any additional customer questions
5. Refers clients to any additional hotel services required, including bell hop, restaurant, room service, or housekeeping
6. Prints bills using Rhombus Computer Reservation system; ensures the accuracy of the bill
7. Uses CreditWhiz machine to record credit card information
8. Takes payment for room (including check, credit card, or cash)

Last Revised: September 3, 1995   Page 2 of 2

Annotations:

- The specific duties and responsibilities are organized almost chronologically—from the beginning of client contact to payment after service. Other organizations would be possible. See ORGANIZATION.
- The letters and numbers of the main subheadings (A, B, C, etc.) are sequential throughout the job description (despite different major headings). This sequential numbering also permits good cross-referencing.
- The parentheses set off an extra piece of information. See PARENTHESES.

The description covers two areas: (1) general requirements and (2) specific duties and responsibilities. General requirements by themselves may be too general—hence, the need for some specific job-related duties and responsibilities.

Résumé, Experienced Functional

▶ *See RÉSUMÉS, pp. 145-160*

Write a job objective that mentions your skills and the job in which you are interested. See RÉSUMÉS. Use a period after the objective.

Use action verbs to describe your skills or tasks. These action verb phrases do not need a final period. See RÉSUMÉS. Use bulleted lists or other format options. See EMPHASIS and LISTS.

List jobs, beginning with your current or most recent one. You need not include supervisors' names; these names should appear on a separate list of references. See RÉSUMÉS.

Periods should not follow the job title, company, and location when these are in a displayed list. See LISTS and PERIODS.

Jason T. Holt
45 Grove East
Cleveland, Ohio 34526
412-555-6784 (W)   412-555-0987 (H)

Job Objective
To use my business, communication, and office skills as a supervisor or manager of office personnel.

Skills and Accomplishments

Supervisory Skills
- Supervised five employees
- Tallied each day's receipts

Communication Skills
- Handled customer service inquiries and complaints
- Tracked down hardware that did not reach customers
- Negotiated with the airline and freight companies to guarantee speedy delivery of replacement hardware

Advanced Office Skills
- Processed invoices and checked company inventory lists for accuracy
- Maintained personnel files on nearly 200 employees
- Word processed letters and reports using WordWhiz and Microdot Write
- Worked as a typist and an office assistant; typing speed 65 wpm
- Used most office machines, including photocopiers, postage meters, and word processors

Work Experience
Customer Service Representative (1994 to 1996)
BMI Regional Service Center, Kansas City, Missouri

Senior Clerk (1991 to 1993)
Acme Trucking Company, Tulsa, Oklahoma

Typist (1987 to 1991)
Midwestern Mortgage Insurance, Kansas City, Missouri

Office Assistant (1985 to 1987)
Suarez & Suarez Investment Company, Joplin, Missouri

Supervisor (1984 to 1985)
Burger Shak Restaurant, Joplin, Missouri

Education
Kansas State College, AA in Business Management (1987), Galena, Kansas
Joplin Senior High School, High School Diploma (1984), Joplin, Missouri

---

Choose a functional format when you want to emphasize your skills and accomplishments (even if you have job experience). In this example, the skills come immediately after the job objective rather than at the end of the list of jobs. Contrast this résumé with the chronological résumé on the next page.

Choose a page layout that is open and attractive; if possible, limit your résumé to one page. See RÉSUMÉS, PAGE LAYOUT, and EMPHASIS.

Résumé, Experienced Chronological

▶ *See RÉSUMÉS, pp. 145-160*

Write an employment objective that mentions your skills and the job in which you are interested. See RÉSUMÉS: Use a period after the objective.

List jobs, beginning with your current or most recent one. You need not include supervisors' names; these names should appear on a separate list of references. See RÉSUMÉS.

Use action verbs to describe your skills or tasks. These action verb phrases do not need a final period. See RÉSUMÉS. Use bulleted lists or other format options. See EMPHASIS and LISTS.

Periods should not follow the job title, company, and location when these are in a displayed list. See LISTS and PERIODS.

For consistency with *Work History*, omit the periods following the items under *Education*. See LISTS.

Jason T. Holt
45 Grove East
Cleveland, Ohio 34526
412-555-6784 (W)   412-555-0987 (H)

EMPLOYMENT OBJECTIVE

To use my business, communication, and office skills in a position that offers challenging opportunities for further training and advancement to the level of supervisor.

WORK HISTORY AND EXPERIENCE

Customer Service Representative (1994 to 1996)
BMI Regional Service Center
Kansas City, Missouri
- Tracked down hardware that did not reach customers
- Worked with airline and freight companies to guarantee speedy delivery of replacement hardware

Senior Clerk (1991 to 1993)
Acme Trucking Company
Tulsa, Oklahoma
- Handled customer service inquiries and complaints
- Supervised various operational tasks assigned to other clerks in the office

Typist (1987 to 1991)
Midwestern Mortgage Insurance
Kansas City, Missouri
- Completed all letters, memos, and forms on the computer
- Improved typing speed; typing speed 65 words per minute

Office Assistant (1985 to 1987)
Suarez & Suarez Investment Company
Joplin, Missouri
- Worked on a variety of word processors (WordWhiz, Microdot Write; familiar with many financial programs)
- Worked with accounts receivable and payable to take care of customer invoices
- Deposited payroll and large checks at the local bank

Supervisor (1984 to 1985)
Burger Shak Restaurant
Joplin, Missouri
- Supervised five employees
- Tallied receipts once per day

EDUCATION

AA in business management (1987), Kansas State College, Galena, Kansas
High school diploma (1984), Joplin Senior High School, Joplin, Missouri

---

Choose a chronological format only if you have a sequence of jobs. In this example, the jobs are listed in reverse order and clearly support and lead up to the employment objective. Choose a page layout that is open and attractive; if possible, limit your résumé to one page. See RÉSUMÉS, PAGE LAYOUT, and EMPHASIS.

Do not include personal information about your age, religion, ethnic origins, sex, or physical disabilities. By law, employers cannot ask about these topics.

Cover Letter, Experienced Applicant

▶ See LETTERS, pp. 75-91

Include your full address and a date in the heading; your phone number is optional because it is included in the body of the letter. See LETTERS.

Use a salutation, followed by a colon, when you know the name of the person who will receive the letter. Do not use *Mr., Mrs.,* or *Ms.* unless you are sure about the reader's preference. See LETTERS.

The body follows the 4-Box organization. The subject line and the first paragraph summarize the purpose. Paragraph 2 outlines the three main points. The rest of the letter expands on the three points. See ORGANIZATION.

Use lists and format options to highlight key points. See EMPHASIS and LISTS.

---

45 Grove East
Cleveland, OH 34526
412-555-6784
December 5, 1996

D.L. Kessenbaum
Operations Manager
Klangen and Company
10 Cornerstone Lane
Dallas, TX 43009-3204

Dear D.L. Kessenbaum:

Submission of Résumé for Consideration for Office Manager Position

I am pleased to send you my résumé in response to the Office Manager position I saw advertised in last week's *Herald Times*. I am confident my experience qualifies me for the position.

In your ad, you stated that you are looking for someone with past experience as a customer representative, strong clerical skills, word processing experience, and supervisory experience.

As you can tell from my enclosed résumé, I meet all the requirements for the job.

Customer Service Experience: I have served as a customer service representative for international accounts with BMI Corporation.

Clerical and Word Processing Experience: I have perfected a wide variety of clerical and word processing skills with BMI Corporation, Acme Trucking, Midwestern Mortgage, and Suarez and Suarez.

Supervisory Experience: I served as night supervisor for Burger Shak.

Now, I would like to combine my skills to serve as an office manager for Klangen and Company. As the enclosed résumé demonstrates, I have the qualifications and experience to meet your needs. I hope I can meet with you to talk more about my qualifications and the position. Please call me at 412-555-6784 to schedule a time when we can meet.

Sincerely,

Jason T. Holt

Jason T. Holt

Enclosure

Always include a cover letter whenever you send someone a résumé. You need not prepare a cover letter if you are submitting your résumé in person. See RÉSUMÉS and LETTERS.

Write your cover letter to respond to the job description or to an advertisement in the newspaper. As in the above example, refer to your source of information and respond to any criteria mentioned. You will repeat some information in your résumé but use the cover letter to add special notes or highlights to the résumé information.

Résumé, Inexperienced Functional

▶ See RÉSUMÉS, pp. 145-160

Write an employment objective that mentions your skills and the job in which you are interested. See RÉSUMÉS. Use a period after the objective.

Use action verbs to describe your skills or tasks. These action verb phrases do not need a final period. See RÉSUMÉS. Use bulleted lists or other format options. See EMPHASIS and LISTS.

Periods should not follow the job title, company, and location when these are in a displayed list. See LISTS and PERIODS.

Mentioning the availability of references is optional. You might take a separate list of references with you when you go in for an interview. See RÉSUMÉS.

Mary Bennett
102 West Central Park
New York, NY 01009
212-555-6578 (W) 212-555-0908 (H)

Employment Objective

To use my communication and teaming skills in a law office receptionist position that offers challenging opportunities and that demands work versatility, dependability, and ingenuity.

Skills and Abilities

Dependable
- Distributed meals to poor families in the West Central Park area of Manhattan
- Ensured each meal got to the right family by a pre-determined time
- Regularly participated on the varsity basketball team

Detail-oriented
- Processed invoices on the computer; filed invoices correctly
- Took customer orders via phone
- Helped the bookkeeper with accounts receivable/payable administration

Good communicator
- Answered up to 10 phone lines at one time for Parcels Plus
- Explained policies to customers and input their orders at the same time

Team player
- Played on varsity high school basketball team for 4 years
- Created basketball program on the computer and distributed it to the Physical Education department on a monthly basis
- Worked well with other food bank volunteers

Work History

Food Bank Volunteer (1996 to 1997)
West Central Food Bank
New York, NY

Clerical Assistant (1995 to 1997)
Parcels Plus
New York, NY

Education

High School Diploma (1993 to 1997), West Central High School, New York City, NY
Varsity Basketball team, 1995 to 1997
Junior Varsity team, 1993 to 1995

References

Available upon request

Use a functional format if you do not have job experience or only limited experience. As in this example, the functional format allows you to expand on your skills and abilities even if they do not come directly from jobs. See RÉSUMÉS.

Do not include personal information about your age, religion, ethnic origins, sex, or physical disabilities. By law, employers cannot ask about these topics. See RÉSUMÉS and BIAS-FREE LANGUAGE.

Cover Letter, Inexperienced Applicant

▶ *See* LETTERS, *pp. 75-91*

Include your full address and a date in the heading. See LETTERS.

102 West Central Park
New York, NY 01009
December 5, 1997

Ms. Etta D. Baldridge
Office Manager
Williams and Wang, Attorneys at Law
446 Sloane Street
New York, NY 10045-2495

Use a salutation, followed by a colon, when you know the name of the person who will receive the letter. See LETTERS.

Dear Ms. Baldridge:

Response to Advertisement for Receptionist

The body follows the 4-Box organization. The subject line and the first paragraph summarize the purpose. Paragraph 2 outlines the three main points. The rest of the letter expands on the three points. See ORGANIZATION.

I am pleased to send you my résumé in response to the receptionist position advertised in last Sunday's *Daily Herald*.

Your advertisement specified you were looking for someone who is dependable, is comfortable performing a variety of tasks, has excellent communication skills, and is a team player. In addition, the candidate needs good word processing skills. My skills, acquired both through job experience and activities, meet or exceed all your requirements.

While working as a clerk at Parcels Plus, volunteering for the West Central Food Bank, and playing varsity basketball, I demonstrated the following skills:

Use lists and format options to highlight key points. See EMPHASIS **and** LISTS.

- **Dependable:** Met all requirements in a timely, consistent manner.
- **Flexible:** Performed additional duties for Parcels Plus and the basketball team as needed.
- **Excellent Communicator:** Answered phones and worked with customers at Parcels Plus.
- **Team Player:** Worked well with food bank volunteers and basketball team members.
- **Efficient Word Processor:** Word processed the basketball team roster and class assignments.

As this letter and my résumé indicate, I am a dedicated worker who will be an asset to your law firm.

I am available for an interview at any time. Please call me at 212-555-0908 or 212-555-6578.

Sincerely,

Mary Bennett
Mary Bennett

Enclosure

Always include a cover letter whenever you send someone a résumé. You need not prepare a cover letter if you are submitting your résumé in person. See RÉSUMÉS and LETTERS.

Write your cover letter to respond to the job description or to an advertisement in the newspaper. As in the above example, refer to your source of information and respond to any criteria mentioned. You will repeat some information in your résumé, but use the cover letter to add special notes or explain unusual information.

Thank You Letter

▶ See LETTERS, pp. 75-91

---

102 West Central Park
New York, NY 01009
December 12, 1997

Ms. Etta D. Baldridge
Office Manager
Williams and Wang, Attorneys at Law
446 Sloane Street
New York, NY 10045-2495

Dear Ms. Baldridge:

Thank you for meeting with me to discuss your receptionist position.

I enjoyed meeting with you the other day to talk about the receptionist position Williams and Wang has available. I was also interested to hear about your experience as a race flagger.

After learning more about the position, I am convinced I could meet Williams and Wang's requirements for a receptionist. Not only do I have the experience answering phones that will make me comfortable serving as a receptionist, but I also have written communication skills that will be an asset to Williams and Wang. As we discussed, I am willing to perform any additional tasks as necessary. In addition, I think that I can play an integral part on the Williams and Wang team.

If you need any more information from me, please call me at 212-555-0908 (Home) or 212-555-6578 (Work). I look forward to speaking with you again soon.

Sincerely,

Mary Bennett
Mary Bennett

Make sure the inside address is accurate, including spelling of names and any preferred titles. If necessary, call and verify the information.

Use a subject line to highlight your main point. As in this example, you can use the optional capitalization pattern, where only the initial word is capitalized.

This letter is so short that it does not follow the 4-Box organization we recommend for most business letters. In this letter, Paragraph 1 is the introduction. Paragraph 2 summarizes the interview. Paragraph 3 closes with the offer of more information. See ORGANIZATION.

Sending a thank you letter whenever you have had a job interview is courteous, and it reminds the interviewer that you are interested in the job. Use the thank you letter to send along your references if you did not have them with you at the interview.

Make your comments personal, if possible. For instance, mentioning the race flagger experience will help the interviewer recall who you were, especially if a large number of people have been interviewed. See LETTERS, RÉSUMÉS, and INTERVIEWS.

Letter, Commendation

▶ See LETTERS, pp. 75-91

348 Landis Drive
Decatur, Illinois 38337
217-555-6881

October 28, 1997

Service Department
ICS
2554 Valley Road
Los Angeles, CA 92055-7553

Attention: Maria Valdez, Service Manager

EAST LAKE HOSPITAL SATISFACTION WITH ICS SERVICE

Thank you for your prompt computer service to our Records Department last week. We are pleased with your support for the following reasons:
  1. Prompt service
  2. Concerned service reps
  3. No-hassle warranty

1. Prompt service
About 4:30 P.M. last Tuesday, our ICS System 520 server went down. I frantically called your service line and talked to Craig. Thirty minutes later, David Lee was at our Records Department. By 5:30 P.M., our system was up again. We simply can't afford to deal with technical problems. The quick attention ICS provided saved us a lot of problems and worries.

2. Concerned service reps
When I called the hot line, Craig seemed to understand my frustration and was very helpful. I have called other companies' service lines, only to be put on hold and transferred several times. When David arrived at the Records Department, he was anxious to solve the problem. He found we needed to replace the System 520 server.

3. No-hassle warranty
We bought the System 520 with the 18-month warranty even though we needed to feel confident the server would work. When I called Tuesday, I was in no condition to squabble over a warranty policy. Neither Craig nor David fussed over details and technicalities of the warranty. The server was replaced simply and quickly and we were in business again.

Your quick action, concerned reps, and hassle-free warranty have made us at ELH very happy with your service. Thank you for being so reliable.

Sincerely,

Debra McBride
Debra McBride
Director, Records Department

DM:sf

As in this example, the attention line replaces the salutation. See LETTERS.

The body follows the 4-Box organization. The subject line and Paragraph 1 summarize the purpose and outline the three main points. The rest of the letter expands on the three points. See ORGANIZATION.

Make the content personal and specific so the letter doesn't sound like a routine form letter. See LETTERS.

Use a commendation letter when you receive good service or when a product exceeds your expectations. Such a letter is a valuable reminder to companies that their customers should come first.

As with any letter, include personal comments or examples. Your readers will appreciate such information and will more likely remember what you have to say than if you write a brief form letter. See LETTERS.

Letter, Complaint

▶ See LETTERS, pp. 75-91

 ATLAS STEEL CORP.

April 28, 1997

Clay Kearns
Vice President, Marketing
ICS
2554 Valley Road
Los Angeles, CA 92055

Dear Clay Kearns:

Subject: Request for Warranty Coverage of the Second System 645 Hard Drive

The Purchasing Department's System 645 server has had several problems with its hard drive. Please investigate this problem, and if possible, extend the warranty.

The System 645 has had the following problems:
1. Performance
2. Warranty

1. The hard drive on our System 645 has gone out twice.

Three weeks after purchasing the system, the hard drive went out. A certified ICS technician installed a new drive at no cost, since it was still under warranty. However, that drive failed about 2 months later. When we contracted with ICS, we were promised a fast, reliable system. This is necessary because we cannot afford downtime. Our department needs a system we can depend on.

2. The warranty should cover the second hard drive failure.

Atlas Steel must have the system operating during business hours. When the hard drive went out a second time, I tried to keep the department going by checking the drive myself. When I called the service line, Kerry told me that because I had opened the machine, the warranty was void and there was nothing she could do. We have paid to have the second drive repaired by an ICS technician at the cost of $992.73.

We are disappointed in the low performance of the System 645 hard drives and feel the warranty should cover the second hard drive failure. Please send a reimbursement of $992.73 to cover our cost for the second hard drive replacement.

We look foreword to a successful relationship with ICS. I hope we can solve this problem to ensure Atlas Steel will meet future hardware and software needs through ICS. Please contact me as soon as possible at 301-555-4388 to discuss how you can help.

Respectfully,

David Chen

David Chen
Purchasing Manager

DC:kj
Enclosures

870 Rosecrans Street   Eire, Pennsylvania 10327   301-555-4388 • FAX 301-555-4390

Annotations:

- The optional salutation (a more formal version) would be *Dr.* or *Mr. Kearns*. See LETTERS.

- The 4-Box organization means that the subject line and Paragraph 1 present the main request. The remaining paragraphs continue the 4-Box format.

- Use informative headings to emphasize main points. See HEADINGS.

- Close the letter with a firm, but courteous repetition of the request. See ORGANIZATION and EMPHASIS.

Complaint letters usually start with a concise statement of the problem followed by a request for action or resolution. The problem statement should be as brief as possible but long enough to make the request understandable. See ORGANIZATION.

Even if written in anger, complaint letters should not sound angry. The tone should be positive and constructive. The writer should present clear evidence of dissatisfaction but should strive to balance the complaint with positive solutions. See TONE.

Letter, Persuasive Sales

▶ See PERSUASION, pp. 132-135

 MARTIN FITNESS EQUIPMENT
Serious Supplies For Serious Athletes
1234 Market Place, Centertown, OK 74101 • 405-555-1234 • FAX 405-555-4321

February 10, 1997

Ann Devi
Head Buyer
TuffMax Sporting Goods
4550 Highway 40 NW
Southfield, OH 44301

Subject: Invitation to Discuss Improved Martin Skating Products

Ann, in our discussion last week, we determined four challenges Martin Fitness Equipment can help you meet. Please consider a visit from one of our new local representatives to explore these challenges.

TuffMax will sell only the most durable and dependable ice skate on the market. Competitive skaters need every edge they can get. Martin skates use a patented blade that has greater flexibility and a more lasting edge than any other skate available. Every aspect of the skates from the leather to the lacings is designed to ensure a star performance on the ice.

TuffMax must consider the quality and cost of all equipment it offers for sale. Martin recognizes the keen financial challenges facing your company. We have supplied skates for professionals since 1931, and our reputation for service and dependability is unequaled. The last five national champions have all used and endorsed Martin skates, and we guarantee that our skates will last longer and provide better value than any of our competitors' products.

TuffMax has a limited advertising budget. Martin Fitness Equipment will be a major sponsor of all national and international skating competitions in the coming year. Our advertisements will be seen throughout these televised events, and this exposure should guarantee an increased demand for our skates.

Annotations:

- The subject line serves to replace the salutation and clearly captures the purpose of the letter. See LETTERS.

- The content follows the 4-Box organization. The specific subject line and Paragraph 1 establish the purpose of the letter. Paragraphs 2, 3, 4, and 5 each discuss solutions to TuffMax's need and objectives.

- Use headings to convey major ideas. Use consistent headings with all headings of the same level. See HEADINGS and EMPHASIS.

A persuasive sales letter uses techniques to gain agreement or to win support for an idea. The most obvious persuasive technique is an appeal based on solid, logical reasons. But most effective persuasive writing also enlists the reader's emotional support. See PERSUASION.

The writer's goal is to know enough about the reader's needs he or she can present effective solutions and benefits. See ORGANIZATION, LETTERS, and TONE.

Letter, Persuasive Sales

Organize your information with your reader's needs in mind. Consider both the logic of your points and the arrangement of these points for maximum effectiveness.

Paragraph 6 closes the letter with a review of the purpose and an offer of assistance. See PERSUASION, LETTERS, and ORGANIZATION.

Restate your most important point. The lengthier a document becomes, the more crucial this summary is.

Ann Devi					-2-					February 10, 1997

TuffMax needs a reliable supplier who can deliver products on short notice. We understand you cannot afford a large inventory of skates and need to have quick delivery on orders to maintain your stock. Our new direct dealer network is set up for customers just like you. We have permanent supply outlets in three states near you, and we can ship any order within 24 hours.

As we discussed, Martin has recently opened a direct dealer office in your area. Our local representative will call on you to discuss further ways of meeting the challenges your business faces and improving your equipment-management capabilities. Please call me at 800-555-1111 with any questions.

Best regards,

Tom Pedersen
Tom Pedersen

TP:gf

This letter illustrates the simplified block format. See LETTERS.

Letter, Proposal

▶ *See LETTERS, pp. 75-91*

Omit *Ms.* or *Mrs.* unless you know Linda Alvarez's preference. And in the salutation, if you don't want to use only the first name, either use *Dear Linda Alvarez* or omit the salutation. See LETTERS.

The content follows the 4-Box organization. The specific subject line and Paragraph 1 establish the purpose of the letter and introduce the three topics for discussion.

Use displayed lists to emphasize major points. No periods are necessary when listed items are not sentences. See LISTS.

Paragraphs 2, 3, and 4 each expand on one of these topics. Paragraph 5 closes the letter with an offer of more information.

 **Andromeda**

7483 Esteles Court
Crescent Valley, CA 94057

714-555-9248

November 2, 1997

Linda Alvarez
Technical Support
TSX Inc.
234 Palo Verde Way
Dallas, TX 70647-3429

Dear Linda Alvarez:

Proposal to Andromeda for the Omega System

Gain greater speed, efficiency, and reliability with your computer system. The Omega System from Andromeda will give TSX Inc. the technical advantage needed to lead the engineering industry. During our phone conversation October 27, we determined the Omega System benefits your company in the following areas:

- Speed
- 3D modeling capability
- Reliability

Speed up your computer-aided design with the Omega System.

Reduce processing delays and ensure your graphics move smoothly. The 90 MHz processor gives you the speed required for computer-aided design. The system's access time is 16 milliseconds.

Support your 3D modeling software efficiently using the Omega System.

Develop complex graphics with clear detail when you use the power of a four gigabyte hard drive — installed by Andromeda professionals. Software for three-dimensional rendering works especially well on the system. Apollo and other applications, such as Intact and Move, are often used on the Omega System.

Rely on the Omega System backed by Andromeda experts.

Ensure your satisfaction with the Omega System because it includes a 9-month warranty. Receive all the benefits Andromeda offers when you purchase a system from us. Andromeda has invested 7 years of dedication in this superior product—approximately 35 percent of engineering CAD applications use an Andromeda system to ensure success.

For more information, please call me at 873-555-4387. I am anxious to help.

Sincerely,

John Rowski

John Rowski
Vice President, Marketing

JR:kn
Enc.

Proposal letters are essentially sales letters. They present details about a product or work to be done. Some proposal letters also give the cost for the service or product.

Highlight the benefits the customer receives from the product or service. In the above letter, faster design capabilities is the first benefit mentioned. The technical information about the 90 MHz processor is the product feature that provides the benefit. Benefits, not features, convince a customer to buy. See PERSUASION.

Letter, Proposal Acceptance

▶ *See LETTERS, pp. 75-91*

Pacific Rim
TRAVEL

July 11, 1997

Sales Department
Discount Computer Co.
3769 Skyline Drive
Kalamazoo, MI 86448

Request: Install a Challenger System as soon as possible

We are happy to tell you we have decided to purchase the Challenger System. Please install the system as soon as possible.

Our travel company uses computers heavily for airline reservations and ticket printing. When we needed a more current system, we looked at several competing systems. We considered the Andromeda Omega, Cannyon's CTM 540, Elid's CTM 555, and several others.

The travel business is very competitive, so cost is an important factor for us to consider. For the type of computer needs we have, Discount Computer Co.'s Challenger is by far the best. Your low price on the Challenger System allows us to buy a new system sooner than we thought.

We would like the system installed as soon as you can, if possible during a weekend. Please call me to make arrangements.

Regards,

Javier Ortega

Javier Ortega
Manager

399 K Street • Los Angeles, CA 92533 • 714-555-0359 • Fax 714-555-0355

Omit the salutation if you don't have an employee's name to use in addressing the letter. See LETTERS. The subject line (request) serves to replace the salutation.

The content of the letter (in the subject line and in Paragraph 1) opens with a **Do** statement, which is a request for action. Paragraphs 2 and 3 provide brief reasons for the choice. Paragraph 4 repeats the request. This pattern is a little different from the 4-Box organization. See ORGANIZATION.

Although not illustrated in the above letter, some acceptance letters list certain assumptions or requirements. These might include delivery schedules or optional equipment. If these are extensive, they could be put in an attached list rather than in the letter itself.

Letter, Proposal Rejection

▶ *See LETTERS, pp. 75-91*

August 17, 1997

Andromeda
Marketing Department
7483 Esteles Court
Crescent Valley, CA 94057

Attention: Carrie Clausen

Response to Andromeda Proposal

After carefully reviewing the Andromeda proposal, we are sorry to tell you that we have not selected your system for use in our stores.

Thank you, however, for making your proposal to Quickstop Markets. Your October 12 presentation was very helpful and informative. As you stated when we met, the computer needs here at Quickstop Markets are complex and specialized.

It was a pleasure meeting you and learning about the products and services that Andromeda provides.

Sincerely,

Karl Beecher

Karl Beecher
Information Systems

KB:ms

232 Davis Drive   Chicago, Illinois 39940-3145   730-555-6755 • FAX 730-555-6755

- As in this example, the attention line replaces the salutation. See LETTERS.

- The introductory phrase sets up the bad news of the rejection. The rejection, however, still comes early in the letter. See LETTERS and ORGANIZATION.

A rejection letter is one of the hardest letters to write because it is hard to know how direct to be. In the above letter, the subject line does not give the rejection—the actual rejection is placed early in the body of the text. Writers should not delay the bad news until the end of a letter. Such a delay fools no one and often will annoy a reader who is interested in finding out what you have decided. See LETTERS and ORGANIZATION.

Letter, Sales

▶ See LETTERS, pp. 75-91

Use *Ms.* with *Anita Jefferson* only if her business card or printed stationery has this title. Otherwise, use her full name without a title; the salutation would be *Dear Anita Jefferson.* See LETTERS.

The content follows the 4-Box organization. The subject line and Paragraph 1 present the proposal (a sales presentation). Paragraph 1 also introduces the three sales benefits. Paragraphs 2, 3, and 4 expand on these benefits. See ORGANIZATION.

DISCOUNT COMPUTER CO.

February 1, 1997

Ms. Anita Jefferson
President
Burrows Courier Service
833 South Bend
Deer Lodge, MT 59722-6773

Dear Ms. Jefferson:

Proposed Computer Sales Presentation

I would like to propose a meeting with you and your staff to show you how our new Discount Computer systems can increase revenue for your business. Discount Computer Co. (DCC) can provide equipment and services with the following benefits:

- Reduced price
- Free trial period
- Available peripheral devices

Reduced Price
DCC offers top quality hardware at a much lower price than the same type of hardware offered by any other brand. This allows you to get more productivity for your money.

Free Trial Period
DCC is so sure of our systems, we offer a deal for first-time customers. You can use any main server free of charge for 2 weeks. We will install the system and help you get it going. Then you can see for yourself how much faster you can manage your records and track your packages.

Available Peripheral Devices
DCC carries terminals, barcode scanners, modems, printers, and dozens of other products. All equipment is discounted to fit your budget. The enclosed price list shows much of the equipment we carry.

You will be impressed by our low prices, the free trial, and all the equipment available from one company. Please call me at 867-555-7580 to talk about the opportunity for a short presentation on DCC computer systems.

Sincerely,

Jeffers Elliot, Jr.
Jeffers Elliot, Jr.
Sales Manager

JE:tf
Enclosure

3769 Skyline Drive • Kalamazoo, MI 86448-3001 • 867-555-7580 • FAX 867-555-7596

This letter is not a pure sales letter because its main purpose is to request a meeting with Anita Jefferson. A pure sales letter—such as the ones that often come in the mail—may ask a reader to buy a product based solely on the letter and on the attached information.

The tone of a sales letter is important. It should be positive without promising too much because excessive promises can make readers begin to doubt the writer's truthfulness. The best advice is to keep the tone personal, friendly, and factual. See LETTERS and TONE.

Letter, Survey Data

▶ *See* LETTERS, *pp. 75-91*

Omit *Ms.* or *Mrs.* unless you know Sonia Cline's preference. In the salutation, if you don't want to use only the first name, either use *Dear Sonia Cline* or omit the salutation. See LETTERS.

The content follows the 4-Box organization. The subject line and Paragraph 1 establish the purpose and introduce the two key problems (slow service and a limited warranty). Paragraphs 3 and 4 expand on the two points. Paragraph 5 summarizes the letter.

Use heading for subsections even when a letter is only a single page long. See HEADINGS.

738 Weston Drive
Albuquerque, NM 86501
862-555-8774

January 23, 1997

Sonia Cline
Manager
Express Printing, Inc.
2930 Monroe Street
Kansas City, MO 97312-3401

Dear Sonia:

Subject: Survey of DCC Challenger Users

Discount Computer Co.'s Challenger has some weaknesses you will want to be aware of before buying a system. As you asked during our phone call on October 20, I did an informal survey with our desktop publishers, graphic artists, and our technical support person. I found two things which seemed significant:

- Slow Service
- Limited Warranty

DCC was slow to service our system.

We needed service when the VGA card on our Challenger system went bad. The technical support person here said he called DCC and was on hold for about 30 minutes. In addition, a DCC service representative could not come out until a week later. We had to use another computer as the server for a week until the Challenger was fixed.

The warranty on the Challenger is only 1 year.

The 1-year warranty was too short to be useful to us. The VGA card on our system went bad during the 13th month, so it was not covered by the warranty. When the card was replaced, we had to pay for the part and the repair.

These two points, the slow service and limited warranty, were mentioned by several of our staff members as being significant problems for our company. I don't know how these factors would affect your company, but I thought I would pass their comments on to you.

Otherwise, the system seems to be sufficient for our use; about 50 people use the system daily. I hope this information helps you in your decision concerning which system to buy.

Best regards,

Jorge Gonzalez
Jorge Gonzalez

JG:pk

This letter records data collected by Jorge Gonzalez, in response to Sonia Cline's call. Such a letter is common in business, when a potential customer checks with references to see if a company's service and products are acceptable.

The general points about the service and the warranty are illustrated in the text with specific examples. These examples make the letter both more convincing and more memorable. See LETTERS.

Memo, Personnel Notice

▶ See MEMOS, pp. 97–103

The subject line matches the light tone of the memo.

The opening sentence states the point of the memo. The opening contraction creates an informal, conversational tone. See TONE and MEMOS.

The bulleted list is a good way to highlight the suggestions. Note that each listed item is parallel in structure. See LISTS and PARALLELISM.

The use of the run-in headings (in all capitals) visually highlights each suggestion. See HEADINGS.

MEMORANDUM

To: All Employees of the Sales Department
From: James Yee, Manager Sales Department
Date: May 30, 1997
Subject: **Keeping Your Work Area Hazard-Free**

Let's all try to do everything we can to make our offices as hazard-free and well maintained as possible.

Offices should be useful places to work, but they also should be safe and hazard-free for us and our visitors. So please take time to ensure your office is free of potentially dangerous situations, especially hazardous equipment. Also, we feel that a neat office is a safe office.

Suggestions:

- **EXTENSION CORDS.** Please use power strips instead of extension cords if you need to plug more than two things into a wall outlet. Not only is the extension cord "octopus" ugly, it is also a fire hazard. Our building supervisor has a supply of power strips if you need them.

- **LOOSE RUGS.** We wouldn't want anyone tripping on loose rug corners. Please make sure area rugs are firmly fastened to the floor. The secret to making rugs stay in place is an invention called double-sided tape. My secretary has a supply of this tape.

- **WIRES.** Please make sure wires such as computer cords, printer connectors, or electrical cords do not cross walking areas. Use duct tape to secure loose wires to the floor or to any firm object.

- **LADDERS.** If you need to reach an item on the top shelf of a bookcase, please do not climb the bookcase or other office furniture. Use a step ladder to get the out-of-reach item. We don't want anyone to fall because of a misplaced step or unstable furniture.

- **GENERAL HOUSEKEEPING.** Neatness and organization take a lot of effort, but they are worth it. We'll all be able to walk the halls without glancing into offices and wincing. Even more importantly, we'll be assured that every area is a safe and enjoyable place to work if all stations are carefully maintained and hazard-free.

Please give some thought to making your office as hazard-free as possible. We have a safe and beautiful facility, and with a little effort from us all, it will remain so.

JY

Personnel notices often require a light touch. Employees rightly object to personnel notices that are too serious, impersonal, or critical in tone (and content). Managers and supervisors sometimes have to send reminders and requests that are potentially negative (as this notice could be). The lighter tone helps writers convey negative information without offending readers.

Memo, Procedure

▶ *See* MEMOS, pp. 97–103

The first paragraph states the scope of the procedure and the circumstances when the procedure should be performed.

Each step in the procedure begins with an imperative (command) verb, giving the action to be taken.

The substeps break down the procedure into smaller pieces. See EMPHASIS **and** HEADINGS.

Parentheses enclose supplemental information. See PARENTHESES.

MEMORANDUM

To: Distribution
From: Susan Ramerez, Manager Records Department
Date: December 28, 1997
Subject: **Procedures for Storing Records at Trolley Street Warehouse**
Reference: Company Policy 230, Records Retention

We have reorganized our record-keeping system. In summary, here are the steps for the new procedure:

- Use the standard storage box and the new transmittal slip.
- Fill in completely the new transmittal slip.
- Send the box to Trolley Street Warehouse.

Please follow these steps when you store records at the Trolley Street Warehouse:

1. Place records in a standard size records transmittal box and include a records transmittal slip. Call 287-9009 to order these boxes. Each empty box contains a blank records transmittal slip.

2. Include the following information on each records transmittal slip:

    - **Description of the files.**
        - ✓ Record the file type (e.g., financial invoice, shift report, billing invoice, employment application).
        - ✓ Record the department described in the file.
        - ✓ Write the dates described in the file (for example: Jan. 1996-April 1996).
        - ✓ Record if the files are being archived with their electronic backup (computer disks).
        - ✓ Record if the files are being archived with any audio or video tapes.

    - **Destruction date.** Record the date when the files will not be useful and should be destroyed. For more information, please refer to Company Policy 230, Records Retention.

    - **Name of the responsible supervisor.**

    - **Your department number (and extension).**

3. Enclose the white and yellow copies of the records transmittal slip inside each box of records when you send the boxes to Trolley Street. The Trolley Street Warehouse will record the number and location of each box on the yellow copy, which will be returned to the department storing the records. Each department should maintain a file of the yellow copies.

Procedure memos should have an action format and use headings, lists, and imperative statements. This format enhances readability and allows readers to find their particular responsibilities and actions. See EMPHASIS and PAGE LAYOUT.

Memo, Procedure

> The reason for the procedures is less important than the procedures themselves, so the rationale comes last.

> Procedures must be updated, so the date of creation or revision needs to appear on each page. See PAGE LAYOUT.

Distribution —2— December 28, 1997

These procedures are a result of the recent reorganization of the records storage area. This reorganization was necessary because too many records were being lost and too many out-of-date records were being stored. By following these procedures we will be able to reference our archived files, destroy our outdated files, and make the best use of our storage space.

SR

Distribution:

Department Heads: Sally Ling, Marketing
  Robert Townsend, Manufacturing
  Jamie Furlong, Research
  Miranda Santos, Customer Service
  Tyrone Brown, Administration

Shift Supervisors: Belinda Walker
  John Rodriguez

Support Staff: Chris Goldberg
  Joanne Chipman
  Melisa Cuado

Memos sent to a large number of readers often have a distribution list. *Distribution* appears in the heading following *To*. *Distribution* also appears at the close of the memo with a list of names of those people who should receive copies of the memo. See MEMOS.

Memo, Recommendation

▶ See MEMOS, pp. 97–103

Memorandum

To: F. Winters, Senior Vice President
From: Harry Roterman, Facility Manager
Date: July 7, 1996
Subject: Recommendation to Conserve Water by Establishing a Regular Watering Schedule and by Planting Low-Maintenance Plants

Please authorize our recommended plan for conserving water by using these methods:

- Establish a regular watering schedule.
- Plant low-maintenance plants.

We are using too much water in our daily operations. Our water consumption and the resulting cost have doubled in the last 6 months. We are not being environmentally responsible when we use more water than we need. We can reduce our monthly cost of operation by lowering the amount of water we use. Our recommendations will help our company use its resources wisely.

Establish a Regular Watering Schedule

Our current practice is to water plants whenever it seems necessary. This practice consumes 150 gallons of water monthly. Using a regular watering schedule will reduce this number to 75 gallons. A regular watering schedule will also prevent over or under watering.

Plant Low-Maintenance Plants

By replacing plants that require constant watering with plants that use small amounts of water, we can save 50 percent of our normal water usage. Plants that do not need to be watered as often will also lower the time employees spend watering plants (which will save us time and money in man-hours).

Summary: Reduce Our Water Use

Please authorize our recommended water conservation plan. Using less water will lower our monthly operation budget. Our company is committed to using our resources in the most efficient manner. We are also striving to help the community by doing our part to conserve water.

Harry Roterman

Harry Roterman, Facility Manager

Side annotations:

- The subject block is specific. The subject block should not be misleading or vague. See MEMOS.
- Paragraph 1 repeats the request and lists its two provisions.
- Paragraph 2 sets up the request by providing sound support for it. See ORGANIZATION.
- Deliberate repetition is a valuable technique. The opening two paragraphs establish the writer's recommendation. This recommendation is restated in the closing summary.

Recommendation memos should open with the recommendation (as above). A writer might wish to provide a brief setup or explanation before making the recommendation, but the recommendation still comes early in the memo. A memo should not lead up to a recommendation in the final sentence or paragraph. See ORGANIZATION and MEMOS.

Memo, Report

▶ See MEMOS, pp. 97–103

Use a full memo block to introduce the writer(s), the reader(s), and the subject. See MEMOS.

Use a subject line that is informative, often with an action requested.

Use Paragraph 1 to expand on the **Do** and **Know** statements. The paragraph then leads into the list of reasons. See ORGANIZATION.

Use a displayed list for important points. No period is necessary unless points are full sentences. See LISTS.

Use headings (often with boldface type) to identify key sections of reports. See HEADINGS.

Use parenthetical citations in the text, keyed to a final list of works cited. See CITATIONS and BIBLIOGRAPHY/WORKS CITED.

Use graphics to communicate important information. See GRAPHICS.

Memorandum   **Date: November 30, 1997**

To: Lester T. Gumbell, Operations Manager

From: Shipping Services Steering Committee (P. Burke, N. L. Naspro, J. Hildalgo)

Subject: **Recommendation to Use Pelican Express as Cajun King Corporation's Shipper**

We recommend using Pelican Express for all of Cajun King's shipping needs in 1998 even though its service charges are slightly higher than the other two vendors' costs. We have selected Pelican Express instead of the two competitors primarily because of its consistent customer service ratings. We arrived at the following four conclusions regarding Pelican Express:

1. Higher customer service satisfaction and reliability ratings than competitors
2. Higher overall shipping costs than competitors
3. Equal delivery flexibility with competitors
4. Freezer equipment superior to that of the competitors'

The three shippers we analyzed included Pelican Express, Blue Ridge Cargo, and Federated Shipping, Inc. As you requested last week, the following report compares and contrasts each of the shipping companies against the four criteria that you left on our voice mail.

1. **Higher customer service satisfaction and reliability ratings than competitors**

    After referring to a consumer review magazine article on regional shipping services (*Business Service Review 72*), we developed a graph of customer service ratings from 1994 through 1997. As you can see from the graph below, Pelican Express' customer service record consistently ranked above the other two shipping services.

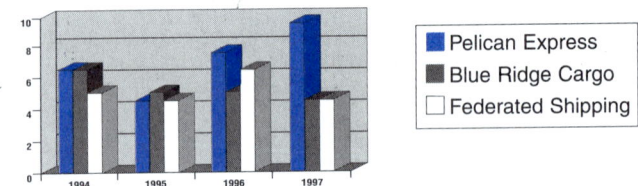

Figure 1: Customer Service Ratings from 1994 to 1997. *In 1996 and 1997, Pelican Express' customer service ratings substantially surpassed its competitors' ratings.*

Cajun King

This memo report presents one type of subject routinely covered in business memos. Memos, by definition, are internal publications and need only have the essential information necessary for internal routing and filing. Usually, a standard introductory block (*To, From, Subject,* and *Date*) is all that is necessary.

Lester T. Gumbell   —2—   November 30, 1997

The reliability factor, as you expressed in our conference last week, is critical to our business of shipping "Crawfish Boil" supplies to customers across the U.S. We asked each vendor (Martin T. Long, Pelican Express; Karen H. Little, Blue Ridge Cargo; Al Olsen, Federated Shipping, Inc.) to do a 30-minute presentation on their services, including reliability. Afterwards, our committee rated each vendor on a scale from 1 to 10 (1 = not reliable, 10 = very reliable). Our score breakdown was as follows:

- Pelican Express   9
- Blue Ridge Cargo   7
- Federated Shipping, Inc. 4

In addition to presentation scores, our support staff called local and regional businesses using these shipping services to ask if they would send us a brief letter commenting on the services provided by each vendor. We received a letter back from each business we called. They unanimously praised Pelican Express' reliability. The other two vendors had positive responses, but also some negative ones.

In one reply, the Manager of Operations at Lickemup Chocolates stated, "We never could have made last year's Christmas order crunch if we hadn't used Pelican Express. They helped us deliver all our orders, even last-minute emergencies" (Pratt).

2. **Higher overall shipping costs than competitors**

We asked each vendor to submit a 1997 cost sheet during the oral presentation. While cost is not the top priority, it is important. We examined all three vendors' costs and discount rates for bulk shipping. In the end, we determined that even though Pelican Express was more expensive than Blue Ridge Cargo and Federated Shipping, Inc., the cost of losing orders due to late shipments (see customer service/reliability) was far more costly than saving a few pennies with the other two services. The table below shows a 1997 cost breakdown for all three vendors:

1997 COST BREAKDOWN TABLE			
UNITS (*lb.*)	PELICAN EXPRESS ($/lb.)	BLUE RIDGE CARGO ($/lb.)	FEDERATED SHIPPING, INC. ($/lb.)
1-50 lbs.	1.60 per lb	1.50 per lb.	1.52 per lb.
51-150 lbs.	1.54 per lb.	1.49 per lb.	1.50 per lb.
151-250 lbs.	1.42 per lb.	1.35 per lb.	1.40 per lb.
251 lbs and over	1.05 per lb..	1.10 per lb.	1.05 per lb.

Figure 2: 1997 Cost Breakdown Table. *Even though Pelican Express' services are more expensive than competitors', customer service ratings show (Figure 1) that clients are still satisfied and continue to give Pelican Express the highest ratings.*

Cajun King

This memo is a report because it arises from a question: Which shipping vendor should Cajun King use in the upcoming year? Businesses routinely have to answer such questions. Often, as in this case, a committee is assigned to do the investigation and to prepare a report for upper management. Management then makes the final decision.

Memo, Report

Use a heading on additional pages that includes the name of the person receiving the memo, the page number, and the date. See MEMOS.

Lester T. Gumbell   –3–   **November 30, 1997**

---

3. Equal delivery flexibility with competitors

The shipping schedules were all relatively the same, although Pelican Express offered an emergency, 24-hour shipping hot line; they claim they can arrange an unscheduled shipment and have it to our customer's door within 6 hours of our request (Continental 84). The other two vendors did not offer this service.

Overall, all three vendors had competitive, regular shipping schedules. Each company had at least 10 in-house pilots, 20-plus operations employees, 10 to 15 airplane mechanics, as well as current licenses and permits.

4. Freezer equipment superior to that of the competitors'

In addition to its high customer service ratings, Pelican Express also has just updated its freezer equipment. The Pelican Express sales representative explained that the company has spent over $350,000 upgrading the freezer capabilities of all its planes. They recently spent $250,000 with Icenhauf, Inc., the leading German air cargo specialist, and $100,000 for training their employees on the new equipment (Howell).

The Blue Ridge Cargo company explained that the last modification to their freezer equipment was over 10 years ago; Federated Shipping, Inc. acknowledged their freezer equipment was relatively new (modified in the last 3 years) but was not purchased from Icenhauf, Inc., the industry leader.

Summary: Rationale for Recommendation

Although Pelican Express did not rank above both other vendors for customer service in 1994 and 1995, it did improve customer service substantially in 1996 and 1997. In fact, while Pelican Express' ratings increased the past 2 years, the other two vendors' ratings slipped substantially. And, even though Pelican Express' services are more expensive than competitors', the customer ratings still continue to increase each year.

Pelican Express has a history of being a dependable, customer-service company and has been an established shipping service in this region for over 50 years. We believe using Pelican Express in 1998 will help our company maintain customers, improve customer relations, and increase sales.

Cajun King

Conclude with a summary. In a business memo, this closing summary will often be the third or fourth restatement of the same information. Repetition in business writing is a virtue. See EMPHASIS, ORGANIZATION, and WRITING.

Reports use information from different sources. In a business context, the information can be published (as in a magazine) or unpublished (letters, phone calls, or sales presentations). Whatever the source, information used in a report needs to be carefully identified and made available for readers to review. Most business writers prefer parenthetical citations, as shown in this report.

Memo, Report

| Lester T. Gumbell | –4– | November 30, 1997 |

We are confident in our choice and look forward to your response. Thank you for the opportunity to prepare this report. Please contact any of the steering committee members if you have questions regarding our selection of a new shipping vendor or data used to support it.

Shipping Services Steering Committee

Janine Hidalgo

J. Hidalgo, Chair
Shipping Services Steering Committee

> Close the memo with a signature block, usually containing the typed name and title of the sender. In this case, the sender is the chairperson of a committee. See LETTERS for examples of signature blocks.

Works Cited

Howell, Paul. Pelican Express sales presentation. 27 July, 1997.

Pelican Express advertisement. *Continental* 27 June, 1994: 31.

Pratt, Sara. Letter to Cajun King Shipping Services. 8 July, 1997.

"Shipping Satisfaction." *Business Service Review* 13 June, 1997: 72.

> *Works Cited* should include all sources mentioned in the report, whether published or unpublished. Give as much information about each unpublished source as possible, such as the writer (or speaker), organization, site, date, and, if appropriate, page numbers. See BIBLIOGRAPHY/WORKS CITED.

Cajun King

All sources used to prepare a report should be identified in a final list of Works Cited, or in some cases, any sources used would be copied and attached to the report. If copies are used, they are called attachments and are numbered as they are mentioned in the report. For example, *Attachment 1: Notes From a Sales Presentation by Paul Howell of Pelican Express.*

Memo, Request

▶ See MEMOS, pp. 97–103

MEMORANDUM

To: All Department Managers and Supervisors
From: Jacqueline Burrows
Date: April 7, 1997
Subject: **Help Us Analyze Our System by Filling Two Requests**

Constant Air needs information about our air conditioning system in order to perform their annual maintenance work. As a result, we are requesting that every department do the following:

- Appoint an air conditioning survey monitor.
- Remove all air conditioning vent blockages.

Appoint an Air Conditioning Survey Monitor

Please assign someone from your department to monitor the air conditioning system between now and May 1. From the monitor's information, Constant Air, Inc., will review and balance the systems in Buildings 3 and 4 to guarantee that all departments can independently maintain the temperatures appropriate for their areas. The duties of the monitor are as follows:

1. **Call Constant Air with questions and reports.** Constant Air's number is 555-3421. Neither the monitor nor any other employee should call Building Services with requests related to the air conditioning.

2. **Keep an hourly log of temperatures at selected points in your department.** Constant Air will identify these points during its initial visit to your department on April 9 or 10.

3. **Prepare a weekly report summarizing the week's events.** Constant Air will bring sample forms for this report to your department when they visit on April 9 or 10.

Please call me (extension 456) if you or your monitor has any questions about this survey.

Remove All Air Conditioning Vent Blockages

Please ask all employees to remove cardboard, Styrofoam, tape, and other material from the ventilation grill before Constant Air's visit. Many employees have tried to control the temperature in their offices by blocking the vents. However, Constant Air cannot obtain accurate information about the current system unless the vents are clear.

Your cooperation in appointing a survey monitor and removing all blockages is greatly appreciated.

A set-up is unnecessary, so the writer opens with the major idea: a request. See ORGANIZATION and MEMOS.

The opening sentence summarizes the paragraph. The word please *is courteous, and it adds a personal touch.*

Each item in the list begins with an imperative verb; therefore, the list is parallel. See LISTS and PARALLELISM.

Although a request, this memo is neutral in content and in tone. The writer minimizes the use of *I*, *my*, and *me*. Instead, she follows the *you* approach. Note how often and how directly she addresses the readers. See TONE.

The paragraphs and sentences are short and direct, and the list allows readers to scan the memo for key points. See LISTS and EMPHASIS.

Memo, Request for Clarification

▶ *See MEMOS, pp. 97–103*

MEMORANDUM

To: Edwin Dilworth, Shift Manager
From: Charlotte Smart, Senior Accountant
Date: November 24, 1997
Subject: **Request for Clarification on Closing Procedures**

I would appreciate your investigating and clarifying the closing procedures that were followed the week of November 12, 1997.

I understand during the week of November 12-17, 1997, the cash registers were not closed properly and the recommended closing procedures were not followed. Here are the facts as I understand them. Please inform me if these facts are incorrect.

Procedures Improperly Completed

Management authorized new closing procedures on November 3. However, starting on the night of November 12 the registers were not secured, and the cash drawer contents were not counted for an entire week. I learned of these procedure omissions after John Sturgees, our company accountant, informed me that the store deposit totals did not balance because store employees were not closing out the registers properly.

Recommended Procedures

Early in November, we established procedures that employees were to follow at the closing of the work day. We analyzed the needs and recommended the following:

1. Total the contents of the cash drawer including all credit slips and checks.
2. Compare the cash total against the printed receipts for the day's business. If they do not balance, record any differences on the balance sheet.
3. Record the cash drawer total on the daily report. Place the daily report and the cash drawer contents in the wall safe.
4. Lock the cash drawer and secure the register.
5. Remove any garbage and clean your work area. Use the cleaning supplies in the back room, if needed.
6. Set the alarm and lock the double doors as you leave the building. Make sure the "Closed" sign is displayed in the front window.

I would like to know why the closing procedures were not performed according to management's recommendation and who was responsible for the failure to follow the new procedures.

CS

Annotations:

- The specific subject line states exactly what needs to be clarified. See MEMOS.
- Paragraph 1 establishes the topic and conveys the purpose of the memo.
- Paragraph 2 sets up the list and leads into the details. See ORGANIZATION and MEMOS.
- Displayed lists are naturally emphatic. Note that listed items begin the same way. See PARALLELISM and LISTS.
- The last paragraph summarizes the memo and restates the request for clarification of the issue.

While basically a request for information, this memo is potentially critical of the reader or people working for the reader. In such politically or humanly sensitive matters, tone is important. The writer must be forceful without being aggressive, direct but not blunt, businesslike but not inhuman. See TONE and MEMOS.

Abstract, Descriptive

The opening sentence states the question studied. The pronoun *we* assigns the study to the authors and makes the sentences active rather than passive. No results or details are given. See ACTIVE/PASSIVE.

Title: Sloppiness is inherited not learned.

We studied the possible inheritance of a "sloppiness" gene in humans to determine whether children can be taught to be neat or whether their tendency to neatness is inherited. The study population included 2,024 identical twins, fraternal twins, and siblings; individuals reared in the same family were compared to those reared in different families. We developed a rating scale for sloppiness. We also questioned families and friends to determine whether individuals stayed the same, in terms of sloppiness, throughout their lives.

Key words: sloppiness, tendency, neatness, inherit, twins, behavior

Smythe, M.L. (1995). *Journal of Gene Psychology* 21:31–37.

Descriptive abstracts give the general content of a study or report, but they do not discuss the actual results. Descriptive abstracts are primarily useful for bibliographic cross-referencing because they provide the *what,* the *why,* and the *how,* but not the actual conclusions or recommendations.

Abstract, Informative

Title: Sloppiness is inherited not learned.

In a study of 2,024 adults, we determined that "sloppiness" is inherited, not learned. Although home situations and lessons imparted during childhood can alter behavior in a limited way, children "born to be neat" stay that way, as do children who "couldn't care less" about the neatness of their surroundings. The study rated sloppiness in adults and compared scores in a variety of genetic and familial combinations. Genetically-related adults reared in different families were more likely (99.44%) to have the same sloppiness rating than were genetically-unrelated adults reared in the same family (77.33%). Also, adults rated by their childhood friends and relatives as "messy" (or neat) were still messy (or neat) as adults; fewer than 0.5% had changed their behaviors.

Key words: sloppiness, tendency, neatness, inherit, twins, behavior

Smythe, M.L. (1995). *Journal of Gene Psychology* 21:31–37.

- The abstract opens with the conclusion written in terms of the question studied.
- The second sentence is an extension of the first, in this case a generalization based on the conclusion.
- The third sentence identifies the technique used for the study.
- The last two sentences give results in numerical terms.

Informative abstracts give the actual information discovered—the results and any pertinent conclusions or recommendations. The primary readers of informative abstracts are those who are familiar with the subject field and who are able to use the content of the abstract without ordering the whole report. Informative abstracts mention research methods and other techniques only if they are likely to be unknown to knowledgeable readers.

Minutes, Action

The subject line is quite specific. See HEADINGS and MEMOS.	September 15, 1997 **MINUTES OF THE SEPTEMBER 15 THIRD-PERIOD CLASS—VIEWING AND DISCUSSING THE FIRST TWO RETURN SCENES**

September 15, 1997

MINUTES OF THE SEPTEMBER 15 THIRD-PERIOD CLASS—VIEWING AND DISCUSSING THE FIRST TWO RETURN SCENES

Attending: Members of the Third-Period, 12th Grade Class
Tardy: Pat Yee
Absent: Jim Householder, Suzanne Simmons
Teacher: Mr. Evan Santiago

ACTION ITEMS

1. Mr. Santiago asked students to choose a partner and prepare to role play a customer service scene. They could use one of the three introduced in the exercise or one of their choosing.

2. Each student was instructed to pick one of the return scenes and prepare to give a 3- to 4-minute summary. This summary will help absent students understand the role of these scenes.

3. Chris Benson is to take minutes tomorrow (September 16).

OVERVIEW OF THE CLASS DISCUSSION

The following are key points presented by the teacher after the class viewed the video:

1. Deal with customers without putting decisions off to a manager.
2. Be courteous and conciliatory toward the customer, regardless of the customer's attitude.
3. Present the store's policy as reasonable and fair.

DISCUSSION

Natalie Memmert's Comment: She suggested the clerk handled the situation poorly. The store clerk should have been willing to work with the customer until he was happy with his service. Natalie felt a happy customer was more important than any store return policy.

Pat Yee's Comment: Pat disagreed. The store's return policy should be followed because it was written to protect the store. If clerks allow exceptions to the rule, the store stands to lose money. Ultimately, the store is a money-making business and needs to protect its revenue.

Side annotations:

- The subject line is quite specific. See HEADINGS and MEMOS.
- An accurate record of attendees is essential.
- Action items emphasize the people, their responsibilities, and the due dates. See EMPHASIS and ORGANIZATION.
- This overview supplies necessary background information (much as corrections to prior minutes would do).
- The numbered list helps to highlight key information. See LISTS.
- This comment highlights the name of the person making the comment, but the heading could identify the issue: *Examples of Customer Service*.

Action minutes highlight (1) actions needed in the future (usually before the next meeting) and (2) activities during the meeting being recorded. Action items do not attempt to capture everything that was discussed, and they deliberately do not record the meeting in strict chronological order.

Minutes, Action

> **Minutes of the September 15 Meeting**   Page 2
>
> The class finally agreed that the problem between the store clerk and the customer could have been avoided if the store's return policy had been presented more clearly.
>
> **EXERCISES**
>
> **Recording Exercise (Students):** Students recorded actual words and phrases that identified problems with Fashion Farm's return policy. Students answered the following questions about the video:
>
> 1. What did the customer want to return? Why?
> 2. What happened during the incidents?
> 3. What problems arose because of the store's return policy?
>
> **Role Play Exercise (Matt Martinez and Pat Yee):** They role-played one of these typical incidents:
>
> 1. A customer tries to return a pair of shoes that has obviously been worn. He or she does not have a receipt, and the purchase was made 4 days ago.
> 2. A customer wants to return a jacket because two buttons fell off after just one wearing. The customer does not have the buttons but does have the receipt. The garment was purchased last month, but the customer claims it was not worn immediately.
> 2. A customer wishes to return an item after Christmas that was given to him/her as a gift. He or she does not have the receipt, but the tag is still on the garment. The item is now on sale for 40 percent off.
>
> **Exercise Question:** Mr. Santiago asked the students how a sales person should deal with or speak to customers, in general (especially angry customers). Matt Martinez suggested that angry customers need to be dealt with sternly because they are more aggressive customers. Pat Yee disagreed and said the best way to deal with angry customers is to counteract their harshness with extreme politeness and courtesy.
>
> Respectfully submitted,
>
> *Jeanne Skrout*
> Jeanne Skrout

These headings highlight the content of the exercises. The person's name is included in parentheses.

The format above, although not mandatory, is visually open and makes the minutes easy for readers to review. See EMPHASIS.

Action minutes record enough information for them to be useful as a record of what the participants discussed. This information is important in case someone besides an attendee has to review the minutes.

Minutes, Traditional Format

The title or subject is specific. See HEADINGS *and* MEMOS.

September 15, 1997

MINUTES OF THE SEPTEMBER 15 THIRD-PERIOD CLASS—VIEWING AND DISCUSSING THE FIRST TWO RETURN SCENES

Attending: Members of the Third-Period, 12th Grade Class
Tardy: Pat Yee
Absent: Jim Householder, Suzanne Simmons
Teacher: Mr. Evan Santiago

REVIEW OF THE FIRST TWO RETURN SCENES

Students viewed two video clips. Students recorded actual words and phrases that identified problems with Fashion Farm's return policy. Students answered the following questions about the video:

The displayed list highlights important questions discussed in the meeting.

1. What did the customer want to return? Why?
2. What happened during the incidents?
3. What problems arose because of the store's return policy?

After viewing both videos, students recorded answers to these questions in their notebooks. The teacher also recorded answers to these questions on the board for discussion.

Short paragraphs enhance readability. See LETTERS.

DISCUSSION

Natalie Memmert suggested the cashier handled the situation poorly. Pat Yee disagreed. The class finally agreed that the problem between the store clerk and the customer could have been avoided if the store's return policy had been presented more clearly.

Each paragraph summarizes a different motion, with some details about the discussion. The writer is following a chronological pattern. The results of the motions come late in the paragraphs.

EXERCISE QUESTIONS

Mr. Santiago asked the students how a sales person should deal with or speak to customers, in general (especially angry customers).

Matt Martinez suggested that angry customers need to be dealt with sternly because they are more aggressive customers. Pat Yee disagreed and said the best way to deal with angry customers is to counteract their harshness with extreme politeness. The teacher settled the argument by presenting these points:

Traditional minutes usually attempt to record most of what happened during the meeting and follow events chronologically. The above minutes begin with a review of the activities and discussion topics. They end with action items (the Assignment) for the next class meeting.

Minutes, Traditional Format

Minutes of the September 15 Meeting Page 2

1. Deal with customers without putting decisions off to a manager.
2. Be courteous and conciliatory toward the customer, regardless of the customer's attitude.
3. Try to diffuse any anger and present the store's policy as reasonable and fair.

ROLE PLAY EXERCISE

Mr. Santiago called upon Matt Martinez and Pat Yee to role play one of these typical incidents:

1. A customer tries to return a pair of shoes that has obviously been worn. He or she does not have a receipt, and the purchase was made 4 days ago.
2. A customer wants to return a jacket because two buttons fell off after just one wearing. The customer does not have the buttons but does have the receipt. The garment was purchased last month, but the customer claims it was not worn immediately.
3. A customer wishes to return an item after Christmas that was given to him/her as a gift. He or she does not have the receipt, but the tag is still on the garment. The item is now on sale for 40 percent off.

The class critiqued the sales person's (Matt Martinez) responses to the customer and discussed whether there was a better approach to dealing with the situation.

ASSIGNMENT

1. Mr. Santiago asked students to choose a partner and prepare to role play a customer service scene. Students may use one of the three introduced in the exercise or another of their choosing.
2. Each student was instructed to pick one of the return scenes and prepare to give a 3- to 4-minute summary. This summary will help absent students understand the role of these scenes.
3. Chris Benson is to take minutes tomorrow (September 16).

Respectfully submitted,

Jeanne Skrout

Jeanne Skrout

The numbered list highlights the criteria. Each item is parallel with the others. See LISTS and PARALLELISM.

The headings, lists, short paragraphs, and brief sentences all contribute to the overall readability, but motions and action items are potentially lost. For this reason, we recommend the action format for minutes (see the previous example). See LETTERS and EMPHASIS.

Newsletter Item

The headline captures the key idea.

The opening paragraph summarizes the who, what, where, when, how, *and* why.

Actual quotations help make the story more vivid and readable.

Headings help break up the text. See HEADINGS.

Honeytree Hotel Opens New Conference Center

The Honeytree Hotel today announced that its long-awaited conference center will open on November 12, 1996. This new facility makes the Honeytree the premiere meeting and special-event site in Jackson County. The conference center will provide a full-service, affordable location for wedding and graduation receptions, proms, and business events.

According to Anna Dentone, Director of Catering, the new facility is " . . . luxurious without being expensive. Anyone looking for an event site can now stay right here in Jackson County. They can host their special events at the Honeytree, the same hotel that has been serving this community for over 20 years."

New rooms for special events

One major feature of the new conference center is the range of meeting facilities—all equipped for the handicapped—that will be offered to the public. At the heart of the conference center is the Chestnut Ballroom, a flexible space that can be used for exhibits, dances, banquets, or meetings. Large enough to accommodate 700 people comfortably, the ballroom can also be subdivided into smaller conference areas. In addition to the Chestnut Ballroom, the 20,000 square-foot conference facility also includes 9 large meeting rooms, each of which seats 50 people.

New chef and menus

As a part of the upgrade of all hotel facilities, the Honeytree has also hired a new chef, Pierre DuParc. Trained in Paris at the École d´ Haute Cuisine, Chef Pierre brings a new level of continental dining to Jackson County. He specializes in events catering and can adapt or modify his menus to meet the individual demands or tastes of the most exacting guest. Although his specialities include classic French dishes such as Veal Oscar and Beef Wellington, Chef Pierre also offers a full selection of low-fat, healthy alternatives.

Recreational opportunities

Every meeting has to end sometime, and now guests at the Honeytree have new opportunities to unwind at the end of the day. As a part of its expansion, the hotel has added a new indoor jogging track and a superb fresh-water pool. In addition, the fitness center has been extensively remodeled and offers the latest in exercise equipment including a jacuzzi, treadmills, weights, and stationary bikes.

If exercise is not too appealing at the end of the day, guests can retreat to the comfortable haven of their rooms. Pampering extras—French milled soaps, luxury shampoos, and extra-thick terry cloth towels—are a standard feature of every guestroom. And after that relaxing bath, a weary guest can kick back and enjoy a private showing of a first-run movie on the room's 19-inch TV.

These new facilities and services make the Honeytree the first choice for meeting and events in Jackson County. If you are planning a special event, either personal or business, call the director of marketing at the Honeytree for scheduling information and price estimates.

Newsletters should be as specific and informative as possible. Thus writers should use direct quotations as well as other specific facts. Newsletters should follow the Seven Quality Standards for Documents, with the main point in the opening paragraph. See ORGANIZATION.

Newsletters should be as readable as possible, with short sentences and simple, direct words. See LETTERS and TONE.

Policy, Customer Service

Jefferson Policies	**2.0 Customer Service**

The policy statement describes the intent behind the general policy and establishes the policy's basic goals.

The contents description previews the rest of the policy and functions as a table of contents. (Policies 2.3–2.4 are not shown in this model.)

2.1 General Policy

Policies Covered:
2.2 *Incomplete Orders*
2.3 *Defective Merchandise*
2.4 *Shipping Delays or Damage*

2.2 Incomplete Orders

2.0 Customer Service

"We serve the customer. We are customer driven; and in concert with our values, we give customers what they seek."

   -*Jefferson Governing Value*

Customer service is central to the Jefferson customer-satisfaction philosophy. We guarantee that our customers will be satisfied with Jefferson products because we want their business now and in the future. Our success depends on it. Remember, the customer is always in the right, even if you disagree.

Should any Jefferson product fail to meet the customer's expectations for any reason, the customer can return it to Jefferson for a full refund or replacement. Jefferson has become legendary because of the quality of our customer service.

Incomplete orders can occur when (Case 1) Jefferson personnel fail to ship an ordered item or (Case 2) the customer has mistakenly failed to order an item but believes that he or she did order it.

In Case 1, the problem is our fault; and we should remedy it in any way the customer requests. We can send the missing merchandise, or we can provide a refund. We should apologize and, if appropriate, offer a complimentary product (up to $10 retail price).

In Case 2, after we have reviewed the customer's order and confirmed that the item(s) were not listed, we can give the customer these options:

- Order the missing items(s) and pay the appropriate retail price.
- Cancel the additional items(s) if they are no longer wanted.
- Order replacement or alternate merchandise, if desired.

Under each of the options, at the discretion of our representative, we can offer a complimentary product (up to $10 retail price).

Policies inevitably must be updated, so the numbering system and revision date need to appear on each page.

Jefferson Time Books
Last Revised: December 1996   4

A divided column format makes reading easier. The use of numbered headings allows easy updating and quick reference. See PAGE LAYOUT and HEADINGS.

Procedure, Incomplete Order

Jefferson Procedures   **2.21 Incomplete Orders**

2.21 Incomplete Orders

When a customer calls and claims that part of an order is missing, use the following procedure to resolve the problem.

1. Apologize for the customer's inconvenience.

2. Ask the customer for the order number.

Locate the Order

3. Search for the order in question. If you need information about searching for an order, see "Search" in the Computer section (Section 5.0) of this manual.

Check for the Missing Items

4. Check to verify that the missing item was listed on the original order.

   If the item was not on the original order:

   4.1 Inform the customer and arrange to ship the new item using Steps 5 through 7.

   If the item was on the original order but never sent, choose one of these options:

   4.2 Cancel the additional item(s) if the customer no longer wants them.

   4.3 Order replacement or alternate merchandise, if desired.

   4.4 Send the missing item using Steps 5 through 7.

Order and Reship the Missing Item

5. Enter the stock number and quantity of the missing product on the new order screen.

6. Press **F14** (Tax and Total). Enter the method of shipment at the customer's request.

7. Press **F10** to save the procedure.

> Remember Jefferson's 100% customer satisfaction policy. You have the authority to satisfy the customer.

Jefferson Time Books
Last Revised: December 1996   6

Annotations (left margin):

- Numbered lists indicate a sequence of action and visually emphasize points. See LISTS and EMPHASIS.

- Headings in the left column restate the order and allow a quick summary of the procedural steps.

- Shaded boxes, a change of typeface or typesize, boldface type, and placement emphasize key points, warnings, or unusual steps or procedures.

Procedures using an action format are as schematic as possible, with headings, lists, and imperative statements. See HEADINGS, LISTS, and ACTIVE/PASSIVE. This format is easy for readers to understand and to use.

Shift Report, Computer Company

The title and associated data allow for careful cross-referencing and storage and retrieval of documents.

The information in these blanks should be as complete as possible.

When hand writing, print as clearly as possible.

Long Beach Computer Systems

Shift Summary

Date: 10/31/94   Store Number: 15

Logged By: J. Reynolds   Department: MIS

Shift Supervisor: N. Nickolaisen   Employees Absent: M. Madsen (vacation)

Interruption of Work

Time	Incident	Action
8:47 am	R. Lopez (Computer #23102), Screen message "Hard Drive Error, D0101."	Sent C. Stevens to diagnose problem.
4:28 pm	L. Britt (Computer #18636), Screen message "Printer memory Error, L1016." While trying to print large files at printer 7277.	Told Britt to print job in small pieces. Next shift scheduled to upgrade printer 7277 memory.

Equipment Problems

Equipment Name & Number	Problem	Action
Computer 23115	Will not print.	Install print driver.
Computer 18636	Will not print large jobs.	Install expanded memory.

Action Items for Next Shift

1. Install expanded memory in Printer 7277.
2. Install print driver in Computer #23115.

Form 578H J/I

Field notes, shift reports, and logs contain essential information. As such, they need to be carefully written and systematically filed. Writers should use ink (or at least a dark lead pencil), and they should attempt to print or write clearly and neatly. If possible, writers should review their notes at least once a day and correct any obvious errors or sloppy writing (such as dotting *i*'s or connecting loops on *o*'s).

Reference Glossary Index

4-Box Organizer, 109–111
  in model documents, 197
    199–206, 208–209

Abbreviations, 1–9
  and acronyms, 1, 129
  and addressing, 84, 90
  and apostrophes, 19
  and copyright symbol,
    68–70
  and plurals, 138
  and registration mark,
    68–70
  and trademarks, 68–70
  for page or pages, 36
  list of, 4–9
  U.S. Postal service address
    elements, 90
  U.S. Postal service for
    states, 84
  use of, 1–4
Abstract, 220–221
Acronyms
  and apostrophes, 19
  and parentheses, 129
  and punctuation, 1
  spelling out, 129
Active/Passive, 10–13
Active voice, 10–13
  (*also see* gobbledygook,
    100)
  and captions, 59–60
Addresses
  and commas, 42
  in letters, 75, 80, 83–85
  in model documents,
    197–200, 206
  in reference lists, 159
  in résumés, 154
  on envelopes, 88–90
Adjectives
  (*also see* Parallelism,
    126–127)
  and commas, 40
  and hyphens, 64–66
  and lists, 96
Adverbs
  and hyphens, 66
  and semicolons, 161–162
  conjunctive, 43, 46,
    161–162
Agenda
  for the interview, 72
Agreement, 14–17
  (*also see* Parallelism,
    126–127)
  and bias-free language,
    22–23
  and hyphens, 65, 67
  in persuasive writing, 132,
    135, 203
Alphabetize
  (*also see* Citations, 35–36)
  bibliographic entries, 26, 28
Apostrophes, 18–19
  (*also see* Plurals, 136–138)
  (*also see* Possessives,
    139–141)
  and abbreviations, 19, 138
  and acronyms, 19
  and contractions, 18
  and hyphenated words, 140
  and numbers, 107, 138
  and passage of time, 19
  and plurals, 19, 138–140
  and possessives, 18–19,
    140–141
  and signs and symbols, 19,
    138
Appearance of type, 63
Article, 167
  (*also see* Capitals, 29–34)
  (*also see* Citations, 35–36)
  (*also see* Titles, 166–167)
  and bibliographic entries,
    26–27
  and quotation marks, 143
  use of brackets, 130

Articles
  and capitalization, 31, 34
Ascender, 123
Attachment notation in
  memos, 101, 103
Attachments, 217

Baseline, 123
Bias-free language, 20–24
  and agreement, 16–17
  in courtesy titles, 84
  in résumés, 198
Bibliography, 25–28
  (*also see* Citations, 35–36)
  in captions, 60
  parenthetical citations, 214
  works cited list, 217
Boldface type, 52, 54
  (*also see* Page Layout,
    115–125)
  in headings, 63, 113
  in letters, 76–77
  in memos, 98
  in persuasive writing, 134
  proofreader symbol, 245
  used as emphasis, 113, 134
Borders, 118
Braces, 131
Brackets, 128–131
  (*also see* Ellipses, 49–50)
  and commas, 42
  in citations, 35–36
Brainstorming, 175–178
Bullets in lists, 94, 96, 110,
    112–113, 123
  in letters, 77
Business documents,
  (*also see* Memos, 97–103)
  (*also see* Page Layout,
    115–125)
  (*also see* Persuasion,
    132–135)
  (*also see* Résumés,
    145–160)

231

Reference Glossary Index

(*also see* Writing, 175–184)
and letters, 75–91
job application, 190–192
job description, 193–194
memo report, 214–217
résumés, 195–196, 198
use of graphics, 55–60
Business tone, 168–172

Capitalization, 29–34
(*also see* Capitals 29–34)
(*also see* Hyphens, 64–67)
after colon, 39
and hyphens, 34
in addressing, 84
in bibliographic entries, 26–27
in complimentary closing, 85
of abbreviations, 2, 84
of articles, 34
of common nouns, 31–32, 34
of conjunctions, 34
of geographical names, 33–34
of headings, 34, 123–124
of listed items, 33, 94, 127
of names of Diety, 33
of prepositions, 34
of proper names, 30–31
of proper nouns, 34, 151
of quotations, 33
of titles, 30–31
of trademarks, 69
Capitals, 29–34
(*also see* Headings, 61–63)
(*also see* Titles, 166–167)
as emphasis tool, 54
proofreader symbol, 243
Captions, 52, 117
(*also see* Graphics, 55–60)
modification and copyright, 70

Charts, 56, 58
identify source of, 70
to emphasize information, 113–114, 124
Chronological résumé, 145–146, 148, 196
Citations, 35–36, 60, 129
(*also see* Bibliography/ Works Cited, 25–28)
(*also see* Intellectual Property, 68–70)
Colons, 37–38
(*also see* Dashes, 47–48)
capitalization following, 33
contrasted with semicolons and dashes, 37, 47
in letters, 80, 83, 85, 197
in memo headings, 101
introducing lists, 37–38, 93–95
proofreader symbol, 244
use with abbreviations, 4
with quotation marks, 144
Color
for emphasis, 54, 113, 123–124
Commas, 39–42
contrasted with dashes and parentheses, 48, 128
in a series, 39, 162
in complimentary closings, 42, 80, 85–86
in displayed lists, 95
in salutations, 42
proofreader symbol, 244
punctuation style in letters, 83, 86
separating adjectives, 40
separating complete thoughts, 40, 162
separating groups of digits, 107

separating introductory clauses, 41
separating items in dates and addresses, 42
separating nonessential clauses, 41
separating parenthetical expressions, 41
separating titles/degrees from names, 42
with abbreviations, 4
with brackets, 42
with conjunctive adverb, 46
with parentheses, 42, 129
with quotation marks, 42, 143–144
with subordinate phrase, 45–46
with transitional words, 173–174
Communication
(*also see* Bias-Free Language, 20–24)
(*also see* Interviews, 71–74)
(*also see* Letters, 75–91)
(*also see* Memos, 97–103)
(*also see* Page Layout, 115–125)
(*also see* Persuasion, 132–135)
4-Box Organizer, 110
and Seven Quality Standards, 114
Complimentary closings, 42, 79–82, 85–86
Compound
adjectives, 66
numbers, 66
sentence, 40, 44
terms, 137
words, 22, 34, 64–65
Computers
(also see Graphics, 55–60)

Reference Glossary Index

(also see Page Layout, 115–125)
and headings, 63
as business tool, 55
software to check spelling, 165
Conclusions
(*also see* Writing, 175–184)
at the beginning of your document, 109
in abstracts, 220–221
Conjunctions, 40, 43–46, 161–162
(*also see* Parallelism, 126–127)
(*also see* Transitions, 173–174)
coordinate, 34, 43–45, 162
correlative, 43, 45
in headings, 34
in titles, 34
subordinate, 43, 45–46
Conjunctive adverb, 43, 46, 161–162
Connected words, 64–67, 126
(*also see* Transitions, 173–174)
Connecting complete thoughts, 44
(*also see* Transitions, 173–174)
with hyphens, 64–67
Content
(*also see* Organization, 108–114)
(*also see* Persuasion, 132–135)
(*also see* Résumés, 145–160)
(*also see* Writing, 175–184)
in letters, 75–79
in memos, 98–101
on envelopes, 88–90
Contractions, 18–19, 141, 171

Coordinate conjunctions, 34, 40, 43–45, 162
Copyrights, 68–70
Correlating conjunctions, 43, 45
Courtesy copy notation
in letters, 86, 89
in memos, 103
Courtesy titles, 84
Cover letter, 160, 197, 199

Dashes, 47–48
and parentheses, 128–131
contrasted with colons and semicolons, 37
enclosing parenthetical expressions, 41
in lists, 94, 96
with quotation marks, 144
Date
(*also see* Citations, 35–36)
in bibliographic entries, 25–27
in job applications, 187
in letters, 79, 82–84, 197, 199
in memos, 101–102
in résumés, 155, 157
use commas with, 42
use figures for, 106–107
Descender, 123
Designing documents
(*also see* Emphasis, 51–54)
(*also see* Graphics, 55–60)
(*also see* Letters, 75–91)
(*also see* Memos, 97–103)
(*also see* Page Layout, 115–125)
(*also see* Persuasion, 132–135)
(*also see* Résumés, 145–160)
(*also see* Writing, 175–184)
tone of, 172

Diagrams, 56, 59, 113
Display typeface, 121
Displayed lists, 92–96, 117
(*also see* Parallelism, 126–127)
and colons, 38
capitalization of, 33
for emphasis, 205, 214–215, 219, 224
in résumés, 146, 195–196, 198
Do statements, 110–113, 206, 214
Document design
(*also see* Emphasis, 51–54)
(*also see* Graphics, 55–60)
(*also see* Letters, 75–91)
(*also see* Memos, 97–103)
(*also see* Page Layout, 115–125)
(*also see* Persuasion, 132–135)
(*also see* Résumés, 145–160)
(*also see* Writing, 175–184)
tone of, 172

Editing proofreader symbols, 243–245
Ellipses, 49–50
Emphasis, 51–54
(*also see* Headings, 61–63)
(*also see* Lists, 92–96)
(*also see* Organization, 108–114)
(*also see* Page Layout, 115–125)
and colons, 37
and dashes, 47–48
in letters, 77
in memos, 97–100
Enclosure notation, 86, 88
Envelopes, 84, 88–91

Reference Glossary Index

Figures
   (*also see* Graphics, 55–60)
   and apostrophes, 19
   and parentheses, 129
   numbers as, 104–107
   plurals of, 138
Fonts, 121–122
   (*also see* Page Layout, 115–125)
Footers, 116–120
   in writing process (prototyping), 178–179
Format
   (*also see* Citations, 35–36)
   (*also see* Graphics, 55–60)
   (*also see* Page Layout, 115–125)
   (*also see* Résumés, 145–160)
   bibliographic format, 25–28
   brainstorming, 175–177
   letter format, 79–88
   memo format, 101–103
Forms
   blank job application, 190–192
   4-Box Organizer, 109–111
   in model documents, 197 199–206, 208–209
Functional résumé, 146–147, 150–153, 195, 198

Garbage-in-garbage-out, 51
Gender distinctions, 20–24, 84, 155
Gobbledygook, 100
Graphs, 55, 57, 118
   (*also see* Graphics, 55–60)
   (*also see* Page Layout, 115–125)
Graphics, 55–60
   copyright, 68–70
   for emphasis, 113–114
   placement, 123–124

Headers, 116–117, 119–120
Headings, 61–63
   capitalization of, 34,
   in letters, 77, 85, 202–203, 209–211
   in memos, 101–102
   in résumés, 146–147, 153, 156
   on additional pages, 85–86, 216
   used for emphasis, 53
Hyphens, 64–67
   and abbreviations, 3
   and apostrophes, 140
   and capitalization, 34
   and technical terminology, 67
   as connectors, 64–65
   in numbers, 105

Illustrations, 56, 59, 70
Informal tone, 168–169, 171
   and contractions, 18
   in letters, 85
Initials
   reference, 86–87, 103
Inside address in letters, 83–84, 89–90, 200
Intellectual property, 68–70
Interoffice correspondence, 97
   (*also see* Memos, 97–103)
Interviews, 71–74
Introductions
   in letters, 76–77, 200
   to graphics, 58–59
Irregular plurals, 136–138, 165
   and apostrophes, 18
Italics
   for emphasis, 54, 63, 77
   in bibliographic form, 25, 38
   in citations, 36
   in headings, 63, 124
   in titles, 167
   replace quotation marks, 143

Jargon, 100
Job
   blank application, 190–192
   completed application, 187–189
   description, 193–194
   interview, 71–74
   résumés, 145–160, 195–196, 198
Joining words, 65
   (*also see* Hyphens, 64–67)

Key
   content in documents, 76–77, 99, 110, 112–113, 197, 199, 209, 214
   facts emphasized with graphics, 55–60
   principle of time management, 182
   to successful brainstorming, 176
   to a successful résumé, 149
   word for alphabetizing, 28
   writing principle (organization), 108
Know statements, 110–111, 214

Landscape format, 118
Language,
   bias-free, 16–17, 20–24, 84
   gender-neutral, 22–24
   nonprejudical, 20–21
   skills, 158–159
Layout
   (*also see* Emphasis, 51–54)
   (*also see* Organization, 108–114)

234

Reference Glossary Index

(*also see* Page Layout, 115–125)
for letters, 77
for memos, 99–100, 211–212
for persuasion, 134
for policy, 227
for procedure, 228
for prototype, 178
for résumés, 146, 195–196, 198
for tone, 172
Letters, 75–91
(*also see* Memos, 97–103)
(*also see* Organization, 108–114)
(*also see* Page Layout, 115–125)
attention line, 85
bias-free language in, 23–24
body, 85
closing, 78–79
components, 83–88
content, 75–79
courtesy copy notation, 86, 88
courtesy title, 84
cover letter for résumé, 146, 160, 197, 199
date line, 83
enclosure notation, 86, 88
envelopes, 88–90
folding of, 91
format
  block, 79–80
  modified block, 79, 82
  simplified block, 79, 81
heading, 85–86
inside address, 83–84, 89
mailing address, 90
margins, 79–81
models, 75
  commendation, 201

complaint, 202
cover letter, 197, 199
newsletter, 226
persuasive sales letter, 203–204
proposal, 205–207
sales, 208
survey data, 209
thank you, 200
organization of, 108–114
page layout of, 115–125
punctuation styles, 80, 83
reference initials, 86–87
return address, 83, 90
salutation, 85
signature block, 85–86
spacing, 79
special notations, 83, 90
subject line, 75–76
Lists, 92–96
(*also see* Bibliography, 25–28)
(*also see* Citations, 35–36)
alphabetized for works cited, 35–36
and colons, 94–95
and parallelism, 126–127
and parentheses, 129
and punctuation, 37–38, 94–95
bullets and numbers in, 94, 96, 210, 214–215, 222, 225, 228
capitalization, 94
for emphasis, 53, 93, 117
in page layout, 123
in résumés, 146, 148–149, 153, 156–160, 195–196, 198
of abbreviations, 4–9
of figures for graphics, 59
of hard interview questions, 73–74

of references, 159–160, 188

Maps, 56, 59
Margins
  in letters, 79–81
  in page layout, 117–118
Mathematical expressions in parentheses and brackets, 131
Measurement abbreviations, 2–3, 104–105
Memos, 97–103
(*also see* Letters, 75–91)
(*also see* Organization, 108–114)
(*also see* Writing, 175–184)
4-Box Organizer for, 110–111
attachment notation, 103
body of, 102
closing, 101
content, 98–101
courtesy copy notation, 103
definition of, 97
design of, 97, 99–101
format, 101–103
heading, 101–102
models, 97
  personnel notice, 210
  procedure, 211–212
  recommendation, 213
  report, 214–217
  request, 218
  request for clarification, 219
organization of, 108–114
reference initials, 103
references, 102
report, 214–217
signature line, 103
subject lines, 98–99, 102
tone of, 168–172

Reference Glossary Index

Mock-up of documents, 58, 178
Model documents, 187–229
Model letters, 75, 80–82, 197, 199–209
Model memos, 97, 210–219
Model résumés, 148, 195–196, 198
Mono-spaced typefaces, 122

Names
  and capitalization, 29–34
  and commas, 42
  and titles, 166–167
  in bibliography/works cited, 25–28
  in citations, 35–36
Newsletter item, 226
Notations
  attachment, 103
  courtesy copy, 86, 89, 103
  enclosure, 86, 88
  special, 83, 89, 90
Notes
  brainstorming, 177
  clustering, 177
Nouns
  capitalization of, 29–34
  plural, 136–138
  possessive, 139–141
  proper, 151
  singular and plural agreement, 14–17
Numerical figures, 104–107
Numbering
  of graphics, 59, 215
  of lists, 93–94, 96, 228
  system for documents, 194
  system of headings, 63, 194
Numbers, 104–107
  and abbreviations, 3
  and apostrophes, 18–19
  and commas, 107
  and hyphens, 66
  and plurals, 107, 138
  beginning a sentence with, 105
  combining with letters, 106
  consistency of, 106
  writing out, 105

Objective
  and needs of readers, 132–133
  in job applications, 187
  in résumés, 145, 147–149, 154–155, 157–158, 195–196, 198
Omitted
  letters in words, 18–19
  quotation marks, 27
  salutation in letters, 23, 206
  titles in letters, 205, 209
  words, 49–50
Organization, 108–114
  (*also see* Emphasis, 51–54)
  (*also see* Letters, 75,–91)
  (*also see* Memos, 97–103)
  (*also see* Transitions, 173–174)
  according to readers' needs, 134
  charts, 56
  of cover letter, 199
  of data, 108
  of job description, 194
  of meeting minutes, 222
  of most important points, 109–114
  of newsletter, 226
  using 4-Box Organizer, 110, 197, 199–206, 208–209, 214
  using emphasis techniques, 113
  using headings, 113
  using the Seven Quality Standards for Documents, 114

Page design, 53, 118, 146
Page format, 58
Page layout, 115–125
  and columns, 116, 119
  and design, 117–118
  and graphics, 117, 123–124
  and headers and footers, 116, 119–120
  and headings and lists, 116–117, 123
  and letters, 77
  and margins, 117–118
  and memos, 100, 211, 212
  and organization, 113–114, 134
  and persuasion, 134
  and policies, 227
  and résumés, 146, 153, 195–196
  and style sheets, 115–117, 124–125
  and tone, 172
  and typesize and style, 116–117, 121–123
  and writing, 176, 178
  using emphasis, 53
Paper
  and résumés, 153
  and tone, 172
  fold, 91
Paragraph lists, 92–93, 96, 126, 129, 146
  and colons, 38
Paragraphs
  and ellipses, 49–50
  and organization, 109–110, 113, 197, 199–206, 208–209, 213–214, 219
  and quotation marks, 143
  in memos, 102

Reference Glossary Index

indentation, 82, 102
length of, 125, 172, 218, 224–226
opening sentence, 218
proofreader symbol, 244
single-sentence for emphasis, 53–54
spacing after, 79, 85
transitions between, 173
Parallelism, 126–127,
 (*also see* Headings, 61–63)
 and conjunctions, 45
 in headings, 62, 153
 in lists, 48, 92, 96, 153, 193, 210, 218–219, 225
 in résumés, 153
Parentheses, 128–131, 194, 211
 (*also see* Dashes, 47–48)
 and abbreviations, 2–3
 and attachments, 103
 and bibliographic form, 26
 and citations, 35–36, 60
 and commas, 41–42
 and dashes, 48
 and ellipses, 49
 and lists, 93–94
 and parenthetical expressions, 41
 and quotation marks, 42
 in résumés, 154
Passive voice, 10–13, 169, 171, 220
 how to convert, 12-13
Period
 and abbreviations, 2, 4
 and ellipses, 49–50
 and lists, 94–95
 and parentheses, 129–130
 contrasted with dashes and semicolons, 48, 161
 following unit of measure, 104
 in résumés, 195–196, 198

proofreader symbol, 244
Persuasion, 77, 132–135, 203–205
Phrases
 and apostrophes, 18–19
 and commas, 39–42
 and conjuctions, 43–46
 and parallelism, 126
 and quotation marks, 142
 in lists, 94
 in résumés, 150–151, 153, 195–196, 198
 transitional, 161, 174
Placement
 (*also see* Page Layout, 115–125)
 of graphics, 123–124
 of headings, 63, 101, 123–124
 of key ideas, 113, 228
 of words for emphasis, 52, 113, 228
Planning
 for interviews, 71, 74
 page layout, 115, 118, 124–125
 writing, 175–177, 182
Plurals, 136–138
 and abbreviations, 2
 and agreement, 14–17
 and capitalization, 32
 and possessives, 140
 in bias-free language, 23–24
 of nouns and pronouns, 136–138
 of numbers, 107
Portrait format, 118
Position
 (*also see* Emphasis, 51–54)
 (*also see* Page Layout, 115–125)
 of graphics, 123–124

of headings, 63, 101, 123–124
of key ideas, 113, 228
of words for emphasis, 52, 113, 228
Possessives, 139–141
 and apostrophes, 18–19
Postal Service abbreviations, 84, 90
Postal Service addressing guidelines, 88–90
Prefixes
 hyphenation of, 66–67
Prepositions
 and capitalization, 31, 34
 and colons, 38, 93
 preceeding a list, 93
Presentation
 (*also see* Graphics, 55–60)
 for emphasis, 52–53, 55
Prewriting, 175–181
Procedures, 211–212, 228
Pronouns
 and agreement, 14–17
 and apostrophes, 19
 and bias-free language, 22–24
 and possessives, 19, 139, 141
Proofreading, 125, 164, 184
 of résumés, 151, 153, 160
 on computers, 165
 symbols, 243–245
Proper names
 and capitalization, 30–32
Proper nouns
 and capitalization, 32, 34, 93
Proportional typefaces, 121–122
Proposal letters, 86, 205–208
 (also see Persuasion, 132–135)

237

Reference Glossary Index

Prototype of document, 178–183
Publication information
  for bibliography, 25–28, 59–60
  for citations, 35–36
Publish
  (*also see* Intellectual Property, 68–70)
  permission to, 69
Publisher
  listed in bibliographic form, 25–26
  listed in citations, 36
Publishing, 184
Punctuation
  correct punctuation to establish credibility, 135
  in lists, 95
  in parentheses and brackets, 128–131
  of abbreviations, 1–2, 4
  of dates, 106–107
  of numbers, 104, 106–107
  on envelopes, 89–90
  open, 83, 85–86
  proofreader symbols, 244
  standard, 80, 83
  styles, 83, 85–86

Question headings, 62
Question marks
  and parentheses and brackets, 129–130
  and quotation marks, 144
Questions to develop
  résumé information, 155, 157–159
Quotation marks, 142–144
  and dashes, 144
  and punctuation, 143–144
  and titles, 143, 166–167
  enclosing direct quotations, 142

Quotations
  and capitalization, 33
  and ellipses, 50
Quoted material
  and brackets, 128, 130
  and citations, 35–36
  and ellipses, 49
  and intellectual property, 69–70

Readability
  and emphasis, 51, 53–54, 97, 117
  and newsletters, 226
  and organization, 113
  and page layout, 117–119, 123–124, 211, 225
  and short paragraphs, 53–54, 224–225
Reference initials
  in letters, 86–87
  in memos, 103
References
  and bias-free language, 20
  and tone, 171
  and writing, 184
  courtesy copy, 89
  for cited information, 25–28
  in letters, 88–89
  in memos, 102
  list of, 155, 159–160, 196, 198
  on job applications, 188
  on résumés, 155, 159–160, 196, 198
Repetition
  (*also see* Emphasis, 51–54)
  in letters, 202
  in memos, 213, 216
  of important ideas, 52–53
Restatement
  and interviews, 74
  and letters, 204
  and memos, 101, 216

  and transitions, 174
Résumés, 73, 145–160
  and bias-free language, 21
  and interviews, 73
  chronological, 145–146, 196
  format, 153–160
  functional, 146, 195, 198
  models, 195–196, 198
Review
  (*also see* Writing, 175–184)
  and organization, 112–114
  and writing process, 175, 178, 182–184
  major points, 112–113
  procedures for documents, 183
  sample interview tape, 73
  Seven Quality Standards for Documents, 114
Revising documents, 182–184
  proofreading symbols, 243–245
Revision date in headers and footers, 119–120, 193, 212, 227–228
Run-in headings, 63, 210

Salutation, 23–24, 79–81, 85, 197, 199, 201–203, 205–209
  and colons, 38
  and commas, 42
Sans-serif fonts, 121–123
Semicolons, 161–162
  (*also see* Commas, 39–42)
  (*also see* Conjunctions, 43–46)
  and dashes, 47–48
  and transitions, 173–174
  contrasted with colons, 37

Reference Glossary Index

in lists, 95
  with quotation marks, 144
Sentences
  active and passive, 10–13
  active/passive voice, 10–13
  and agreement, 14–17
  and bias-free language, 20–24
  and capitalization, 29–34
  and emphasis, 51–54
  and numbers, 104–107
  and parallelism, 126
  and punctuation, 37–50, 64–67, 161–162
  and tone, 168–172
  in letters, 78
  in lists, 92–96
  in memos, 100–101
Series
  and lists, 92–93
  and parallelism, 126–127
  and semicolons, 161–162
Serif fonts, 121–123
Seven Quality Standards for Documents, 114
Sexist language
  (*also see* Bias-Free Language, 20–24)
Signature block, 85–86
Signature line, 103
Singular
  (*also see* Agreement, 14–17)
  (*also see* Plurals, 136–138)
  agreement of subject and verb, 14–15
  and abbreviations, 2
  and apostrophes, 18
  and bias-free language, 23–24
  and possessives, 139–140
Spacing, 79
  single-spaced, 61, 79, 85, 102

Spellchecking software, 165
Spelling, 163–165
Style
  and tone, 168–171
  in letters, 79–83
  in writing (style sheets), 124–125, 178
Subheadings
  (*also see* Headings, 61–63)
  and capitalization, 34
  in memos, 99–100
  in writing, 178–181, 183–184
Subject, 97–99, 101–102
  and active/passive voice, 10
  and agreement, 14–17
  in letters (subject line), 23, 75–77, 85
  in memos (subject line), 98–99, 101–102
Subordinate phrase (or clause), 45–46
Subordinating conjunctions, 43, 46
Subtitles
  and colons, 38
Summaries
  and 4-Box Organizer, 110, 204, 213, 216
  and organization, 113
  and transitions, 174
Symbols
  (*also see* Abbreviations, 1–9)
  (*also see* Apostrophes, 18–19)
  as trademarks, 68–70
  copyright, 68–70
  revising and proofreading, 243–245
Tables, (*also see* Graphics, 55–60)
  as emphasis, 113
  examples of, 215

for visual aids, 114
Teamwork, 175–184
Telephone numbers on résumés, 154–155, 159
Template
  (*also see* Page Layout, 115–125)
Text
  (*also see* Citations, 35–36)
  and headings, 61–63
  and numbers, 104–107
  and persuasion, 132–135
  in letters, 75–91
  in lists, 92–96
  in memos, 97–103
  in résumés, 145–160
Thank you letter, 74, 200
  (*also see* Letters, 75–91)
Time
  and colons, 38
  and numbers, 104
Titles, 166–167
  and abbreviations, 3
  and bias-free language, 20–24
  and capitalization, 34
  and commas, 42
  and quotation marks, 142–143
  in citations, 35–36
  in letters, 83–85
  in memos, 101–103
  in résumés, 145, 151, 155–160
  of graphics, 59–60
  used in bibliographies, 25–28
Tone, 168–172
  in letters, 77–79
  in memos, 101
  models
    commendation letter, 201
    complaint letter, 202
    cover letter, 197, 199

239

Reference Glossary Index

newsletter, item, 226
personnel notice, 210
persuasive sales letter, 203–204
proposal acceptance letter, 206
proposal letter, 205
proposal rejection letter, 207
recommendation memo, 213
request for clarification, 219
request memo, 218
sales letter, 208
thank you letter, 200
Trademarks, 68–70, 119
Transitions, 173–174
   and active/passive voice, 11–12
   and commas, 40
   and conjunctions, 46
   and semicolons, 40, 161–162
Typefaces
   and headings, 63
   and tone, 172
   document design, 118, 121–125
   on envelopes, 89
   used for emphasis, 54, 117, 228
Typesize, 63, 121–124, 228
Typewriters
   and bullets, 94
   and dashes, 47
   and mono-spaced type, 122

Underlining
   and bibliographic form, 25
   and citations, 36
   and headings, 63
   and quotation marks, 143
   and titles, 25, 36, 167

   for emphasis, 52, 54, 63, 76, 98, 113
   in letters, 76
   in memos, 98
Uppercase
   in abbreviations, 2
   in headings, 116

Variable typeface, 121
Verbs
   active and passive, 10, 13
   agreement with subjects, 14–17
   and colons in lists, 38, 93
   and connected words, 64–65
   and hyphens, 64–65
   in procedures, 211
   in résumés, 148, 150–152, 195–196, 198
   parallel forms in lists, 96, 126–127, 153, 218, 193
Vertical page layout format, 118
Visuals
   (*also see* Emphasis, 51–54)
   (*also see* Graphics, 55–60)
   (*also see* Page Layout, 115–125)
   and emphasis, 95, 113, 223, 228
   and graphics, 113
   and letters, 77
   and memos, 99
   as intellectual property, 68–70
   for headings, 63, 210
   use of color in, 54
Visual aids, 114, 116
   (*also see* Graphics, 55–60)
   and abbreviations, 4
Voice active/passive, 10–13

Warnings
   in a procedure, 228
Word-processing, 165
   and small capital letters, 2
Wordiness and tone, 170
Words
   (*also see* Abbreviations, 1–9)
   (*also see* Capitals, 29–34)
   (*also see* Spelling, 163–165)
   and capitalization
      in lists, 93–94
      in titles, 167
   and emphasis, 54, 113
   and hyphens, 67
   and parallelism, 126–127
   connected, 64–66
   direct and simple, 78, 100
   in subject lines, 76
   plural forms, 136–138
   tone, 168
   transitional, 173–174
Works cited, 25–28
   (*also see* Citations, 35–36)
Writing, 175–184
   (*also see* Bias-Free Language, 20–24)
   (*also see* Citations, 35–36)
   (*also see* Letters, 75–91)
   (*also see* Memos, 97–103)
   (*also see* Résumés, 145–160)
   and active/passive voice, 10–13
   and citations, 35–36
   and emphasis, 51–54
   and headings, 61, 113
   and intellectual property, 68–70
   and organization
      4-Box Organizer, 110–111
   and repetition in, 216
   key writing principle, 108

Reference Glossary Index

principles of, 108
using Seven Quality Standards, 113–114
using transitions, 173–174
and page layout, 115, 124–125
and parallelism, 126
cover letters, 197, 199
evaluating and revising, 182–184
first draft, 182
numbers, 104–105, 107
pre-writing, 175–181
proofreading and publishing, 184
résumés, 145–160, 195–196, 198
using persuasion, 132–135, 203
using proper tone, 168–171

Zip Code, 9, 83, 88, 90, 154

Revising and Proofreading Symbols

Symbol		Meaning of Symbol	Example	
In Margin	*In Text*		*Marked*	*Corrected*
	⤴	Delete or leave out a word, letter, or punctuation mark.	Leave out this word word. Leave out this /letter. Leave out this period.⤴	Leave out this word. Leave out this letter. Leave out this period.
	⤴ (with close)	Delete or leave out a letter and close up the word.	Every t/ime I run for office, I lose.	Every time I run for office, I lose.
	⌒	Close up space entirely.	The secretary's work load is heavy.	The secretary's workload is heavy.
	∧	Insert a word, letter, or punctuation mark.	Insert this∧ *word* Insert th∧ letter. Insert this punctuation mark∧letter, or word.	Insert this word. Insert this letter. Insert this punctuation mark, letter, or word.
	#	Insert or add a space.	Insert #space here.	Insert a space here.
ⓛⓒ	/	Lowercase a capital letter.	L̸owercase letter	lowercase letter
ⓒⓐⓟ	≡	Capitalize a lowercase letter.	My attorney, Mr. andrews ≡	My attorney, Mr. Andrews
ⓢ.ⓒ.	=	Small cap letters or words. (Small caps are small capital letters.)	The deadline is immediate.	The deadline is IMMEDIATE.
ⓒ+ⓢⓒ	≡ =	Regular capitals with small caps.	The deadline is immediate.	The deadline is IMMEDIATE.
	∧—	Change or replace a word.	It belongs to my/sister. *brother*	It belongs to my brother.

Symbol		Meaning of Symbol	Example	
In Margin	*In Text*		*Marked*	*Corrected*
	/	Change or replace a letter.	referance	reference
tr	∽	Transpose or change the order of words or letters.	the disk replacement the replacement dsik	the replacement disk the replacement disk
	⊙	Add punctuation: period	The president ordered the work⊙	The president ordered the work.
	⁁	comma	The president, John Harvey⁁ordered the work.	The president, John Harvey, ordered the work.
	⊙⊙	colon	Follow these rules⊙	Follow these rules:
	⁁	semicolon	I paid the bank⁁ however, they sent another bill.	I paid the bank; however, they sent another bill.
	?	question mark	Do you know the answer ?	Do you know the answer?
	!	exclamation mark	I don't care !	I don't care!
	=	hyphen	a cross=country car race	a cross-country car race
	⌄	apostrophe	the girls⌄team	the girls' team
	⌄ ⌄	quotation marks	He said loudly, No.	He said loudly, "No."
	¶	Begin a new paragraph.	This sentence ends the paragraph.¶This sentence begins a new paragraph.	This sentence ends the paragraph. This sentence beings a new paragraph.

244

Symbol		Meaning of Symbol	Example	
In Margin	*In Text*		*Marked*	*Corrected*
	no ¶	No new paragraph.	This sentence does not complete the paragraph. no ¶ This sentence must be linked to the previous sentence.	This sentence does not complete the paragraph. This sentence must be linked to the previous sentence.
ital	⎯⎯	Mark text to be set in: italics	The Ram is an excellent magazine.	*The Ram* is an excellent magazine.
underl	⎯⎯	underlined	the memo must be	the memo <u>must</u> be
b.f.	〜〜〜	boldface	Distribute the memo immediately.	Distribute the memo **immediately**.
sp	◯	Spell out the abbreviation.	The Jackson-Miller (Co.)	The Jackson-Miller Company
stet	....	Ignore corrections and let original stand.	It displayed a ~~light~~ yellow background.	It displayed a light yellow background.

245